Voices from an Evil God

BARBARA JONES

BLAKE

Published by Blake Publishing Ltd.
98-100 Great North Road, London N2 0NL, England

First published in Great Britain in 1993

ISBN 1 85782 065 7

British Library Cataloguing-in-Publication Data:
A catalogue record for this book is available from
the British Library.

Typeset by BMD Graphics, Hemel Hempstead

Printed by Cox & Wyman, Reading, Berkshire

Cover picture by Chris Furr

1 3 5 7 9 10 8 6 4 2

To my friend Kate Wharton.

Acknowledgements

Special thanks to Bill Frost, who shared the many headaches associated with this book.

Heartfelt thanks also for a hundred different reasons, to: Barry Askew, Graeme Gourlay, David Grey, Eddie Jones, Bob Hill, Margaret Maisey, Andrew Mathias, Raz Mireskandari, Beverley Molter, Jon Thurley and Gerald Wynne.

Contents

Introduction

The first few difficult hours I spent with Sonia Sutcliffe, in April 1984, threw no more than a glimmer of light on what lay behind her husband's series of murders and attacks on women.

Peter Sutcliffe is behind bars for life. He will never be released.

Sonia was completely withdrawn, traumatised by her husband's trial three years earlier and his conviction on thirteen charges of murder and seven murder attempts. It caused her physical pain to speak of his life imprisonment. In the many halting conversations we had in the early days of our relationship, Peter Sutcliffe emerged as much more than a man who had lost his mind and murdered women with a frenzied bloodlust. He was an enigma, an inexplicable and perhaps unfathomable combination of caring husband, loyal employee, and serial killer; he was also intelligent, controlled and plausible.

Sutcliffe had never been interviewed, had never spoken a word to a journalist, and I decided that, however long it took, I was going to meet him and talk to him.

It took four years. I finally saw Peter Sutcliffe

at Broadmoor, Britain's top security hospital for the criminally insane, on 23 August 1988. Sonia took me there, having first invented a false name for me to put in the visitor's book at the reception desk. She and her husband had dreamt it up together. Thus, for two years, signing in and out of Broadmoor more than twenty times, I was stuck with the unlikely tag of Giotta Katalos.

The first occasion was the only time that I saw Sutcliffe with Sonia. After that he asked me to come alone, and then we talked for hours until I began to understand something of the man behind the terrifying label of the 'Yorkshire Ripper'.

Sonia and I had come to a financial arrangement over a book I was to write about her life with Peter Sutcliffe. The contract she made with me, in the form of two handwritten receipts, was to haunt her much later, at the highly publicised libel trial in December 1990 when we faced each other across the High Court.

Peter Sutcliffe also wanted me to write his life story, although he didn't ask for money. He wanted only the opportunity to show the world that he was not an evil monster but someone who deserved sympathy and understanding. His grotesque attempts at self-justification intruded upon every interview I had with him. All the time, the real Peter Sutcliffe was emerging.

My relationship with Peter ended as soon as I

felt I had sufficient material to write this book. That coincided with the date in the summer of 1990 when I received the writ that was to draw me into High Court confrontation with Sonia. By then I had known her on and off for six and a half years, in a relationship that was discreet, almost clandestine. There were coded phone calls, meetings in places where we would not be recognised by others and notes passed via Broadmoor's secret postal system.

Despite her judicial separation from her husband she has remained devoted to him, and he to her. She has hated his enemies, fought for his rights, and missed his daily presence. She told me that she had come to understand his crimes 'spiritually and intellectually'. He was her 'uncut diamond'. She still lives in the house in Bradford that she shared with Sutcliffe during the period when he murdered eight of his victims; it was her home, and 'nothing bad' had ever happened to her there.

The question instinctively asked of Sonia Sutcliffe is: Did she know? Did she know her husband was the Yorkshire Ripper?

After years of intensive thought and study, I truly believe she had no inkling. She was not asking herself, in the way that many other women were at that time, whether the Ripper might be someone she knew. She was utterly absorbed with her new home and her demanding job as a teacher.

She reacts stormily to suggestions that she must have read about the murders and must have speculated about the killer's identity. She insists that she did neither, and that she was not in the habit of avidly reading garish headlines in the newspapers. She has always claimed that she felt deep shock when Peter told her himself: "It's me, luv. I'm the Yorkshire Ripper."

Nevertheless, Sonia Sutcliffe emerges as a staunch supporter of her husband. For me, listening to a woman who continually defended her husband's horrendous crimes was as uncomfortable as it was odd. She was not claiming that he had not murdered. She was claiming that he was a good and lovable person and that, by implication, his victims were not.

It was this extraordinary relationship between the Sutcliffes that drove me to discover more. Years later, when I felt I might have reached the roots of their relationship, I heard of another twist that had me reeling. In 1986, when her husband had been incarcerated for five years, Sonia Sutcliffe conspired to help him escape from Broadmoor.

I have irrefutable evidence that she agreed to help Sutcliffe and a fellow patient cut their way through the iron bars on the windows of their top security hospital ward, use grappling hooks to scale the walls surrounding Broadmoor, and meet a getaway car stationed several hundred yards away.

Sonia and Peter Sutcliffe discussed this plan during visiting hours at Broadmoor and were convinced that it would work. It was to be his task to find a practical way out of the place, and hers to ensure his successful disappearance once he was out.

Their bizarre plan failed, although Sonia insists today that her husband had got as far as obtaining a hacksaw. Security, for patients and visitors, was then increased and by the time Sutcliffe and others were transferred to the newly-built wing of Broadmoor, thorough checks had been introduced at the hospital's reception. The couple conceded that their chances of a reunion were lost.

Years later, though, in the late spring of 1992, Broadmoor Hospital authorities announced that a hacksaw blade had been found in Peter Sutcliffe's room. No details were given, but in national newspapers and on television news it was strongly suggested that the blade had been brought in from outside. Senior hospital staff insisted that it would have been impossible for a patient to obtain such a thing in any other way. Newspapers were quick to remind the public that in the summer of 1991 a child rapist called the Wolfman had escaped from the hospital after cutting his way through bars with a hacksaw blade.

Having moved large numbers of patients to the expensive new wing, with its state-of-the-art security devices, it was all hugely embarrassing for Broadmoor. Hospital spokesmen stressed that there had been no possibility of a break-out by Sutcliffe, despite the existence of the hacksaw blade, but the implication was that the blade had been hidden among Sutcliffe's belongings for a long time – prior to his move to the new hospital wing.

To Broadmoor's further embarrassment, a screwdriver went missing a few weeks after the discovery of the hacksaw blade, along with a knife from the day centre and a fork from the patients' activity centre. The Prison Officers Association demanded a full enquiry.

Sonia Sutcliffe has remained silent on the subject. She had, in any case, been concentrating for some time on other projects since realising that she was not going to get her Pete out of Broadmoor. Soon after she and her husband had ditched the 'over-the-wall' escape plan, she launched a campaign of litigation that was to make her a wealthy woman.

She started by taking the magazine *Private Eye* to court over a libel she claimed they had committed soon after her husband's conviction. She claimed they were wrong to say she had been negotiating to sell the story of her experiences as the wife of the Yorkshire Ripper to a newspaper. She claimed she would never do that, and that she had never received money for her story. Sonia was awarded record libel damages of £600,000, reduced on appeal to £160,000. She went on to win other large sums of money in out-of-court settlements with other newspapers. She has always maintained that she has never been paid by a newspaper for her story.

There is irrefutable evidence that she received £12,000 in secret payments from the *News of the World* dating back to 1981, the year of her husband's sensational trial. Until then, she had refused all offers from newspapers who had sent their journalists flocking to her door immediately after Sutcliffe's arrest. Among other substantial offers was one of £130,000 from the *News of the World*. Sonia turned this down, but maintained contact with the journalist who made the offer.

Barry Askew was the new editor of the *News of the World*. He was more persistent than the others, held the most senior post among them, and adopted a caring attitude towards Sonia Sutcliffe which she liked and appreciated. By the end of Sutcliffe's trial she had met Askew often and had accepted practical help from him in getting safely in and out of the Old Bailey. A few months after the trial, she agreed that payments made via a devious route, involving four other journalists, should find their way into her personal possession. All four men are named in a sworn affidavit that is to be handed to the office of the Director of Public Prosecutions.

These affairs came to light early in 1992 and could not be made public sooner. Sonia Sutcliffe may well come to regret her foolhardy and self-righteous attitude towards those who have written about her. Knowing her as I do, I would not expect remorse to be any part of her reaction to these new revelations. Remorse has never been a part of her husband's reactions to his crimes and Sonia and Peter Sutcliffe are as one in their attitude to his crimes and to his victims, and to the world in general outside their relationship.

It was this relationship, as well as the enormity of Peter Sutcliffe's crimes, which inspired this book. While I came close to both of them as biographer and confidante, the balancing act between us was often challenging and difficult. I certainly never came close to liking either of them.

The shock of hearing the details of just one murder never left me, while the litany of Sutcliffe's continual complaints about his treatment in court, in prison and in hospital, was like an often-repeated obscenity. His demands to be 'understood' by the families of his victims were an insult. So why go on listening to it? Why indulge his taste for Jaffa Cakes and canteen tea while he preached about justice not having been done; about those in authority failing him; about the retrial he deserved on 'theological grounds'? The answer is this: it must be valuable for someone like me – not a doctor, a priest, psychiatrist or police officer, but simply an experienced journalist with a useful working knowledge of human nature – to take the opportunity to learn about and illuminate such extremes of behaviour.

Emlyn Williams, asked why he wrote about the notorious Moors Murders in his book *Beyond Belief*, said that it was right to learn all we could about humankind, and that included mass murderers and social lepers as well as great men of letters and world leaders. Williams also said, however, that his study of one real-life murder case was quite enough for him; he was happy to return to writing fiction.

I know how he must have felt. The extraordinarily casual way in which Peter Sutcliffe would discuss details of his killings was, for me, a chilling experience every time. Two hours spent in his company in Broadmoor's depressing shabbiness left me emotionally exhausted and I would leave each meeting with a heavy heart and a sense of outrage that I would like to have shared with the victims' families and the survivors of the seven murder attempts.

Of course, Peter Sutcliffe is criminally insane; the workings of his mind not only beyond belief but beyond repair. His schizophrenia is of Jekyll and Hyde proportions. For six long years he was able to appear 'normal' in his everyday life. Long-distance lorry driver by day, he haunted the streets by night.

INTRODUCTION

He had a mission to fulfil and he carried out his work with ruthless efficiency, for the 'voices' in his head would accept nothing less. This study of his psychotic violence is not undertaken for its own sake. If it adds just one chapter to the sum of criminal knowledge then it must be worthwhile.

CHAPTER ONE

Retribution

It was the eyes they noticed first. The seven survivors of his frenzied attacks had all told police of his 'crazy stare', which had been reproduced in thousands of photo-fit posters during the six-year hunt for the killer they called the Yorkshire Ripper. Now, in Court Number One at the Old Bailey, the full force of that evil stare can be felt by the jury, the lawyers, the court clerks, and the judge himself.

Peter William Sutcliffe, aged thirty-four, is looking fixedly at a point above the head of Mr Justice Boreham. And he continues to look back at it throughout his two-week murder trial, the unwavering gaze a text-book symptom of his paranoid schizophrenia. Sutcliffe himself understands such unnerving power. From the witness box he relates stabbing his final victim through the eye 'because she seemed to be looking at me with an accusing stare'.

This admission comes at the end of two days of cross-examination, and contributes to a total of twenty life sentences. The judge says he hopes that life imprisonment for the Ripper will mean precisely that. The man in the dock – the Bradford lorry

1

driver who killed thirteen times and left another seven women for dead – now says nothing, although earlier he spoke of 'voices in my head which said "Kill, Kill, Kill",' and of his God-given mission to cleanse the streets of prostitution.

When sentenced, he stands impassively at the rail of the dock, still staring straight ahead, dressed in the pale blue shirt and cheap grey suit he has worn every day of the trial. That was Friday 22 May 1981, the last the public was to see of Peter Sutcliffe before he began his life sentence.

———— o ————

Ten years later he still wears the same cheap suit. The bulbous brown eyes still stare intently, the gaze never shifting. If you believe, as this man says he does, that the eyes are the window of the soul, then you look here upon a soul dedicated to evil.

Then the voice, unexpectedly high-pitched, breaks the spell, for it is thin, monotonous and complaining; the voice of a man who has sinned and yet, incredibly, believes himself sinned against. Peter William Sutcliffe, patient number 75879, is sitting at a stained formica-topped table in Central Hall at Broadmoor Hospital. He has been in this institution for seven years now, the protracted arguments over his sanity, or lack of it, at last resolved.

According to the doctors, he is clinically insane, a paranoid schizophrenic, although Sutcliffe disagrees. Certainly the man sitting across the table looks as 'normal' as the bloke next door, and with his friendly smile he can appear physically attractive, almost cuddly. That is the chilling and baffling contradiction which lies at the very heart of his mission to murder and maim. He tells me in all seriousness that the court should have accepted his submission that he killed through 'diminished responsibility on theological grounds', a bizarre defence not to be found on any statute book.

Sutcliffe still maintains that the murders went against everything in his nature. By all accounts, particularly his own, he was kind and caring – a model son-in-law and a model employee. Today in Broadmoor he sets time aside to help fellow patients who can neither read nor write, answering their letters for them and reading to them. He also cuts their hair. 'I'm the self-appointed barber of Block Three,' he grins proudly, revealing the gap in his front teeth. It is the same wolfish smile that stared from newspaper front pages at the time of his arrest and trial.

Yet a whining tone will creep into every conversation. The trouble is, you see, that no one really understands. 'I suppose the public believe what they've read in the newspapers – that's all wrong. I'm not a beast. That isn't me at all.

I'm concerned about other people – I've always been good to my neighbours, particularly when they're in trouble. No one seems to understand what it's like when a person is taken over, given a mission.'

Sutcliffe's continual lament has a glib unattractive quality: 'It's really awful for anyone to be in pain. I wouldn't be responsible for anyone's agony, ever. Those people I attacked, well it wasn't really me, I mean the real, caring me. That me was in conflict – a good Catholic fighting an avenging angel acting on orders from God. I'm no mass killer. I'd been told what my mission was, like a soldier in a war. I couldn't disobey my orders. They came from the highest authority.'

In a letter home to his father while still in prison at Parkhurst, Sutcliffe asked: 'Do you, any of you, even imagine that I had any choice in the matter? I can tell you the mind is a very strange thing and I would have thought you would all have complete faith in me and what I have tried my best to interpret! Something that I have always seen as a "divine phenomenon".

'You all know me far too well to accept that I could ever be a nasty or malicious person. Haven't you seen how the gutter press have done nothing but wage diabolical campaigns...'

To Peter Sutcliffe, the murders are always 'the tragedy', while his victims are always 'those people'.

If it were not for thirteen murdered women, seven more left for dead, and twenty-three children who will never again enjoy a mother's love, his words would sound ridiculous, even farcical.

As it is, his words can never be anything but deeply sinister, coming as they do from the mouth of Britain's most feared killer, a mass murderer who confounded the combined efforts of two entire police forces for six years. Women throughout the country went in fear of the Yorkshire Ripper, a criminal invested with what appeared to be superhuman powers. He stalked, he killed and then melted away like the mist that can hang so ominously over the Yorkshire Moors.

His first victims were prostitutes, wretched figures on street corners in the more squalid parts of cities like Leeds, Bradford and Wakefield, but then the Ripper began killing at random – a sixteen-year-old shop girl, a nineteen-year-old building society clerk, a university student. The police hunt, already the biggest in British criminal history, was stepped up, but still the murderer continued his blood mission, apparently invincible.

Public speculation about his identity was intense. He was certainly mad but at the same time more than a match for the combined brainpower and expertise of top police officers. It was generally supposed that he was a severely disturbed loner, possibly unemployed and certainly with a record of violent crime. He would have an unmistakably dangerous look and it would not be a complete surprise to his neighbours when he was finally arrested. So it was all the more chilling when the monster proved to be 'the bloke next door'. Neighbours saw Peter Sutcliffe going to work as a long-distance lorry driver; they saw him mending his car in the driveway of his house; they saw him taking his wife out shopping. He was not obviously mad or dangerous. He was about as ordinary as they come.

The man who now sits in the visitors' hall at Broadmoor high security hospital has managed to preserve that ordinariness. His behaviour now is as unremarkable as it appeared then; his conversation, always self-centred, is banal, even tedious. The late Sir Michael Havers, the Attorney General, described him to the jury at his murder trial as 'an unremarkable person leading an unremarkable life'. The dreadful reality, though, is that Peter Sutcliffe, 'the bloke next door', exists in the same mind as Peter Sutcliffe, the Yorkshire Ripper – a working-class lorry driver and a mass killer both vying for control over one sick and fragmented personality.

Sometimes the 'ordinary' Peter Sutcliffe can talk in a flat, matter-of-fact way about the activities of the extraordinary Peter Sutcliffe. While sipping tea from a white china cup and saucer and munching his way through a packet of Jaffa Cakes, he will casually describe and justify his murders. He has always claimed they were inspired by 'voices in his head', although strenuously objecting to any suggestion that he was, or is, mentally ill. He has steadfastly refused to take medication. 'If I took drugs the doctors gave me and the voices stopped, that could be dangerous for me. I'd have to admit I was mentally ill, and I couldn't live with that,' he explains.

Although it is almost impossible to listen impassively, suppressing the natural response of distaste and revulsion, it is important to do so, for this is Sutcliffe talking off guard. He is neither trying to deceive a jury into believing he is insane, nor lying to police officers; he is not trying to gain a reduced sentence, or even public sympathy. He is simply sitting here, sipping tea and talking about his favourite subject – himself.

He says that during his six years of killing he believed that like the Old Testament prophets, he'd been given a mission to rid society of all that was corrupt, all that was evil. His mother, a devout Roman Catholic, had instilled in him a near-superstitious religious faith, made up of images of fire, brimstone and retribution. The voices had chosen him as their instrument. 'There have been crusades, holy wars, ever since history began. Thousands and thousands have been killed. I was on a crusade too – against prostitutes. But I thought

7

I was saving their souls.'

Today he claims he has finally recognised that the 'voices' were not from God but from the Devil. He has come to this conclusion through the teachings of Jehovah's Witnesses, contained in literature sent to him at Broadmoor by a friend – a somewhat bizarre source of revelation, given that for many years he remained a Catholic, attending Mass every Sunday in the hospital's chapel.

'Like I said, the instructions came from God. Really, it could have been anyone with the same religious beliefs. If I'd not been brought up a good Catholic this might never have happened. From the start I was taught the difference between right and wrong. It stands to reason that sex for money, sex without love, is wrong.'

———— o ————

A sad little notice, posted in the visitors' waiting-room, warns against anyone bringing in items that could aid escape, such as rope, cutting tools, money, etc. Any food brought in for patients may be cut up and searched, it says.

All Broadmoor staff are qualified nurses, whose priority it is to maintain maximum security. Each warder, dressed in a dark blue uniform with a white shirt and black tie, carries a bunch of keys at the end of a dark brown, woven leather strap tied at the waist. Even the chaplain, with his dog collar, black robes and kindly smile, jangles as he walks.

Some of the 'screws' have been at Broadmoor longer than many patients. They regret that the solid four-storey blocks, their tiny windows criss-crossed with bars, that made up the original hospital, are to be closed down as patients move to the newly built collection of units in the same grounds. Structural problems held up the move, and for some time the only new part in use was the entrance lobby and the visitors' waiting-room.

The voluntary workers, whom patients have irreverently nicknamed the 'Fiends of Broadmoor', have a brand-new kitchen nearby, from which they dispense tea and snacks to visitors.

There is a long bleak walk from the waiting-room, with its royal blue, foam-filled furniture and its dog-eared Sunday colour supplements, well past their read-by dates. We are accompanied inside the hospital grounds by an escort party, through one locked gate after another. Occasionally a straggling group of patients appears, en route for one of the many workshops, schoolrooms, canteens or kitchens where they have daily jobs to do.

The final locked gate is at the shabbily painted entrance to a main corridor. The canteen for male patients is immediately inside; toilets for inmates and staff are on the opposite side of the corridor. The high walls and ceilings are painted a garish orange offset with cream. Our footsteps produce a shuffling echo as we make our way to the Central Hall. Some visitors chat to their immediate companions during the five-minute trek. Others are too sad or preoccupied. Anyway, no one wants to chat to me, for they've known since my arrival at the reception desk that I am here to see the one patient they all despise – the Yorkshire Ripper.

Although 550 patients are confined in Broadmoor, no more than thirty or forty visitors turn up at any visiting time. Some of the inmates have no visitors at all, but for those who do, each two-hour visit is an all-important lifeline. Every patient jealously monopolises the attention of his visitor. Yet in the grim and dreary Central Hall, where we huddle around small tables, many eyes stray towards Sutcliffe. I have seen the naked hatred in them, not just for him but for me too. Whatever the crime or unthinkable family tragedy that has led to a son, husband or brother being held in Broadmoor, none can compare with the calculated killing spree that brought Peter Sutcliffe here. He cannot be forgiven, not even by those who have seen other horrific effects of insanity, and nor can his visitors. He has a list of twenty-five visitors posted at the reception desk.

There seems to be little respect from the patients for the kindly volunteers, nor for the social workers whom they call 'social smirkers'. Since the preoccupation of each Broadmoor patient that I have met – five in all, including Sutcliffe – is the possibility of release, the only way in which they see themselves as being helped at all is towards that end. Many of them write persistently to the charity Mind, which offers legal advice to those unfairly treated by the courts or institutions. If help towards a release is not forthcoming, resentment sets in.

Sutcliffe depends to a large degree on Sonia's efforts when it comes to official complaints or attempts at an application for an appeal and re-trial. He knows there will be no release for him, ever, so will not waste time chasing the impossible. He restricts his campaigning to a continual call for improved living conditions, such as being allowed to use artists' materials for painting and drawing or, at one time, being moved nearer to his Yorkshire home so that he might have more frequent visits from Sonia and his family.

He told me insistently that I must claim back my travelling expenses to Broadmoor, as many other visitors do. There is a simple system which involves filling in a form on arrival and handing it to a hospital officer. Sutcliffe's insistence was not out of concern for me; it was just another small gesture that he could make against authority. They might have taken away his freedom, but there was no reason why they should not also be forced to pay for my visits. I never did claim the expenses. For one thing, I had used a false name to get in and I didn't want to compound any infringement of the rules.

In many ways, the daily life of Broadmoor suits Sutcliffe. He is the ultimate, institutionalised patient – submissive, respectful and non-assertive. He is keen to point out that he has lost his liberty and is 'doing his punishment' for the crimes he committed, and that appears to deal totally with any question of remorse. He does not say it is unfair for him to be incarcerated. He accepts that this is the only possible punishment for him. But he does say that permanently losing his freedom should be sufficient recompense for the public and for those to whom he caused suffering. He should not be expected to suffer further. Some of his fellow patients seem to disgust him. He says they squabble and that some of them are 'very mad and hysterical', keeping him awake at night by screaming. Petty jealousies inevitably take on great importance. Sutcliffe says he is envied by others because he receives a good deal more post than any other patient, and many more visitors. Many of them bring gifts, and there is a strict system by which these are distributed that draws every other patient's attention to it.

Visitors must deposit gifts – usually fruit, biscuits, cakes or other treats – at the reception desk. Brown boxes are handed over by the hospital staff, to be filled and labelled by visitors. A mechanical cart is driven over to the reception area just after visiting hours begin, and the brown boxes are taken to the wards. Patients wait, each morning and afternoon, to see if something has arrived for them. I have taken fruit, and sometimes flowers that Sutcliffe has asked for, and always wondered what other patients made of this once they reached the ward.

I found out when my flowers were delivered to the wrong patient, a friend of Sutcliffe's whom I had occasionally visited. He told me he was extremely embarrassed at being called to the staff office on the ward, and having to return to his room carrying a bunch of white chrysanthemums. He said Sutcliffe, by contrast, enjoyed the experience.

Sutcliffe told me he often had quantities of fruit, orange juice and biscuits stored in his personal locker and this sometimes caused resentment from other patients. 'This black chap came into the passageway once when I was getting something from my locker. He told me to give him some of my things, and stood over me in a threatening sort of way. I was having none of that. I said to him, straight out like, "This is my stuff and I'm keepin' it. What do you want to make of it?" He soon scuttled off. You've got to look after yourself, you know. Even if you're not a violent person by nature, you've got to protect yourself in here.'

Sutcliffe is quite vain about his personal strength and also, I discovered, about his looks. Today he is very much plumper than in 1981 when he was tried and convicted. His ambling gait is partly due to his bloated figure. I have seen him eat heartily during a visit that started at 2 pm, despite having only just finished lunch on the ward. Yet, when I told him half-seriously once that another patient had agreed with me that he should diet, he looked displeased, almost angry. I have only seen him angry twice, a discomfiting experience despite the presence of the 'screws'.

The topic of his weight, which I soon dropped, was one occasion. Another was more serious: he was intensely disappointed that Sonia had cancelled a series of visits. He had even gone to the lengths of getting his social worker to telephone her to ask her to come. And, of course, he also asked me several times to put pressure on her. Now she had 'let him down again' and his eyes darkened as he spoke about it. I saw his fists clench, and he thumped the table to emphasise his point. He was like a child in a tantrum, but rather more serious. I looked quickly down the room to see how far away the hospital officers were sitting. They were chatting among themselves and looked relaxed, but then one of them met my gaze and I realised that they never really let their attention wander.

Once there was a noisy argument at a nearby

table, and I looked on anxiously while a patient jabbed his finger angrily at a couple who looked like his parents, and shouted at them. One of the 'screws' came over to quieten him, and when that failed he was quickly dispatched back to his ward, cutting short his visit by more than an hour. His parents, helpless and upset, were escorted to the main entrance.

Patients generally respect the rules. When 'time' is called at the end of a visit, they don't need to be told twice that they must get up and prepare to return to their wards. Many look back to smile and wave, but do not question the authority of their escorts. I have seen them chatting to the 'screws', and one of the patients I have visited occasionally asked for their permission to have extra tobacco bought by me, for example, and handed over some handkerchiefs he had asked me to buy for him and which I had not put in the 'tuck box' at the reception desk. The 'screws' themselves are always friendly towards visitors. No doubt they recognise the vital importance of visits to individual patients. After calling 'time' in Central Hall, they always give a formal thank you.

Some middle-aged parents faithfully make the long trek to the hospital each week, usually on a Sunday, and one can only guess how they feel when their son sometimes spends the entire two-hour visit in sullen silence. Wives and small children also often visit on a Sunday, and turn Central Hall into a noisy sort of crèche. It seems hard on the children to be growing up with a lasting image of their father as a prisoner in this strange place, but the mothers have obviously decided it is better for them to see him here than not at all, and the visits clearly mean a lot to the patients.

Some patients, of course, will be rehabilitated and allowed home. Broadmoor has a special half-way unit which prepares them for a return to the outside world. They will first be allowed a job serving in the canteen during visiting hours, and then a job outside the hospital. Those serving in the canteen always took a pride in the job they were doing. The tea they served came from an urn and was sometimes stewed and unpleasant; the stainless steel teapots always leaked; the table tops were indelibly marked by previous spillings; and all the china was regulation issue. But the 'waiter service' was impeccable. The 'trustys' were a friendly, smiling bunch, and they shared pleasantries with Pete whenever they came to our table.

Once, in the reception waiting room, I met a former patient who was back at Broadmoor to visit old mates. He told me it was impossible to describe how important visits were, and he came back down to Berkshire from Liverpool whenever he could. I wondered how he felt when gate after gate clanged shut behind him as he took on his new role as a visitor.

Sutcliffe was not difficult to befriend. For the first time in his life, he was 'somebody' in his terms; no longer the inconsequential lorry-driver who would otherwise have remained in total obscurity. He is quite comfortable with himself and has almost come to expect a show of warmth and affection from his visitors. He would probably be surprised and rather hurt if what he encountered instead was revulsion. His own revulsion is reserved for the corrupt society that tolerates prostitution; the press who have, he says, badly misrepresented him; the judiciary, for refusing to accept the theological justification for his killings; the families of his victims, for demanding compensation; and the police, for their ineptitude in tracking him down. Meanwhile, his insensitivity and arrogance are, quite simply, maddening. They colour everything he says to other inmates and to his visitors, as well as the letters he writes to the outside world.

On our first meeting, I had not really known what to expect, fearfully anticipating a sullen, monosyllabic psychopath whose few spoken words would make little sense. Instead, I looked across Central Hall to see a smiling, self-assured figure sauntering towards me, flanked by burly warders. The grey suit worn at his trial was now too tight and his purple Seventies shirt, with its long, rounded collar, looked decidedly dated. He might have been on his way to a Golden Oldies night at a Bradford pub.

Sutcliffe began talking to me straightaway, surprisingly articulate, as he explained that a work-to-rule by staff had cut short visiting hours and that problems in the hospital had been exacerbated by a pay dispute. He seemed to be on good form, even attempting a little joke when we were offered a drink by one of the canteen staff. I said I'd like a gin and tonic, and he was quick to join in, saying he'd like a large one.

Soon, though, I could hear the complaining whine in his voice, when he showed me photographs of paintings he had done in Parkhurst Prison, bemoaning the lack of facilities in Broadmoor. He had wanted to paint portraits of others on his ward, saying that the insane were a rich source of inspiration, but the authorities refused, explaining that artists' materials could be harmful.

Sutcliffe disassociates himself from any suggestion that he could be mentally ill. Incredibly, he also tries to disassociate himself from the label he must live with for the rest of his life. 'They're wrong to call me the Yorkshire Ripper. I didn't chop up any of those women. But the newspapers seem to be able to print what they like about me. There was only one of them where I acted like Jack the Ripper. I had no choice.'

This was a reference to one of the most gruesome murders he had committed.

———— o ————

Jean Jordan was one of life's victims and Peter Sutcliffe's sixth. At the age of sixteen, she ran away from her home in Motherwell, arriving penniless in Manchester, where she drifted into prostitution. It was easier than working in a shop or factory, and the pay was better.

'Scotch Jean', as she became known among the other girls working the sleazy clubs and street corners, lived with a hotel porter she'd met soon after coming to Manchester. Together with their two young children, they occupied a flat in a 'sin bin' estate in the city's Moss Side area. Their relationship was unusual to say the least. Jean would disappear for days at a time with her girlfriends, while her common-law husband, Allan Royle, also went missing for similar periods.

On the night of 1 October 1977, Jean Jordan was 'out with the girls', in other words working one of her regular patches south of the city centre. Her last customer, and the last person she ever saw, was Peter Sutcliffe.

The Ripper claims he had been drawn to Manchester that night by something he'd read. A priest had complained in his parish magazine about the number of prostitutes on the streets and the story had reached the local Press. Here, in cold print, were the words the 'voices' had been ramming home for what seemed like so long now. His mission was in Manchester.

Sutcliffe studied a local map to locate the Moss Side district, the city's redlight area. He saw several girls 'plying their trade' and targeted a girl he described as 'slim and not bad-looking'. He asked her if she wanted business, and she said she would meet him further down the road. She had been about to get into another car, but changed her mind and got into Sutcliffe's car instead.

'I supposed this was the biggest mistake she ever made. She told me she was going to go with the other man until she saw me,' he said.

After haggling with his victim for a minute or two Sutcliffe agreed to pay £5 for sex, and Jean climbed into his Ford Corsair car to begin the last journey of her life – to a windswept patch of allotments and waste land adjoining the Southern Cemetery at Chorlton.

Once at their destination, Jean Jordan led the way through the undergrowth. She had not gone very far before the Ripper struck her once from behind with a hammer. The force of that single blow would probably have been enough to kill but, not content, he went on to strike her skull another ten times until his violence spent, he crouched panting over the corpse. The predator and the dead prostitute were not alone though, other couples used the area too – working girls and their clients, as well as courting couples – and as the Ripper savoured the kill he saw car headlights come on and heard the sound of an engine being started.

Breathing hard, the Ripper dragged the still-warm body of Jean Jordan towards some bushes. The car's red tail lights disappeared, but seconds later another one arrived and the killer's nerve broke. Leaving Jean concealed in some under-growth, he scuttled back to his car, started the engine and headed for the city centre.

For nine days the body of Jean Jordan lay undiscovered on the bleak waste ground above the cemetery. The area was visited only after dark, and then only by those with little interest in foraging through the undergrowth. Jean's common-law husband Allan had returned home after a drinking binge to find the children alone in the couple's flat, yet he hadn't been anxious. Why should he be? Jean was often away with the girls for days at a time.

However, one person was concerned about the twenty-one-year-old prostitute. Each day since the killing Peter Sutcliffe had been waiting to read or see on a news bulletin that her body had been found. His concern wasn't simply psychotic pride in his evil work and the mission he'd been given by the 'voices'. Sutcliffe was terrified that he had left behind his first clue, a piece of evidence so crucial that even the detectives he held in such contempt could not fail to recognise its significance.

In his haste to leave the scene of the crime the Ripper had forgotten to retrieve the £5 note he'd given to Jean for sex. The note was new and had been in his wage packet just one day before he'd carried out the frenzied murder. There was no alternative; he had to go back, no matter how great the risk.

On Sunday 9 October Peter Sutcliffe set out from his new home in Garden Lane, Heaton, on the best side of Bradford. There had been a house-warming party, at which his father and mother and several of his brothers and sisters had enjoyed an unusually successful family get-together with Sonia. She normally found it difficult to mix with the Sutcliffes, but on this occasion there had been no friction. As the party broke up, Sutcliffe – considerate as ever – insisted on driving his parents back to their home in Bingley, making small talk on the way while his mind raced ahead to the grim task that awaited him on the edge of a Manchester cemetery.

His father and mother safely delivered home, Sutcliffe headed for Manchester. It was late, the roads were clear and he made good time. Once at the waste ground, he set about finding the nine-day-old corpse. It didn't take long. He stripped the body and searched every item of clothing for the incriminating bank note. It wasn't there. Fear and fury gripped Sutcliffe as he pulled at the dead girl's boots, the last possible hiding place for what he must recover – still no £5 note. Where was Jean Jordan's handbag? She had been carrying one when he picked her up. The Ripper pulled aside the undergrowth, searched through bracken and hedges, but still the handbag couldn't be found.

By now the fear had been replaced by a cold and murderous rage. The corpse was mocking him. The dead girl could prove his undoing. With a sharpened screwdriver Sutcliffe set about the remains of Jean Jordan. There was a certain method in his madness, for if her corpse was horribly disfigured and mutilated in a way unassociated with previous Ripper killings, his pursuers could be put off the scent.

Sutcliffe worked in a frenzy on the already decomposing body. Eighteen or twenty times he stabbed her breasts and chest then, warming to his work, he found a large piece of broken glass with a cutting edge and slashed the body from the right knee diagonally to the left shoulder. Finally, he tried to separate Jean's head from her torso. This wasn't one of the Ripper's trademarks, rather the signature of some new criminal lunatic: in the absence of a head, who would see the telltale hammer-blow wounds?

The Ripper slashed at Jean's neck with the shard of glass. It proved unequal to the job but as always he had come prepared – he had brought a hacksaw blade. Still he couldn't separate the head from the body. Frustrated, cold, tired from his exertions and scared now that he might be interrupted, Sutcliffe decided to give up and return home without the piece of evidence he feared could lead the police to his door, as indeed it would.

Sutcliffe's own version of these grisly events is illuminatingly schizoid. When I've talked to him about the death of Jean Jordan, Sutcliffe has restricted himself to complaints about the unfairness of being called the Ripper. Yet in a tape-recording of a conversation with another inmate, made in 1987, he relates the circumstances of the killing with a cold enthusiasm and a gloating attention to detail.

> *Sutcliffe*: 'I read on Sunday about me trying to chop somebody's head off. Well that's a fuckin' fact, because the one, the one time I did that, I went back to Manchester and I knew there were a brand new fiver. And when I were on my way home I just fuckin' realised that. So I had to go back. But I went back nine days later. I went back nine days later to find it, but I couldn't find it anywhere. To

Manchester, you know, where this woman was. Under some bushes, like, you know. I went back there to get the fiver. I went through all that and – the fuckin' stink. I was sick on the grass.'
Patient X: 'And she was still there nine days later?'
Sutcliffe: 'Yeh, yeh, yeh. I were fuckin' sick. It were fuckin' horrible...'

There is no hint of remorse in Sutcliffe's tone during the recording, only bravado in front of a fellow violent inmate of whom he is frightened, and distaste at the smell of Jean Jordan's decomposing body after he'd slashed open her bloated stomach.

In contrast, when recounting the appalling details of his crimes to me, he has never once used coarse language. The Sutcliffe persona that comes across on twenty minutes of tape-recorded conversation is quite different to the version I see during visiting hours in Central Hall. On the ward, among fellow patients, he is tough, earthy and possibly threatening. During visits, he is gentle, affable and painstakingly polite. The only obvious flaw at these times is the whine in his voice.

Having already developed a deep loathing for the Press, he will repeatedly blame them for calling him the Yorkshire Ripper. No amount of patient explanation of the nickname's origins, or reminding him of the fact that the label was used long before he was identified or arrested, will convince him that it is justified.

He says: 'The original Jack the Ripper was a cold-blooded murderer who set out at night with a little black bag of surgical instruments. He crept through London streets, hidden by the fog, and stalked women until he could kill them and dissect them. He removed their internal organs and dismembered their bodies. I've never done anything like that. What I did I was compelled to do, on the orders I was receiving. I didn't have any choice, you see. I believed I had to carry out the orders, and tell no one. That was the real tragedy, not being able to tell anyone.'

He has told me how he would fight against the compulsion to kill – even on one occasion stopping his car outside a Catholic church and going inside to pray to be released, but failing. 'I believed I had been chosen, and I had to go on with the killing.'

To emphasise how the brutality of the murders went against his true nature, Sutcliffe describes how he put his victims out of their misery as efficiently as possible. He says it was 'humane', like the slaughter-house method when pigs are put down.

'It was always over quickly, most of the time it was less than a couple of minutes. I don't think any of them felt any pain. I would always strike them first on the back of the head before they had a chance to experience any fright. That would stun them, then I usually dragged them out of sight and finished them off by stabbing with a knife. I didn't actually wish any of them harm in a personal way. I didn't know any of them, so I couldn't have anything against them personally. I didn't even speak to most of them.'

All this was delivered in a reasoning tone of voice, as if by someone who has been badly misunderstood and now deserves a fair hearing.

Sutcliffe asked me once if I had ever visited a slaughter-house or knew anything of the way that pigs are killed. He said if I'd seen that, I would understand how one blow to the skull would stun, and there would be little or no external bleeding. This, he says, is how he avoided telltale bloodstains on his clothing except for a few times when he had to dispose of a pair of trousers on a garden bonfire. The frenzied mutilation of poor Jean Jordan's body, for example, ruined the smart trousers he had been wearing earlier that evening during the house-warming party.

All the time he talks, Sutcliffe's bulbous eyes are on my face. It is impossible to escape the glare, especially as one cannot move away, once seated with a patient in Central Hall. I feel trapped, as if under a too-bright spotlight, but the effect is even more unpleasant for the eyes burn into mine – not questioning, not accusing, not even threatening;

just burning. The sensation is so discomfiting that I learned always to sit beside him rather than opposite him during a visit, so that our eyes were not locked together so intensely.

I would invite him to pour the tea from the stainless steel canteen teapot, which usually involves some mopping-up afterwards, and to open the packet of Jaffa Cakes. Anything to distract him from the eyeball-to-eyeball examination.

Once, by way of a change, and because I had missed lunch and was hungry, I asked if there was something hot to eat from the canteen. Without thinking, I ordered a steak and kidney pie, and Sutcliffe asked for one too. When it came, however, I simply couldn't touch it. The thought of sharing that sort of meal with the Yorkshire Ripper had completely taken away my appetite, so I had to say I didn't like the look of it, leaving him to eat both helpings while I glanced away.

One day, in the heat of the summer, we were all invited to sit at tables outside Central Hall, in the landscaped grounds of Broadmoor Hospital. Sutcliffe didn't want to do this, nor did most other patients, for nearly all their conversations are overheard and monitored by the 'screws', and the way that the tables and chairs had been set up outside looked as if they would be closer than ever. We had no choice, however, so everyone trooped outside, and most conversations were held at just above whispering level. It was here, in the sunshine, that I noticed for the first time how badly scarred Sutcliffe's left eye is, from an attack in Parkhurst Prison when another inmate lunged at him with a broken glass coffee jar. A two-and-a-half-inch scar across the top of the left eye now makes it appear slightly smaller than the right eye. The scar continues down his cheek, hidden by the black beard' but emerges for a further five and a half inches under his jawline – the result of a total of eighty-four stitches. Sitting there in the glare of the sun, he narrowed both eyes and explained that his right eye had been damaged by welding equipment when he worked as a teenager at an engineering factory in Bingley, his home town.

We talked about Sonia, and Sutcliffe complained that she no longer visited so frequently. This upsets him a great deal, and on this occasion, just for a moment, I thought he was actually weeping. He wasn't. His eyes were streaming from the chronic hay fever he has suffered from since childhood. His skin looked sickly and sallow as a result of nine years' incarceration and an uninspired diet. Often he will stay on the ward for days, writing endless letters after carrying out his duties of cleaning the bathrooms and toilets. No fresh-air fiend, he will breathe only the pungent mix of disinfectant, overcooked vegetables and other people's sweat, common to all institutional life.

The result is unpleasant, particularly when added to Sutcliffe's most self-loathed problem – his feet smell. Other members of his family used to mock him for putting his shoes outside on a windowsill at night and fastidiously washing his socks, but in Broadmoor he cannot even do this.

At close quarters, under the merciless glare of the midday sun, Sutcliffe looks at his worst – overweight, pallid, and unsavoury. But not frightening, although he sometimes boasts about his power to frighten. He told me with relish how he once scared a woman psychiatrist who was examining him while on remand at Armley jail.

'First off, she told me to strip completely and turn round slowly in front of her. I said she must be a Peeping Tom. I said she ought to strip too. I was only joking, though. She was a bit too chubby for me. When we got talking, she asked me if I considered I was a danger to all women, or just to prostitutes. I said if she thought I was dangerous, she shouldn't be in my cell alone with me. I told her all I had to do was to pick up her ballpoint pen and I could stab her through one eye and pierce her brain. She turned pale, and a few minutes later the screws arrived to ask if she was all right. She'd obviously pressed the panic button in the cell. I just laughed, I did.'

He laughed now, while he remembered it, and I thought of his last victim, student Jacqueline Hill whose dead, staring eyes had provoked him until he took his sharpened screwdriver and stabbed her through one eye, piercing her brain.

CHAPTER TWO

Chosen

The enduring image of Peter Sutcliffe at his most murderous is of a dark, thick-set man moving stealthily through the shadows of an ill-lit street, ready to strike and desperate to kill. A terrifying, almost demonic, figure, hell bent on his mission, with hammers, screwdrivers, knives and a hacksaw blade all concealed in his clothing. His target – simply the next solitary woman he saw.

For six years this nightmare haunted the nation. Women everywhere went in mortal dread of the Ripper; husbands and families feared him on their behalf; detectives began to believe he was evil incarnate, and would never be caught. The Ripper was a character from a horror film, come to life. He prowled the midnight streets, a part of the darkness, a ruthless killing machine.

———— o ————

It is difficult to imagine, then, any link with the severely underweight baby boy born shortly after 10p.m. on 2 June 1946 at Bingley and Shipley Maternity Hospital. At that time the mortality rate for newborn babies was high, and doctors feared that the 5-lb infant would not survive the night. But Peter William Sutcliffe, as he was to be christened, had the all-important will to live. He clung on to life successfully, and went home in his mother's arms ten days later. It was almost as if some unseen protector had given him the strength he needed and had marked him for a purpose, a future mission.

If that was the case, however, there was certainly no outward sign of it over the next nineteen years. The whole of Sutcliffe's childhood and most of his teenage years were officially 'irrelevant and uninteresting', according to psychiatrists. There was no major trauma, no single incident that was psychologically devastating, no display of disturbed behaviour and no family history of mental illness.

His was a typical northern working-class upbringing. His father, John Sutcliffe, earned his living in the textile industry. The mills had brought prosperity and were the major employers in that corner of West Yorkshire. The work was hard and monotonous, often involving night shifts, while the days were spent in a struggle to sleep against a noisy background of children playing in the streets, neighbours calling in for a chat, and John's wife downstairs surrounded by endless washing and household chores.

It was not surprising, then, that John Sutcliffe liked a drink or two at the end of the working week.

A physically impressive man, he played for a local football side and was an accomplished all-rounder in the cricket team. Despite the responsibilities of a growing family, he also found time to perform with local amateur dramatic and operatic societies. Altogether, he was a larger-than-life character, but just as he could be amusing and good company outside the home, he could be moody and bad-tempered with his own family. Peter Sutcliffe remembers his father as an impatient, unpredictable man: 'If you weren't interested in cricket or football, then he wasn't interested in you.'

He claims his father picked on him, and when he recalls one particular incident, it is almost as if he has shed thirty years. In the words that an eleven-year-old would have chosen, and with the same inflection in his voice, Peter Sutcliffe tells of sitting close to the television in the family's front room.

'I were sitting right up close to television. I suppose it were on quite loud because I never heard me Dad coming into the room. The next thing I knew he'd thrown a beer glass right across room. It hit me on the side of the head and hurt me. There were blood pouring down me face. I didn't know what had happened, first off. Then I were really frightened because me Dad started shouting and carrying on at me. He said he'd been telling me to turn the telly down, but I never heard him.

'Me Mam came into the room then, saying "what's all the fuss about, our Pete?" I told her, "Mam, he's just thrown this at me, for nothing." It were just like me Dad to come back from the pub, drink more beer, and then take his temper out on me.'

John Sutcliffe had been exasperated with his son's slow development and physical weakness almost since the day he had been brought home from hospital. Sensing his father's disappointment, the boy was drawn ever closer to his mother, clinging to her both emotionally and physically. She did nothing to loosen the ties. Sutcliffe says now: 'I had my mother all to myself for two years. That's why there was always such a special bond between us, a much stronger bond than she had with my five brothers and sisters.'

Kathleen Sutcliffe was, by all accounts, a hard-working, long-suffering woman of Irish descent. She tirelessly washed, cooked and cleaned for her husband and six children, without complaint. She gave the family its stability and insisted her sons and daughters were brought up as Catholics, just as she had been. It was under pressure from her that the family made its first move, from a stone cottage on the outskirts of Bingley to a new council house in Manor Road, Cottingley, when Peter was four and a half, his sister, Anne, two, and his baby brother, Michael, just months old.

The Sutcliffes' new home was palatial by comparison with the old. Whereas one had reeked of damp, the other smelled of new paint and recently dried cement. The contrast could not have been greater for a family accustomed to living in conditions that could only have been described as somewhat primitive.

The Ferncliffe estate itself perched incongruously at the edge of bleak moorland, with uniform streets clinging to a steep hillside where once sheep had grazed. Similar estates were going up all over the country in the post-war years, as the Government made housing one of its priorities. The Sutcliffe children were more fortunate than most in avoiding an innercity upbringing. The moors were their playground, rather than some derelict building or bomb site, while instead of smoke-polluted urban air, they breathed in the healthy freshness of the moors and the Yorkshire Dales to the north.

When he was just four, Peter was sent to St Joseph's Roman Catholic primary school in Bingley. A photograph taken at the time shows a tiny figure, painfully small for his age, staring through plastic-framed NHS spectacles at a world populated by giants. The child looks bewildered, perhaps even frightened. There is no hint of the self-confident smile seen in photographs taken in later years once the 'voices' had begun shaping his destiny.

The child did little or nothing to distinguish himself at St Joseph's. He certainly didn't excel academically, but managed to avoid the scrapes many of his age found so irresistible. According to his school reports, he was an unremarkable child, quite bright sometimes, a little shy perhaps, but always obedient. It was no surprise to the boy's teachers when he failed to win an eleven-plus place at St Bede's Grammar School. Like so many who passed through their hands, he was to end up at the local Roman Catholic secondary modern school, Cottingley Manor.

Sutcliffe's father, John, has said that on visits to St Joseph's he had looked over the playground wall to see his son standing alone, watching the other children. The boy, he decided, was going to be a loner. Peter Sutcliffe has a different version of events, claiming that his father came to the school only once, to pick him up for a dental appointment. 'He saw me waiting in a corner of the playground, wi' me coat on and ready to go,' he says. 'He got it all wrong as usual, and went on about me having no friends.'

Sutcliffe says he had plenty of friends, just like all the other boys. It was they, he insists, who told him not to bother with exams. 'You don't want to go to the grammar school,' they said. 'It'll be more fun if we all stick together and go to Cottingley Manor.' With no encouragement at home for any serious schoolwork, he took the easy option.

What talent Sutcliffe possessed – and he is certainly a gifted, if untutored, artist – lay dormant during his years at Cottingley Manor. For a period he truanted regularly, hiding in the loft of the family's council house reading comics before he was discovered.

At home he played with neighbours' children. The Bus Shelter Gang, as they called themselves, conducted their games in the street. Wendy Turner, who lived locally at the time, recalls that Peter Sutcliffe set himself apart from the gang's more boisterous activities. 'He avoided all the scuffling, and never got into fights.'

If the boy had ambitions to get a good job after leaving school, they were never to be realised, and his artistic talent remained hidden or went unrecognised. Sutcliffe made no attempt to capitalise on his intelligence, assessed by doctors at the time of his trial as well above average. He was, according to his headmaster, Gerald Battersby, 'a very ordinary boy who did not stand out at school in any way at all'. So when he left Cottingley Manor at fifteen, Sutcliffe's future seemed depressingly predictable. With no formal qualifications his options were limited, but then the same was just as true for many of his contemporaries.

Two years earlier, in the summer of 1959 when Sutcliffe was thirteen, the family had outgrown its first council home on the Ferncliffe estate and had moved, not very far, to another house just across the Aire Valley. Kathleen Sutcliffe's mother whom the children called Grandma Coonan, was now a near neighbour and young Peter Sutcliffe became a frequent visitor to her home. He had lived with her as a small child while his mother was pregnant with Anne, and the boy and the old lady were to remain very close. Like Kathleen, Lottie Coonan was a devout Catholic, under whose influence Peter regularly attended Mass and became an altar boy. With five other young children to look after, his mother was frequently too busy to go to Mass with him but Lottie was not.

The new house was larger than the old but, even so, Sutcliffe and his younger brother, Mick, had to share a bedroom until they left home. As with all large working-class families, the kitchen was the focal point of this noisy, busy household.

The contrast between Peter and his brother was marked. Mick was big, brash and boastful; by comparison Peter was quiet, self-conscious and watchful. In later years, as Mick began to take an interest in girls, his elder brother would listen avidly to details of his sexual escapades. He rarely volunteered anything about his own experiences.

By the time he left school at fifteen, Peter had begun tinkering with motor cycles. He showed some aptitude and it was not surprising that his first job was to be with a local engineering firm, Brearley Fairbank, although he left after only seven months without completing his apprenticeship.

For a brief period he worked alongside his father at the mill, then for the next year and a half Peter worked at Fibre Products in Bingley. After that time he claimed his health was being affected by the work – fibres were getting into his lungs – and he quit, saying he needed a job 'out in the open air'. He achieved that ambition in 1964 by becoming a grave-digger with the local council at Bingley Cemetery. It was in the same year that he suffered the first profound emotional shock of his life.

Sutcliffe's grandmother, Lottie Coonan, was now living with the family at 57 Cornwall Road, where she had her own bedroom but enjoyed being a part of the bustling household. Now eighty, her health was deteriorating and her hearing and eyesight were poor. Peter vividly remembers an incident which he believes led to her death. Speaking of it in Broadmoor Hospital today, he claims he once thought he was directly responsible for this.

'I was totally broken up about it. I blamed myself. She had very poor eyesight. She was coming down the stairs, clump, clump, clump. My sister had a little baby kitten, a little fluffy kitten. She was playing with it, and it ran to the bottom of the stairs and my grandma was three steps away. I was sat in

41

the kitchen and I could see the bottom of the stairs where they curved round towards the front door. I saw her foot coming down, and there were just two more steps. I shouted out: "Grandma look out, there's a little kitten there!" Her reactions were slow and she carried on coming down, she couldn't see properly. She crunched it right on its head, crunched it. It was dead and there was blood gushing out of its mouth all over the front door step. I was only eighteen at the time. I said to her: "Grandma, that was really stupid and clumsy." I had never said a wrong word to her before. But seeing the kitten dead and everything, I just let myself go.

'She was dead within a week. She was eighty, but there was nothing wrong with her. I was her favourite. Just before she died she was calling out, asking for me. I told her I was sorry I'd spoken to her like that. All she could say was: "I'd have given anything not have killed that little kitten." She was really sad. She just went to bed and never got up again. She had a blood clot and I believed it was triggered by what had happened.

'I was there when she died. Me Mam was there as well, just the two of us. Grandma was calling out for her husband who'd died donkeys' years before. She said: "Tom, I'm coming." It was very sad for me. But she wanted someone to be there. I saw her when she was dead before the undertaker came, and I saw her again in the coffin. She was buried in the cemetery and I spent a lot of time going to her grave and taking flowers and plants. I used to say some prayers and make sure the grave was neat, with the grass clipped round it.'

There's no doubt that Sutcliffe was deeply affected by the death of his grandmother, but there is an unhealthy relish in his tone when he recounts the experience now, and it is unsavoury anyway to hear a mass murderer affecting such selective grief when he has brought so much suffering and sadness to others.

Lottie Coonan was buried in the Catholic plot at Bingley Cemetery. Once Sutcliffe began working there in 1964, the year she died, he could tend the grave regularly.

Although his grandmother's death weighed heavily on his mind, he was beginning to find life generally quite agreeable. He was making friends among his workmates, earning enough to buy the Teddy Boy-style clothes he and his contemporaries in the town still considered fashionable, and could also afford to indulge his growing passion for motor-cycles. Sutcliffe was to buy a succession of powerful motor-bikes, some of them the envy of the crowd he associated with. They also drew admiring glances from the grammar school girls who would chat to the grave-diggers during their lunch break.

There was a camaraderie among those working at the cemetery, perhaps inspired by the grim nature of the job. During the hours of daylight the cemetery was an almost pleasant place to be, but as twilight gathered, Sutcliffe and the others would retreat to the light and warmth of their 'mess room', where they brewed tea, played darts, swapped stories and teased each other mercilessly on occasions. Sutcliffe says he remembers some 'great laughs' there.

Much has been said about Peter Sutcliffe's strange and sinister behaviour at the cemetery, his ghoulish sense of humour. At the time of his trial those who had worked with the Ripper described some of his more distasteful graveyard pranks. Sutcliffe's friend, Laurie Ashton, recalled one particularly strange incident. 'One time, while we were re-opening an old grave, Pete brought out a skull and chased some girls from the Bingley Grammar School close by with it. He seemed to find it a great joke. Another day he wanted to return to the mortuary adjoining the cemetery to examine a couple of bodies. He thought that was funny too.'

Other workmates have told of Sutcliffe climbing into a newly dug grave to open up a coffin. They claimed he would lift the cloth placed over the corpse's face and stare intently into its eyes for minutes at a time. Sutcliffe is said to have enjoyed working with bodies. He would secrete himself among coffins in the cemetery chapel, covered with a shroud, and when his workmates appeared would groan hideously and slowly lift it. 'It gave us quite a nasty fright,' said one former workmate, Gary Jackson.

Another colleague at the time, Eric Robinson, recalled Sutcliffe stealing rings from corpses. 'He told his sister she could have one for her wedding, but when he said where it came from she jumped back in horror. He thought that was a big laugh.'

Robinson said he was convinced that the Ripper killings 'were bred in that cemetery'. He said Sutcliffe was so keen to look at the corpses in coffins about to be buried that he would jump down into the grave and open them, sometimes before the family and other mourners had filed out of the cemetery gate. He said Sutcliffe was particularly interested in the very old graves, some of them from the seventeenth and eighteenth centuries. 'I heard he used to get in among the skeletons and root around. I think he got a kick out of it. He used to throw the bones around.' Robinson said Sutcliffe enjoyed his occasional stints as a mortuary attendant, when he would wash bodies on the slab and clean knives and scalpels used during post-mortem examinations.

'One night after we'd been out drinking together

he brought out a key for the mortuary and suggested we went and looked at the bodies. I didn't fancy the idea at all.'

Ashton said Sutcliffe enjoyed washing down the bodies for undertakers, and would often go into the mortuary alone after dark. 'God knows what he was doing in there. I think they should have the whole graveyard reconsecrated. There may be dead people in there who still need laying to rest.'

Sutcliffe denies his worst reported excesses while working at the cemetery, although he will admit that he took part in some high-spirited pranks. He now adopts a hushed and reverential tone when talking of his job at the graveyard and vividly remembers taking part in funeral services. As the minister intoned the words '.... earth to earth, ashes to ashes..', he would fling the first handful of soil down onto the coffin in the newly dug grave.

'I saw some terrible things when I worked there. I'll never get over them even though I've seen some bad things in my life. There was this schoolgirl, Joyce Creasley, from the grammar school next door. She died of a brain tumour, she was only sixteen. She had a boyfriend of the same age. He just wouldn't leave the graveside. We lowered the coffin down and he just burst into tears and went hysterical. I was doing the 'ashes to ashes' business, sprinkling the earth onto the coffin. He jumped into the grave. I just couldn't stop him.

'The boy kept saying, "I want to be buried here with her." It was horrible. I didn't like to forcibly restrain him, but I had to get him in some sort of armlock. I shouted to a chap bringing earth on a dumper truck. I made the boyfriend go with him, and the police were called. I just carried on digging. I heard afterwards that the boy wasn't arrested or anything, but it were very unpleasant.

'Afterwards I found out from one of the lads that I knew the girl. I hadn't known her name but he told me it was Joyce. I knew a few of them who used to come and chat to us if we were digging anywhere near the boundary wall between the cemetery and the school. They used to call out: "Here, Mister, can we come and see what you're doing?" I used to say, "No, you'd better stay over there. You wouldn't like what you'd see."

'I found out that this Joyce, who used to chat to me a lot, had been at school one day and just fallen down. The teachers thought she'd fainted, but it were a brain tumour. She just fell down dead in front of everyone.'

Talking to the girls over the cemetery wall was about as close as Peter Sutcliffe got to the opposite sex during this period. Generally his evenings and weekends were spent in the company of his mates. Sutcliffe and his friends, most of them fellow grave-diggers from Bingley Cemetery, would travel on their motor cycles to pubs and cafes. They were on the lookout for girls, but most evenings would be spent listening to pop music on the juke box or discussing engines.

Sutcliffe was shy with girls, although he dressed to attract attention and spent hours in front of a mirror barbering his beard and trimming his bushy black hair, so that at first glance he was quite strikingly good-looking.

Quieter than most, he was still one of the lads, and says today that he was always willing to join in if there was any trouble. He believes the aftermath of one particular gang fight, which took place in 1966, a year before he first heard 'the voices', may have done him permanent injury. 'I've told doctors all about it. I even mentioned it at my trial, but no one took me seriously. They all think they know better than I do. None of them bothered to investigate it properly.

'Five of us on our bikes went out to Dick Hudson's pub on the moors above Gilstead. A coach-load of about fifty lads came in the bar and later this fight broke out in the gents' toilets. Us lot decided to leave. But one of this lot came up to me in the car park. I was sitting on me bike. It were a BSA 250 that night. I knew he wanted trouble because he felt safe like, there were so many of them. I put me head down quick just as he were aiming a punch, and his fist smashed into my crash helmet. He reeled backwards, swearing. I jumped off me bike, had him down and gave him a kicking, a right good kicking. My mates were putting the boot into some of the others in the car park. But then loads more of them came streaming out of the pub, so we decided to call it a day.

'We rode off on our bikes. I suppose I went too fast down the steep hill we used to call the Woolpack. One of my tyres was a bit flat and as I turned sharp right the bike skidded and I flew over the handlebars. My mates picked me up and took me to a house nearby. I was passed out, unconscious. When I came round I saw my helmet. It were smashed, like an eggshell. The woman in the house told me I'd been unconscious for ages. But I soon felt better so we never called an ambulance. Now I wish I'd gone to the casualty, or at least seen a doctor. I had headaches for a long time after, really bad ones.'

Sutcliffe has remained resentful that the jury at his Old Bailey trial was instructed to attach no significance whatsoever to the accident. Prosecuting counsel, Sir Michael Havers – then Attorney General – told the court that despite the accused man's claim that he'd been knocked unconscious in the crash, doctors examining him disagreed. He'd not been unconscious, said Sir Michael, and had not suffered brain damage.

While the relevance of the motor-cycle accident will always be disputed, Sutcliffe and the doctors who examined him are at one over the significance of the hallucinations which overtook him at Bingley Cemetery the following year. Sutcliffe's first experience of the voices that were to haunt him and later inspire such murderous violence appears to have come without any external stimuli whatsoever. There was no tremendous shock or physical trauma, no series of events so catastrophic that he could simply no longer cope with real life. The truth of his slow but sure slide into paranoid schizophrenia is perhaps more chilling.

His psychosis was a sort of cranial time-bomb, ticking away undetected, year by year, until it exploded with a killing force that would leave thirteen women dead and mutilated. To all intents and purposes, he still functioned normally but his hold on reality was growing more and more tenuous.

Sutcliffe says now that he had been suffering mild depression for some time before hearing the voices, before his personal time-bomb was detonated on a hillside in Bingley Cemetery. A close friend, Ronnie Wilson, had lost his father and mother within days of each other. Sutcliffe knew the family well, he and Ronnie both being Catholics and having been to school together, and he shared his friend's grief.

Wilson's father had died of a brain tumour and his mother gassed herself shortly afterwards.

Sutcliffe remembers visiting the Wilsons' home in Ryecroft Avenue, Cottingley before the double tragedy and seeing his friend's father standing weakly against the wall, shaking his head from side to side. Sutcliffe, who'd called to invite Ronnie out for a game of snooker, recalls his friend saying: 'Dad, Dad. Please sit down. You must sit down before you harm yourself.'

It was such memories that Sutcliffe claims were occupying his thoughts as he dug a new grave one summer's day in 1967, next to the plot where Ronnie Wilson's mother had been buried. As he bent over his spade the clock stopped – and the time-bomb exploded in his head.

'I heard a mumbling voice. I looked up but didn't see anybody. I though it was the others, calling from behind trees, first off. Then I got out of the grave and walked up a steep slope. I walked to the top, but there was no one there at all. I heard the same sound again. The "voice" seemed to be coming from the top of a cross on a gravestone. It was an echoing voice, vague and distant, and it repeated itself two or three times, and it was direct from the stone itself. I'll never forget it.

'I read the inscription on the tombstone. It was in Polish, and I didn't understand it. I remember a strange word that might have meant JESUS. Somehow I translated the main inscription to mean "We Be Echo". I decided it was some sort of message from God. I was working in a cemetery, but it didn't frighten me. It was just a job.

'The mumbling voice had a strange effect. I felt I was privileged to hear it. It had started to rain and I remember looking from the top of the slope over the valley and feeling I'd just experienced something fantastic. I looked across the valley, and all around, and thought of Heaven and Earth and how insignificant we all were. But I felt so important at that moment. I had been selected.'

CHAPTER THREE

Secrets

The time-bomb that had been ticking away in Peter Sutcliffe's head, and which was to explode, not fiercely, but with the muffled sound of 'voices' from the heavens, would thrust him into his own private world. It was to be a secret, exclusive place, accessible only to him, the chosen one. God had selected him for a special mission.

In the bustling mill-town community where Sutcliffe still lived his real life, as opposed to this fantasy existence soon to come, there was probably only one other person who inhabited such an intensely private world, though of a completely different kind.

Sonia Szurma was the daughter of East European refugees who believed that they must protect her from the vulgarities of working-class life in the north of England and, accordingly, isolated her and her sister, Marianne, within their council house home on the outskirts of Bradford.

The two girls did not mix with other children. They spoke a mixture of Ukranian and Czech at home, had their clothes made for them by their mother in a style curiously different from the clothes of other local girls, and spent their evenings in the pursuit of knowledge through their father's discussions with them and his readings to them. Sonia, in particular, would accompany him on long walks, during which he laid down the lofty principles she was to follow all her childhood and into maturity.

It was quite against her father's rules when Sonia, aged sixteen, went to a disco in a local Bradford pub one evening, having told her parents she was attending an opera performance. There, amid the noise and the music, Sonia met a man who was her total social opposite, and was attracted to him. Thus the private worlds of Sonia Szurma and Peter Sutcliffe collided on St Valentine's Day, 1967. It was later that same year that Sutcliffe was to undergo the major spiritual experience of his life, when first he heard the 'voices' calling to him in Bingley cemetery.

In the space of a few months the dull routine of Sutcliffe's daily life was overtaken by two major influences – one of them deeply emotional, the other deeply disturbing, and ultimately sinister.

———— O ————

By the age of twenty, Peter Sutcliffe had developed few social graces but until now he had hardly needed them. Minimal good manners were required at home, and his idea of a sophisticated night out was to put a leather jacket over his gaudy suit, get on his motor bike and head off on a pub crawl with the lads who worked with him at the cemetery. The grave-diggers would have a laugh and a joke spiced with some flesh-creeping humour from their day's work, and most of them would make a rough-and-ready approach to the local girls they met. Despite his rather flashy good looks, however, Sutcliffe would hang back during these exchanges, for he had a poor repertoire of flirtatious remarks and was awkward about opening any sort of conversation with a girl.

If he found it difficult to chat up the other girls, he found it almost impossible with Sonia Szurma, who sat apart from the crowd, smiling thinly at him. She wore home-made clothes and little make-up. Slim and angular, she walked awkwardly on wooden-soled shoes, but her thatch of curly dark hair and large, thoughtful, grey eyes were striking, almost glamorous. Sutcliffe was intrigued. 'Trying to get to know her was like trying to climb Mount Everest. She was remote and unattainable. I was fascinated by her from the start.'

The two of them nervously attempted conversation in the noise and smoky fug of the back bar at the Royal Standard pub in Manningham Lane, Bradford, one of the grave-diggers' favourite haunts. The juke-box churned out Sixties rock music and the teenagers danced under dimmed lights. The big solid Victorian pub, with its stained glass and highly decorated wall mirrors, was regularly crammed with youngsters. Set on the outskirts of the city, it was a natural meeting place and starting point for a tour of Bradford's pubs or clubs.

Outside, the cold and damp gleamed from the rooftops and brick-work of blackened terraced houses, and from the rutted cobblestones of mean side-turnings where sodium street lamps barely lit the gloomy alleyways and uninviting backyards. On Manningham Lane itself, a main arterial road leading eventually to the moors beyond Bingley and Shipley, the prostitutes stood in desultory little groups, hidden in the shadows between the street lamps.

Sonia's parents would not have wanted her to be part of the crowd who visited the Royal Standard. It went against everything in her upbringing – and they had put her upbringing before everything else in their lives. She knew instinctively that this Peter Sutcliffe, whom she had just met and whom she intended to see again soon, would not be warmly welcomed by her family. It was to be some time before he was formally introduced to them.

Sutcliffe, however, could not wait to bring his new girlfriend home to meet the family. When he did, the culture shock for Sonia was so great that she did little but perch on the edge of her chair and make sparse conversation in a voice that rarely rose above a whisper. It is almost certain that she had never before entered a household like the one at 57 Cornwall Road, Bingley. Taken there on the back of Sutcliffe's powerful Norton Dominator bike, she had her first glimpse of a way of life familiar to 99 per cent of ordinary northern families. Yet to her it was like being in a foreign country. Instead of the order and formality of her own home, with its unused front parlour and strict regime, there was the untidy litter of belongings strewn about by six boisterous boys and girls. Kathleen, their mother, had given up the unequal struggle for any sort of orderliness, finding that the daily cleaning, washing and cooking took up all her time and energy.

John Sutcliffe, loud-mouthed head of the family, found his usual blunt approach to newcomers to be unsuccessful with Sonia. Although in many ways a stereotypical Yorkshireman, he was like an alien being to her. She disliked him from the start and despite eight years of courtship with his son, there was never a bond of any kind between them. Just as Sonia found nothing to respect or like about him, he found nothing to amuse, entertain or attract about her.

John Sutcliffe was eventually to meet her parents and visit her home, but he remained baffled by the feelings of superiority which she made so obvious. He never understood how she could lay claim to such a high degree of respect and dignity, and an elevated social status. All he could see was that the family were poor, lived a quiet, almost repressed, life with the door firmly closed to outsiders, and had failed to absorb any of the fun and neighbourliness that was there for the taking on a sprawling council estate like theirs.

The fact was that the Szurmas believed they were different from their immediate neighbours. If they had not been forced to flee their homeland, they might have been wealthy. Even without that wealth, they still remained convinced of their social and intellectual superiority, aware that they did not belong among uneducated, unsophisticated members of the lower orders. They were different, their children were different, and council house or no council house they were going to stick to their own culture and shun the rest.

Bohdan Szurma was barely thirty when he was offered refugee status in England in 1947 at the end of a painful war spent partly as a Ukranian incarcerated in concentration camps for two years. He had attended Prague University and had planned to become a lecturer. He met and married a pretty local girl who was training to be a nurse.

When the choice between a bleak, blank future or a new life in the West was put to him, Bohdan Szurma made the same decision as many thousands of his countrymen. Politically homeless, they saw no future but drudgery in Eastern Europe. They accepted the chance of freedom in Britain, even though it meant a lowly, state-owned home to live in and a menial job in the cotton mills.

The offer was not open to married couples, so Bohdan travelled to Bradford and the mills alone. His wife, Maria, was left behind to try to persuade the authorities that she, too, deserved the chance of a new life abroad. She still remembers the fierce questioning she underwent from a short-tempered commandant in charge of the selection process. 'I told them I was from the Ukraine, and named the town where I said I had been born. Of course I had never really been there in my life. He produced a map of the country, and asked me to show him my birthplace. I simply couldn't. I broke down in tears and confessed that I was married, I was missing my husband and I wanted to join him in England. I was amazed when he gave in, and said I could go too. I'll never forget that moment.'

The new life that the couple had dreamed of was centred around one of the poorest, most run-down council estates in Bradford, in the innercity suburb of Clayton. After living in rented rooms for some time, young Mrs Szurma had become pregnant, whereupon the couple were turned out and finally rehoused by the council.

Number 44 Tanton Crescent was on a turning at the top of the estate, a drab cream-painted square box with draughty metal windows, a scrappy front garden, and a view of a wind-blown rubbish tip at the rear of uniform rows of houses.

Bohdan Szurma, tall, upright and powerful-looking, was soon defeated by the tedium and rigours of his poorly paid job at the mill. He was to suffer continuous ill-health until he finally gave in and spent all his days at home, drawing state benefit and acknowledging that his dream of freedom and a good life in the West had not, and never would, come true. He became reflective, quiet, brooding, withdrawn.

His wife was bustling, talkative and excitable. With their two daughters, born within eighteen months of one another, the couple ran a household that was in every way different from that of their neighbours, and took a pride specifically in that.

The food Mrs Szurma cooked was based on the soups and stews she herself had eaten during her childhood in Czechoslovakia, while her husband made his own wine. The kitchen was the hub of the family. There, where the only heating came from an antiquated gas oven with the door continually open, condensation ran in unhealthy rivulets down the cold window-panes and the dark red and cream paintwork on the walls and doors. An oilcoth covered the kitchen table, where Sonia and her sister sat on wooden chairs to do their homework under their father's watchful eye.

The family hardly ever spoke English at home.

Bohdan Szurma encouraged his daughters to be artistic and musical. He played the violin himself, solemnly, a dignified, increasingly stooped figure putting on a fairly accomplished performance in the unheated, pristine front room of the house, for all the world as if it were his salon, his musician's studio.

When his daughters came home from the local junior school, he would set his own homework for them. Marianne was a skilful, natural little pianist, while Sonia was the 'artistic' one. They did not need, and were not allowed, any play-time or entertainment outside their own home.

Sonia says she was so close to her father, as a child, that for several years her mother 'simply did not exist'. They would leave the house together and walk for hours, sometimes in silence. 'I was very slim and tomboyish, more like a son to him,' she says. 'Marianne was more girlish, more feminine. My father taught me everything, his wisdom and his learning. I respected him, and still respect him, more than anyone else alive.'

Sonia learned her high moral standards from her father. He also instilled in her, among other things, a steadfast belief that, as a family, they were morally, intellectually and in every other way better than others.

The two girls were so isolated from the rough, down-to-earth way of life going on around them that they grew up with different speaking voices from almost everyone else in Bradford. Sonia has a deliberately cultivated 'posh' accent, overlaying the undeniable flat northern vowels. The words come out breathily and haughtily, so that when Peter Sutcliffe's family met her they thought she was 'right stuck up'. Her sister, Marianne, has an unmistakably Eastern European accent, guttural and unattractive, which Peter Sutcliffe swears is an affectation.

So firmly did Sonia believe in her family's intellectual and cultural standing that she says she shunned the Sutcliffes from the start. 'Pete and his sister, Anne, were so like their mother. The rest of the family is riff-raff. I completely disassociated myself from them, always. Pete came into *my* world.'

She believes that she takes after her father in 'every way'. 'I have his strength and self-discipline, and a wealth of education passed on by him. He studied medicine and other subjects at university, and he came from a high-class wealthy family. But he joined the resistance movement in Prague, and lost everything. Perhaps if my parents had been able to stay, life would have been very different. We might have gone to live in France. Even so, I don't feel I have lost anything. I had a wonderful education from my father. And, thanks to him, I am classless, not stuck in a rut.'

She said her father was her main inspiration, whereas her mother was the soft, sentimental one. 'Marianne and I have inherited things from both of them. It's wonderful for us.' She said her mother showed her emotions, which was probably more healthy. 'I bottle them up like my father does.'

She remembers that even as a five-year-old, when she simply longed for a Lego set for Christmas, she fought off her disappointment over the presents she received instead, brought it under control and would not allow herself to express it. 'I would never actually ask for something, certainly never beg for it, like other children.'

She talks of her special closeness to her father, but says with a note of disappointment that he has not told her everything about himself – his experiences in the concentration camps or his romance with Sonia's mother. She says, curiously, that she 'could never attempt to write his life story'.

It was her mother, whom Sonia calls Ma, who insisted on a practical career. Her own harsh memories of wartime poverty prompted her to discourage Sonia's dreams of becoming a sculptress when she left school. Later, Sonia's pieces of hand-made pottery, exhibited around the house, came to be a source of great amusement to Peter Sutcliffe's family, who smirked and sneered at them, wondering out loud what the various shapes were meant to be. Sonia took this as yet another example of their uncouthness and lack of culture. She had nothing but contempt for the way John Sutcliffe had ignored his children's lack of progress at school. It was apparently no surprise to her at all that none of the Sutcliffe children had attained a single qualification between them by the time they left school. 'Pete and I were miles apart, educationally, I know, but we hit it off right from the start. We were always close. He is very well read, and he's taught me many things, just as I was able to pass on to him my knowledge of art and history.' Sonia took Sutcliffe to the celebrated Tutankhamun Exhibition at the British Museum in 1971, where they stood in a queue for several hours. It was part of his 'education'.

Whatever Sonia's lofty concept of her childhood and upbringing, her mother's is an endearingly sentimental version. Mrs Szurma remembers that even as a schoolgirl in Prague, England was always 'the land of my dreams'. Consequently, she worked hard at her English lessons in the hope that she might one day visit 'that wonderful free country'.

She goes on: 'By the outbreak of the Second World War that was to irrevocably change so many lives, fate played a part in enabling my childhood wishes to come true. In 1945, with that terrible war thankfully at an end, my newly married husband and I had both suffered unmentionable tragic personal losses. But we were alive, and we had each other. Even though my husband had barely survived the concentration camps, and when finally freed was given only six months to live, there was now hope and a future to look forward to.

'So, we were to be sent to England. Like any new couple starting out in life together, we were apprehensive but thrilled at the prospect of being given a chance to start again in a free country. We knew we had to try to put the past dreadful six years of war behind us and build our future. When we arrived in England, our only possessions were the clothes we had on us. But the English people were very kind and helped us to feel welcome.'

She says their world was complete when their daughters were born: 'Each day brought new pleasures and happiness, with the two girls taking their first steps and becoming a constant source of delight and joy. Like any caring parents, we only wanted the best for our daughters. No sacrifice was too great.'

Mrs Szurma enjoyed making and knitting all the girls' clothes, and says they 'looked a picture'. She was very proud when people commented on how nice they looked. 'But all too soon, they started going to school. I remember the first day when I took them and then cried to myself all the way home.'

They were very good children, she says, and worked hard at their lessons. No one was prouder than Mr and Mrs Szurma when they received first prizes every speech day. From very early days it was apparent that the elder daughter, Marianne, had a natural gift for music, and everything was done to encourage her with private lessons. She passed all her music exams with ease, and at eighteen took her teacher's diploma beginning her studies at the Royal Academy of Music, in London, where she had been awarded a place. She then pursued a successful career, performing and teaching.

Mrs Szurma is particularly proud of her younger daughter, Sonia, displaying a mother's fond over-statement when she discusses her achievements: 'Sonia's gifts lay in the fine arts, especially in sculpture. She has exhibited her works and even her earliest pieces, being very original, have always been greatly sought after by art collectors. In addition, Sonia had a special talent for teaching – a job which she carried out to her own high professional standards. Many were the parents who expressed their personal gratitude for what Sonia had achieved with their children, both gifted and disadvantaged.'

Like every other mother, she dreamed of her children one day meeting and finding a partner for life, and she was 'very happy' with both of her daughters' choices. 'In their own way, I knew they would make good husbands and provide for my girls' futures.'

When Sonia brought her 'young man' home, Mrs Szurma and her husband were favourably impressed by his manners, courteousness and respect for his elders, and they learned that he was well thought of by the many people who knew him in his home town of Bingley.

'Pete was made very welcome in our home and became the son we never had,' she says. 'He willingly helped us in all sorts of ways. No job was too much trouble for him. He encouraged me to learn to drive and patiently taught me, for which I am grateful to this day. He was able to repair most household appliances for me and also any problem I had with my car. Once when I broke down in Scotland, he came all the way from Bradford to rescue me, even though it was the middle of the night. This act is typical of his kind nature and generosity to others.'

Mrs Szurma recalls that she could not have been happier when they finally 'named the day'. 'Then began the preparations. I searched in Leeds and Bradford and at last found the most beautiful material ever. It was silver. Only this was good enough for my daughter. I set about designing an exquisite creation. As the material was so difficult to work with, I literally made the dress on Sonia's body, panel by panel. The end result was magnificent. To crown it, my husband's prize red roses – freshly picked from his well-tended garden

– were made into a full bouquet. Sonia looked a dream. When she walked out of the house on my husband's arm, the sun broke out of the rain-clouds and reflected all the colours of the rainbow in her dress.' Bursting with pride, Mrs Szurma adds that 'only one queen in the history of England was ever married in silver'.

The wedding of Peter William Sutcliffe and Sonia – christened Oksana – Szurma took place on 10 August 1974, her twenty-fourth birthday.

It had been Sutcliffe's grandmother who most actively encouraged him and his brother, Mick, to keep up their attendances at Mass, but once he left home, Sutcliffe had 'lapsed'. He would always describe himself as Roman Catholic, but it was not until his arrest and period of remand at Armley Prison that he began to go to Mass again regularly.

By the time he was moved to Broadmoor he was extremely devout once again, and would often remind me of the importance of the Catholic Church. Sonia, too, was persuaded to enter the Church, a measure of how keen she was to please him by that stage.

At the time their wedding plans were being made, however, it was Sonia who was making all the decisions, and it was her wish that neither of his brothers, but a friend, Ronnie Wilson, should be their best man. It seems unlikely anyway that Mick would have accepted if he had been invited. His dislike of Sonia was clear from the start.

The gradual loosening of Sutcliffe's close family ties was almost complete, and with the wedding, slipped another notch. Peter had, as Sonia says, come into her world.

However, her world, at that crucial time, was not the fairy-tale wonderland that her mother's account of things would suggest. Mrs Szurma's memories of the years leading up to her daughter's marriage to Sutcliffe are at best romantic, at worst highly selective, for it was during their uncommonly long courtship that both Sonia and Sutcliffe were to experience their own lasting private torment.

In 1972 Sonia suffered a complete mental breakdown which hospitalised her for weeks, and interrupted her teacher training studies for four years.

The breakdown was a public affair, with Sonia running into the street in her nightclothes, claiming that she was the Second Christ. She had to be physically restrained and taken to a psychiatric hospital, and has been under the supervision of doctors ever since.

Ironically, Sutcliffe's own breakdown was an intensely private affair. Increasingly influenced by 'the voices', which were controlling part of his mind, he was becoming a willing participant in the evil activities to which they drove him. By the time he married Sonia, he had already carried out a serious attack on a prostitute and had developed a mad and murderous hatred of them that was to remain undetected by anyone close to him for more than ten years. He never sought the help of doctors, and to this day refuses medication.

Sutcliffe claims that the immediate effect of the 'voices' calling to him in the graveyard had been a calming one. He had been suffering mild depression, and for two years the 'voices' reassured him and helped to lift his spirits. Fiercely possessive of the 'voices' inside his head, he believed they were a miraculous phenomenon, giving him the self-esteem he lacked and making him feel important. With no insight into his developing mental illness, he told no one and saw no reason to seek help.

During cross-examination at his trial, he was to tell Sir Michael Havers, prosecuting counsel: 'The first two years were the best. There were no signs of the purpose or why I had been chosen to be here. None whatsoever.'

Sir Michael asked him if he was in love with Sonia at the time he first heard the voices. Sutcliffe said he was and that he trusted her. He also loved and trusted his mother.

> *Sir Michael:* 'This was the most stunning thing in your life and you did not tell Sonia?'
> *Sutcliffe:* 'No.'

> *Sir Michael:* 'You didn't tell your devoted
> mother?'
> *Sutcliffe:* 'No.'
> *Sir Michael:* 'You didn't tell anyone until
> years and years had gone by...?'

Sutcliffe agreed with him that this was 'very odd'.
Sir Michael asked what the voices were telling
Sutcliffe.

He replied: 'That I should have faith and that I
should believe and that there was no need to be
so depressed.'

> *Sir Michael:* 'So, for all these years this
> great miracle – to you it must have been
> a miracle – was kept entirely to yourself?'
> *Sutcliffe:* 'Yes.'

He said he had had blackouts and depression
since his motor-bike accident in 1966, but that he
was frightened of going to the doctor. 'I was in
control. I thought to go to the doctor would
probably result in a brain operation or something
like that, which I did not want.'

In November 1967, Sutcliffe was sacked from
his job at the cemetery for persistently bad time-
keeping, and took a job with the Water Board.

The benign two-year period, when his schizophrenia was inexorably taking hold, came abruptly

and unpredictably to an end one summer's day in 1969 when Sutcliffe came home from his labouring job, to run into his brother Mick, bursting to impart a gleeful message.

Sonia, by now Sutcliffe's regular Saturday night date and his serious girlfriend, had been spotted by Mick in the passenger seat of a red sports car driven by a flashy-looking Italian boy who was a local ice-cream salesman. Sutcliffe was utterly devastated. Even now, he remembers the pain and feeling of betrayal that overtook him when he learned that Sonia had rejected him and was seeing someone else.

'I decided what to do. The next day I left my work at the Water Board a couple of hours before going-home time. I just walked out at about 4.30 p.m. I hung around outside the tech. college in Bradford where Sonia was studying for her A-levels. I saw her walking down the road. Along one side of it ran a high brick wall. As she turned a bend in the road, she suddenly spotted me waiting for her. She could see the look on my face. She stopped, and turned towards the wall. There wasn't anywhere for her to go; she just couldn't face me.'

Sutcliffe has never shown his feelings easily. No one in his family or close circle of friends remembers him ever losing his temper or even coming anywhere near it. Anger was an emotion he could not express. Even then, consumed with bitterness and anxiety, he did not lose his temper with Sonia.

'I asked her, asked her about a million times, if it was true she was seeing someone else. I told her it was no good lying to me. I begged her to just tell me what was going on. I literally followed her all the way home, pressing her for an answer. I was beside myself. I couldn't deal with it – with not knowing, that was the worst.

'She wouldn't answer my questions. I knew it was true anyway, I just wanted her to say something to me, either to reassure me or tell me it was over between us. I went away feeling worse than ever. When Sonia doesn't want to talk about something, there is nothing anyone can do to persuade her.'

That night, the 'voices' talked to him instead. 'They were stronger and louder than ever, drumming inside my head. They reasoned with me – "you must take this out on someone. You must get your own back. Don't take it out on Sonia. You could lose her. Take it out on someone else."'

Driven by manic revenge, Sutcliffe toured the streets around the Royal Standard pub where he and Sonia had spent many evenings together, locked in private conversation. He was at the wheel of a battered Morris Minor, having grown out of motor-bikes and into second-hand cars. He was not looking for the companionship and bright lights of the pub where there would be friends to drink with and talk to. Sutcliffe was suddenly a man with a mission. Psychiatrists were to explain later that he had been pushed over the brink on which his sanity had been hovering for some years. Any deep emotional trauma might have triggered him. That night, it was the threat to his relationship with Sonia. For the first time, he was completely out of control, yet at the same time completely in control of his outward behaviour, showing the classic deviousness of the schizophrenic.

The dark side of his mind rejected any notion of joining his friends in the pub. Instead, he entered the low-life world outside in Manningham Lane, where the girls were waiting for business in the shadows between the street lamps. They were the ones who were going to suffer. He was going to take it out on them, get his own back.

Many times, Sutcliffe and his pals had driven around the streets where the girls plied their trade. They were truly creatures of the night, not the kind of girl you would recognise in Bradford's shopping centre, nor on the top of a bus. On the streets, though, they were instantly recognisable by their clothes and the way they stood. Their skirts were that bit shorter, their make-up that bit more garish, their manner that bit more provocative than the girls you saw in the shops or on the bus. They were blatant, shameless, disgusting.

Sutcliffe and his friends would leer at them,

shouting rude remarks from the safety and warmth of a car, through the wound-down window. They would make crude offers of money and then drive off laughing.

That night, Sutcliffe cruised up Manningham Lane, past the Royal Standard, until he drew level with a petrol station on the other side of the road. There, in the shadows, he saw a girl waiting for customers. She was alone. He wound down the car window and made a crude offer of money, but this time he did not drive off laughing. Instead he invited her in with him and agreed on sex for £5. What happened next, he has always claimed, strengthened his disgust of prostitutes and hardened it into hatred, leading him later into murder.

He tells the story now in a flat matter-of-fact voice: 'I picked up the girl outside a garage, and I realised later that the men who worked there were her "protectors". I'd given her a £10 note and she said she'd give me my change later. We got to her house and went inside. There was a huge Alsatian dog on a mat in front of the fire downstairs. She started going upstairs and I realised I just didn't want to go through with it. The whole thing was awful. I felt disgusted with her and myself. I went upstairs behind her and into the bedroom. I even unzipped her dress, but I told her straight out I didn't want to do anything with her. She could keep the money, just give me my change.

'She said she'd have to go back to the garage where I'd picked her up, to get some change, so I drove her there. I just wanted to get away. I felt worse than ever about Sonia and everything.'

Back at the petrol station, the girl went inside the pay kiosk and didn't emerge for a while. Sutcliffe says a rough-looking man came up to him carrying a wrench. 'He said, "If I were you I wouldn't get out of that car. You'd better get going." I would have had a go at him, but he was holding the wrench in a menacing sort of way. Then I saw the girl come out with another big-built bloke. They walked off together, having a laugh. I just felt stupid, I drove home more angry than ever.'

Sutcliffe claims he saw the same prostitute in a city pub a few days later, and went up to her to ask for his £5. She laughed at him and told all her friends in the bar about making a fool of him. The first flicker of humiliation and anger he felt then was to smoulder deep inside him. Prostitutes – 'scum', the 'voices' called them – were now in sharp focus as the target for his hatred.

At his trial, the jury heard that Sutcliffe had told psychiatrists he had had 'hundreds of messages from God' over the years following his experience in the cemetery. The messages were not always religious. The 'voices' told him that prostitutes 'could not justify themselves in society'. Sutcliffe said he had been frightened and had tried to fight the 'voices', although after first hearing them from the Polish gravestone, he had also felt 'privileged'. He had returned to the grave several times but never heard anything there again.

Doctors told the court that this had been Sutcliffe's first schizophrenic experience. The fury that gripped him two years later, when he was humiliated by the prostitute in Bradford, led to the development of his 'primary schizophrenic delusion', the obsession that was to lead to mass murder. From the moment he felt the girls in the bar were laughing at him an irrational hatred of all prostitutes grew in his mind. It was stoked by the 'voices' urging him to seek revenge – not just for Sonia's rejection of him, but now for this extra humiliation.

When Sutcliffe first explained to Sonia what he claimed was the original cause of his murderous revenge, she asked him: 'Are you saying then, that it is in some way my fault?'

He told her: 'No, I am not saying that. I am just telling you how it all began.'

Some time soon after his encounter with the prostitute in Manningham Lane, Sutcliffe carried out his first attack. By now he was making a habit of driving into the red light areas of Leeds, Wakefield or Bradford after a drinking session with his pals, and was noticeably more interested than before in taunting the girls 'doing business' at the kerbside. He would refer to them as 'old bags' or 'cows' at the same time remaining curiously wary, almost frightened of them, if they approached the car.

The habit was becoming an obsession. Sutcliffe would drive his friends home after a night out, then go back alone to Manningham Lane or Lumb Lane, which was parallel to it, to cruise slowly past the girls on his own in a state of excitement that had nothing to do with sex and everything to do with his personal paranoia.

One Saturday afternoon, after the pubs had closed, he was sitting in his friend, Trevor Birdsall's van, eating fish and chips and providing a running commentary on the behaviour of the girls plying their trade in the street nearby. This had become a regular feature of his outings with Birdsall, as the police were to hear later.

Following his row with her over the Italian boy, Sutcliffe's relationship with Sonia was still a source of deep anxiety at this stage. She was still seeing both of them, and Sut-cliffe was increasingly obsessed with 'punishing' other women.

He told Birdsall he would be 'back in a minute' and disappeared up St Paul's Road, a side turning near where they were parked. He came back after a short while, running down the road and clearly out of breath. He took something out of his pocket and emptied it out of the van window as they drove off. He had finally embarked on his mission.

Years later he was to boast about it, using the incident to sneer at the ineptitude of the police who discovered the assault, interviewed him at home, and then dropped the case. In hindsight, they had come desperately close to checking and controlling the future activities of a man who was to slip from their grasp a further eight times, with the most tragic consequences.

Sutcliffe's boasting comes in the form of another conversation with a fellow patient at Broadmoor:

> *Patient X:* 'So you were under the impression that God was . . .'
> *Sutcliffe:* Instructing me to clear the streets of them all.'
> *Patient X:* 'Right. So that went on for how long?'
> *Sutcliffe:* 'Oh, five years, didn't it? Oh, but wait a minute. It started in 1969. They were careful to cover this up in court. They knew all the fuckin' facts that I, in broad daylight on a Saturday afternoon with people everywhere, I jumped out of the car and whacked one with a sock with fuckin' rocks in, and knocked her down in the street. And everybody, they daren't come near me, you know. A bloke tried one move. 'Fuckin', come on then, you

know, but he wouldn't. I just went and got back in the car and somebody took the number, and the police came and seen me at the house where I was, where me mother and Dad lived. Listen, they came to see me. They interviewed me and I was as cool as a cucumber you know. Nothing fuckin' bothered me. I didn't bat an eyelid, like. They just, they said right, do you know this is a very serious thing, you know. You could get a sentence here like, you know. I hadn't done any time before that or anything. A clean record, you know.'

Patient X: 'Yeh, I know.'

Sutcliffe: 'In 1969. And he says, he says right so I'll need to take a statement Mr Sutcliffe, right. Just for the sake of it, he says. But after he tried to worry me a bit, you know, worry me a bit, he said after about an hour – there were two coppers – and he said well he said, that's a police statement. But don't worry about it, he said, you're not going to get charged... you're not going to get charged. They were, now wait, wait, this is the police. I said, why not? I couldn't believe it, you know.'

Patient X: 'But why did they cover

that up?'
Sutcliffe: 'Because they didn't want the court to know that that could've been used in the hunt to catch me earlier.'

When the two police officers knocked at the door of 57 Cornwall Road, Bingley, the day after Sutcliffe's attack on the prostitute they found a pleasant, helpful young man prepared to answer their questions. He took them into the front room, reassuring his mother that it was 'something to do wi' one of me motors' and telling her to stay in the kitchen while he sorted it out.

The police told him he was 'very lucky'. The girl did not want to press charges for assault, not only because she was a known prostitute but also because her common-law husband was serving a sentence for assault himself and she simply wanted nothing more to do with the incident. The officers undoubtedly believed that Sutcliffe had been drunk and in high spirits that afternoon. Opportunist attacks on Bradford prostitutes were not unusual. They closed the file on Sutcliffe and it gathered dust for more than twelve years.

Further questioning might have exposed the fact that Sutcliffe had taken to carrying around in his pocket a sock filled with small stones – there was nothing 'opportunist' about that sort of behaviour.

Having escaped any sort of official punishment

for what had been a serious attack, he now believed he was invincible. The 'voices' were guiding him, protecting him. He could put his trust in them, and they were telling him that 'whacking' one girl on the back of the head was not sufficient for the mission he had been given. In future he must go properly equipped and they would continue to protect him from the police.

About a month later, in September 1969, he stepped up the activities that would eventually turn him into a mass murderer. He abandoned the sock filled with stones, taking instead a hammer and a long-bladed knife, and set off for the area of Bradford that had become his regular hunting ground.

'I were driving me old Morris Minor, and I were looking for a prostitute. I knew this were the mission I had to carry out. The voices told me it wasn't good enough just to attack them. I had to do it properly. I had to kill.' Whatever happened, he would be able to lie his way out of it. The 'voices' would tell him how to handle it.

He parked his car at the side of Manningham Lane and got out, leaving the headlights on and the engine idling. Hiding the hammer and the knife inside his jacket, he slipped into the shadows that darkened one of the tiny front gardens despite the yellow rays of a street lamp.

A policeman doing the rounds of the red-light

district didn't like the look of Sutcliffe's abandoned car by the side of the road, and turning his torch on the nearby gardens, he discovered a man crouching behind a privet hedge, holding a hammer. Sutcliffe agreed to accompany the officer to the police station, where he stuck to his story that a hubcap had flown off his car's front wheel and he had been looking for it, carrying a hammer with which to secure it back into place. It was true that a loose hubcap had been a nuisance for some time.

He had slipped the long-bladed knife down a gap between the side of the vehicle and the mudguard cover inside the police van that came to collect him. It was never discovered. 'For all I know, it's still there.' He finds it an amusing notion.

Sutcliffe spent his first night in a police cell. At the magistrates' court next morning he pleaded guilty to going equipped for theft. He was fined £25. 'I've never worked out what I was supposed to be stealing with the aid of a hammer.' His plump shoulders shake with laughter.

He reasons that he had every cause to believe from then on that the 'voices' were protecting him, and that they were more intelligent than any police officer. This would not be put to the test until a further six years had elapsed – years during which there would be considerable turmoil in his life and his burning hatred of prostitutes would be turned down to simmering point.

Sonia had finally agreed to stop seeing the other man, although when referring to that friendship in later years she remarked coldly that she 'saw nothing wrong with studying the Italian language'.

Sutcliffe's obvious distress at her rejection of him remains today an important component of their relationship. He becomes unhappy, then by turns disturbed, angry, almost suicidally anxious, when she fails to visit him at Broadmoor, for although he tells her he accepts that she may one day fall in love with another man, in reality Sutcliffe is incapable of facing up to that possibility.

Once, in the face of undeniable evidence that she was romantically attached to someone else, Sutcliffe insisted that Sonia simply needed someone to talk to and that the friendship was platonic. If he didn't believe that, he says, he would tell her not to visit him again. 'I'd rather finish it myself than go on being deceived. I believe in one man and one woman being together and no messing about.'

It is not only the memory of painful rejection that haunts him, but a crisis in his parents' marriage which he witnessed at first hand.

Soon after he and Sonia had got back together again properly and she had stopped seeing the Italian boy, they were invited by John Sutcliffe to meet him at a local hotel, the Bankfield, one evening. This was sufficiently unusual to be downright mysterious, and the mystery deepened when the couple bumped into Sutcliffe's sister, Maureen, on their arrival. It turned out that John Sutcliffe had discovered his wife's unfaithfulness with a local police officer, and wanted to shame her in front of the family with a full-scale confrontation. The lounge bar where they all sat together was as inappropriate a place as anyone could possibly choose for what should have been a private discussion. However, it was John Sutcliffe's style to play-act in front of his own children and the outsider, Sonia, and he had tricked his wife into arriving there in the belief that she was to meet her policeman lover. Instead, he exposed her unfaithfulness to her children, and to anyone else who happened to be in earshot.

Sonia regards this piece of mischief as 'a dirty trick' to play on Kathleen Sutcliffe, a woman she has described as 'an angel'. She did not blame her at all for seeking solace from the drudgery of her own life and the tyranny of her husband. Sonia's firmly held views on morality and marriage seem to be suspended when she talks of her mother-in-law's infidelity.

She recalls with distaste that uncomfortable evening at the Bankfield, a rather grand setting, by Bradford standards, for what turned out to be a tacky and embarrassing occasion.

Over the next couple of years John Sutcliffe

himself developed a romantic friendship with a woman neighbour on the Cottingley estate, partly in order to get his own back. Peter Sutcliffe remembers going to the woman's house, banging on the door and insisting that his father came out. 'The neighbours all looked out 'cos they all knew me, like, and asked what was going on. I told them, me Dad's messing about wi' this Wendy Broughton and it's causing me Mam no end of upset. I were going to stick one on him, like, if he came out. But he never did. He went to live with her in the end. She was deaf and dumb, and she'd been a friend of me Mam. Her husband had left her. It were terrible for all of us.'

The odd situation continued for some months with Sutcliffe senior living half in one home and half in the other. Later, he was to move back with his wife, Kathleen, boasting that he had taken his revenge.

Peter Sutcliffe's behaviour at this time, if at all unusual, went unremarked while the family crisis continued, although as the one closest to his mother, it seemed natural that he would be the most upset. He was in and out of work, mostly in labouring jobs, and was keeping up old friendships with his biker mates and drinking companions. He was also seeing Sonia.

He displayed no outward sign of his psychosis, the primary explosion and its first manifestation –

'voices'. They were now taking control of his mind and, as the fuse burned down more quickly than ever, time was running out. Yet even if there had been any visible signs, they would almost certainly have been obscured by the crisis about to engulf Sonia.

She had gained a place at the Rachel McMillan Teachers' Centre in Deptford, south London, and started a training course, hoping to specialise in art. It had meant leaving home, the council house in Tanton Crescent where she had always felt protected and secure, for the first time. She was separated from her parents, and more significantly, her father's influence, but she was not separated from Peter Sutcliffe, over whom she now exerted the strongest possible emotional control. She needed him to be with her in London, however impossible that seemed, and he went as far as he could to comply.

Sutcliffe would drive down at weekends, often sleeping in his car near the students' lodging where Sonia lived. He even attempted a complete move to London but it was a disaster. He describes his efforts to set up home there: 'I'd never been away from Yorkshire in my life, but I was willing to give it a go. I'd get jobs working on cars, which I was good at. But I needed somewhere to stay, and that was hopeless.'

Sonia's brother-in-law, an English-educated

Indian called Haleem, offered him accommodation in a terraced house he was renting out to immigrants, in Wembley. Haleem said there wasn't really any room, but 'because I was more or less family, he would let me sleep on the floor of the sitting-room. Early each morning the other lodgers had to walk over me to get to the kitchen where they washed. It were terrible. I were willing to put up with almost anything, but I couldn't stand much of that.'

Sutcliffe was soon back at home in Bingley, leaving Sonia feeling more isolated than ever. She was under stress at college, finding it hard to agree with her teacher's methods and ideas, particularly in the art and sculpture classes, and continually wanting to do things her own way.

'There was one woman teacher who would set us a piece of work – for example, telling us to shape our work around the theme of nature – she wanted a conventional end-product. Something instantly recognisable. I wanted to have a free hand, and my results were usually in the abstract range.' Sonia describes a confrontation between herself and the teacher, claiming that she 'won', but that one of the other students was so upset that she left the class-room in tears.

At one point, Sonia had lodgings in what she describes as a typical Kent farmhouse. 'It was the sort of home I really wanted. Everyone used to come into the big warm kitchen still wearing their wellington boots. But the rest of the house was like a palace. I decided that when I qualified I'd like a place just like that. It was my dream.'

She added: 'But we never did it. Pete could never leave Yorkshire. It was his home and the only place he had contacts.' This expression of disappointment seems to imply that Sutcliffe was the weak one in the partnership, unable to put down new roots and lead a life with Sonia independent of his family and his home in Bingley, yet the reverse was becoming increasingly true. It was Sonia who was unable to lead a satisfactory life away from home.

She says herself that at that time she was really enjoying only one activity – a rather unusual diversion – flamenco dancing, complete with castanets, taught by a Spanish lady in Swiss Cottage. 'I just loved my dancing lessons, and the dresses we wore. The tempo was so exciting, and the whole thing a fascination to me.'

Today, flamenco dancing is just a memory, but Sonia stays in touch with her teacher, aged seventy-nine. They exchange letters, and the old lady was a source of encouragement and strength to Sonia when her husband was arrested and charged with murder.

Unhappily for Sonia, there was no one near at hand to help her when she suddenly and dramatically suffered a mental breakdown during her second year at college. She had sent a mysterious telegram to Sutcliffe, telling him: 'Meet me at King's Cross station.' There was no time, no date, no other detail.

'I were completely baffled by it, and then worried about Sonia. I left work and took the telegram straight round to Tanton Crescent. Her Dad took it off me and told me he was her legal guardian and it was his responsibility to go to London and find out if she was all right.'

There, at Bexley Hospital, Bohdan Szurma discovered his daughter in a near-catatonic state. He heard that police and ambulancemen had been called to her lodgings after she had been seen outside in the street in the middle of the night, obviously hallucinating. Sonia had told doctors that she believed she was the Second Christ, insisting there were stigmata on the palms of her hands, and convinced the world was coming to an end. 'All the machinery was breaking down,' she said. She was diagnosed as schizophrenic, and would need a long period of treatment.

Bohdan Szurma took one look at his daughter and experienced intense suffering himself. He carried her bodily from the psychiatric ward, and took her back home to Bradford, where she was admitted to the Linfield Mount Hospital. Agitated and deeply disturbed, on admission, she had to be held down by two nurses and complained of hearing voices talking to her.

Sonia remained at Linfield Mount for more than three weeks, receiving very few visitors. She was erratic and aggressive, subject to dramatic mood swings. Her parents would see her every day and when they felt her condition had improved, they finally agreed to let Peter Sutcliffe see her too. In spite of their reservations, they were impressed by his obvious concern for their daughter and his genuine desire to help.

When he first entered the drab and gloomy hospital ward, he was horrified by what he saw. 'She reached out to me and put her arms round me tightly, so tightly I could hardly breathe. She looked so fragile and vulnerable, and yet her grip was so strong. She seemed to be absorbing strength from me. I could feel it leaving my body and transferring to her.' Sutcliffe claims that this has happened many times since, when one or other of them has been in turmoil.

His devotion to Sonia during the depths of her breakdown brought him so much closer to her parents that they were happy to agree that the couple could see each other regularly. They trusted him now, and the doctors confirmed that his hospital visits were helping her to recover.

It would be four years before she could return to her teacher training course and resume her studies. Long before then, however, in the summer of 1974, Mr and Mrs Szurma were delighted when Sutcliffe asked for their permission to marry Sonia. They had seen for themselves his sincere affection and concern, and were convinced he would make her a good husband.

They had become so fond of him they insisted he and Sonia should live with them. It was an extraordinary gesture from a couple who rarely, if ever, allowed any outsider into their home. This outsider was, superficially, the perfect son-in-law, easy-going and companionable, helpful around the house. In reality, he was a lethal psychotic, biding his time untill the 'voices' told him he must murder.

That time came while he was living with his in-laws at 44 Tanton Crescent, Bradford, during which period Sutcliffe was to commit his first five murders. Each time, he struck within an hour on either side of midnight.

Voices

With her innate love of ancient culture, Sonia had hoped to spend her honeymoon in Greece, where she wanted to see the Parthenon, the Acropolis and all the other important sites she had only read about in Greek mythology. However, political upheaval in Greece made the plan impossible. She found this particularly exasperating, especially as she had spent weeks studying the language. So it was with some disappointment that the couple decided to go to Paris instead, and their experiences in the world's most romantic city were not altogether what they had hoped for.

There were two incidents during their short honeymoon, which were not only to reinforce Sutcliffe's intense hatred of prostitutes, but also to underline the 'messages' that had been hammering inside his head for almost seven years. He said later – a further seven years later – that everything his 'voices' had been telling him about women on the streets was confirmed during the period when his killing instincts lay dormant.

Even here, on his honeymoon, he was disgusted at the brazenness, the lewdness, of approaches from those who sold sex for a living. One time he was walking hand in hand with Sonia when a prostitute came up to them and made obscene suggestions. The couple hurried away. On another occasion, as Sonia waited for him outside a railway station, she was propositioned by a man who thought she was a prostitute.

Sutcliffe, the newly married man with a steady job as a furnaceman and about to start a new life, was inwardly more convinced than ever of the need to clear the streets of sin. He was the one chosen to do it, he was a man with a mission, and the incidents that upset Sonia and marred his honeymoon were further proof that he must act soon.

Sutcliffe remembers other aspects of the few days he spent with Sonia in Paris. For example, he saw her gift for languages put to a severe test and the results amused him. She told him that it was a skill inherited from her father, who, she would boast, could speak seven languages fluently. Sutcliffe's own father would scoff at this, remarking wryly that 'It was a pity English wasn't one of them'.

At dinner one night, Sutcliffe discovered that his new wife was not as proficient in French as she had led him to believe when, after they had studied the menu for some time, Sonia ordered a dish of *poisson*, claiming it was a chicken dish. It turned out to be fish-head soup, and they both gulped in dismay when it arrived, although Sonia ate hers with great effort, attempting to keep her dignity. Sutcliffe did not laugh openly, he says, for Sonia was never amused by jokes at her expense. 'I had to laugh inside. I said to her, "You'll never eat that, luv," but she did. She's got such pride.'

The honeymoon was brief, and the prospect of a new life at Tanton Crescent was a welcome one. To all appearances the couple were like any others starting out, both working and saving to buy their own home one day. For now, their place was traditionally with her parents, his in-laws.

By the time they returned from honeymoon, Sutcliffe was more certain than ever that the 'voices' were right; they seemed to have arranged circumstances around him to make the mission both easier and quite inevitable. Because he was working the night shift at Anderton Circlips as a furnaceman, Sonia and her parents would not always be able to keep tabs on him. Also, more significantly, he was able to renew his friendship with Trevor Birdsall, who lived near Tanton Crescent. The two men returned to their old habits, touring the red-light districts after a pub crawl.

In between times, Sutcliffe was playing the part of the perfect son-in-law, a role that came naturally, for he had always been thoughtful, gentle and caring at home, in favourable contrast to his rough-and-ready brothers. Maria Szurma had really taken to him and even Bohdan Szurma, aloof and imperious towards outsiders, warmed towards him. The two men, separated by language, culture and age, would sit up talking late into the night, Mr Szurma telling Sutcliffe about his early life in the Ukraine and his war years in Prague, while Sutcliffe listened and chatted. However, Sonia, waiting for him upstairs, would grow restive. 'She used to storm downstairs and demand to know if I was ever coming to bed. She didn't like to be excluded, ever, not even by the two of us.'

Sonia was to become increasingly demanding of Sutcliffe, particularly once they had moved to a house of their own, but for now it was simply his time and attention that she wanted. She had no idea she was being excluded from a part of her husband's life that was all but taking him over – his obsession with prostitutes or the 'voices' in his head that were louder now. She was preoccupied with her own convalescence and her determination to return to her chosen career, doing some student teaching as her health steadily improved.

Sonia and Peter would walk together on the moors above Bradford, both feeling at home in these surroundings, which might seem wild and desolate to others, for they had lived all their lives in that outer rim of Bradford where city sprawl ends and bleak open spaces begin.

They had been told by Mr and Mrs Szurma to treat the house in Tanton Crescent just like their own home. Sutcliffe remembers one day when he put that invitation to the test.

'We'd set off in't car for the moors where we planned a longish walk. On the way out of town we saw a girl at a bus-stop with her mother. It were an old schoolmate of Sonia's and I said, why don't we pick them up and take them with us for a walk? We all went off together and it were a right nice afternoon. On't way back to town I asked them in for a cup of tea, like, just as I would've done in Cornwall Road where people were in and out all't time.

'We parked outside and I saw Sonia's Mam and Dad at the front window. I said, "Oh, good they're in, then." But when we went in the back door they'd completely disappeared. It were right odd, right peculiar. I didn't know what to say. We had a cup of tea in the kitchen, and then they left. It turned out the Szurmas were hiding upstairs all't time. They said they wanted to know in advance if folk were coming to the house, like. But I had a few words then. I said all I was doing was treating it like me own home. Everything went right tense after that. The atmosphere were terrible.'

His own noisy, and mostly cheerful, family home in Cornwall Road was a regular refuge for him, especially handy as it was only a short distance from his workplace, and his mother still frequently cooked for him. When workers at Anderton's were laid off in early 1975, Sutcliffe was among them, and the weekday visits to his family stopped, although he and Sonia often turned up there on a Sunday afternoon.

Both prudent savers, the couple agreed that Sutcliffe should spend a chunk of his £400 severance pay on a course leading to a Heavy Goods Vehicle licence, the first step towards a job as a long-distance lorry driver.

He and Sonia had aspirations. She would persevere to qualify eventually as a primary school teacher, specialising in art and pottery, while their joint savings would go towards the nicest home they could afford. The tension at Tanton Crescent had put pressure on them to move as soon as possible and by early summer 1975, when Sutcliffe gained his HGV licence, the pressure was intense, although largely unnoticed by bustling little Mrs Szurma, who, to this day, sees the family relationship, and her daughter's marriage, in a soft focus of her own, with all the sharp, unwanted edges obscured.

Long after Sutcliffe's arrest and trial, she sat in the drab kitchen at Tanton Crescent describing a cosy scene that clearly once pleased her greatly, but is sinister in retrospect. Her hands fidgeted constantly as she talked.

'Pete used to come home from his night shift, and always took off his dirty work clothes at the door. He'd kiss me, put his overalls in the washing right there, and we'd have a chat and a cup of tea together. I always felt we understood each other because some of the time we shared the same working hours, when I was doing a night shift as a nursing auxiliary at the local hospital. We used to chat for hours about this and that. I realise now that sometimes his overalls must have been blood-stained, and I'd been drinking tea with him without a clue about what he'd been doing.' All this was said with more sorrow than fear; bafflement mixed with genuine affection and regret that there would be no more Pete, no more late-night chats with the loving son-in-law, who, for a brief time, lightened up home life at 44 Tanton Crescent.

As the chatty, outgoing partner in her own exceptionally private relationship, she saw nothing unusual in the exceptionally private relationship between Sutcliffe and her younger daughter. She sometimes worried vaguely that Sutcliffe was 'so good-looking' that he might get involved with other women, but she also witnessed the growing inter-dependence between them. There was intense love, but also heated rows.

They remained social opposites: he with no career prospects beyond those of a lorry driver, she with the highest possible goals of teaching and achieving national recognition as a sculptress and potter.

It was during this crucial time, less than a year

after their marriage, that Sutcliffe was giving in to an increasingly dangerous compulsion. He was touring pubs in Bradford, Leeds, Halifax and Manchester with Trevor Birdsall and a neighbour from Tanton Crescent, Ronald Barker. The drinking sprees would regularly end in a detour on the way home, the red-light areas, giving them a chance to taunt the girls on the streets.

Ronald Barker, an insurance company rep, told the jury at Sutcliffe's trial that he always wanted to go home after their drinking sessions, but 'Pete always seemed to want to go round the red-light districts. These excursions would last between a quarter and half an hour. Peter never said why he wanted to go.'

He was asked by Mr James Chadwin QC for the defence: 'Did he ever strike you as an aggressive man?'

To which Barker replied: 'I'm sorry, no. That didn't enter my head.'

He was frequently in Sutcliffe's company between 1975 and 1977, and remembered Sutcliffe drawing his car into the kerb alongside a prostitute and taunting her with offers of money, then driving off, but he was not with Sutcliffe on the night of 4 July 1975, when he first attempted a murder.

Sutcliffe's attacks have been described as opportunist: a girl alone on a deserted street, the night's shadows to hide him, but he is adamant:

'Whenever I attacked, it was a compulsion. I were in agony for the few days before the attack, I were really suffering. I were compelled to plan every detail, then set off with one thing in mind. Nothing could stop me, and I could not stop myself.'

On the night of 4 July his intention – his 'mission' – was to kill, and the 'voices' were urging him to do the job properly. 'I fought against it. I stopped the car and held on to the steering wheel and tried to force myself to turn round and go home.'

Instead, he drove alone into the centre of Keighley, a town some miles north west of Bradford, to follow up a pattern of behaviour he had started several weeks earlier. He had heard from workmates at Anderton's that Keighley was 'crawling with prostitutes', and he had been drawn towards an attractive woman in her late thirties. She was Anna Rogulski, a friendly and outgoing Irish-born divorcee, whose marriage to a Ukranian had been annulled. Sutcliffe had approached her twice before, once in a public square outside the town hall, and once in a coffee bar where she worked.

On the night of 4 July, he hid from her in the shadows of an alleyway near the Ritz cinema. She had returned home from a night out drinking, and went to call on her boyfriend in North Queen Street. Sutcliffe watched from a doorway as she banged on the front door without success. Earlier

on that evening he had already asked her if she was
'in business' and been rebuffed.

'I was certain she was a prostitute – scum. I was
being given instructions on what was the best
moment to attack. I waited till she turned to walk
back home. Then I hit her on the back of her head
with a hammer. I knew that was safest. I knew she
wouldn't see me. It was all over in less than ten
seconds. I didn't mean her to suffer. I meant her
to die.'

Anna Rogulski was not a prostitute, and she did
not die. She was found in the early hours of the
morning by a passer-by. At Leeds Royal Infirmary
she was given the last rites in the Catholic Church,
but survived twelve hours of brain surgery. Her
auburn hair was shaved for the operation, and she
said later that it was grey when it grew again.

Although she had been slashed across the chest,
Sutcliffe had been interrupted before he could stab
her to death. She never remembered any details of
her attacker's appearance, and when she was named
as the Yorkshire Ripper's first 'official' victim by
police two years later, she angrily denied it, not
wanting to be associated with his prostitute victims.
'I'm fed up with being associated with the list of
women killed by this man,' she said. 'I've been
afraid to go out much because I feel people are
staring and pointing at me. The whole thing is
making my life a misery. I sometimes wish I had

died in the attack. My main concern is to have my name cleared. Although the police agree I have never been a prostitute there is a dreadful slur attached to any woman linked with the Ripper's attacks. I am respectable, and I want the record put straight.'

Miss Rogulski was eventually awarded £15,000 by the Criminal Injuries Compensation Board.

Sutcliffe had not fulfilled his 'mission'. 'I had a pathological hatred for prostitutes. I was seized in a grip, difficult to explain, occasionally getting depressed with splitting headaches at times. Sometimes I didn't want to go on living. I didn't tell people because it would pass off.'

He says he tried to kill himself soon afterwards. 'I drove my car up to the moors to the place where the druids used to meet. We called it Altar Rock. As I tried to accelerate off the rocks the engine stalled. I believed it was another positive sign from the voices that I was to go on with my mission. I was to abandon the thought of suicide.'

———— o ————

While Sutcliffe claims he was suffering metal turmoil during this period, he does not dispute that the pub crawls and the inevitable aftermath – a cruise round the city backstreets – continued as usual. Just six weeks after the attack on Anna

Rogulski, he ventured as far as Halifax on a drinking spree with Trevor Birdsall, and later that night he attempted to murder a woman while his friend waited in the car. 'I didn't think anything of leaving him there while I went after her. I felt as though I'd never be caught. I felt as though I were being protected, and I were.'

During their round of the Halifax town pubs, the men had been drinking in the Royal Oak. There, Sutcliffe came out with his usual running commentary of contempt against some of the women in the bar. One of them was forty-six-year-old Olive Smelt, an office cleaner who was out for the evening with some friends. Sutcliffe was openly insulting to her in the pub, and told Birdsall: 'I bet she's on the game.'

As they drove home towards Bradford, they were still less than a mile from Halifax city centre when Sutcliffe saw a woman walking down Woodville Road. She turned into a narrow lane, and he recognised her from the Royal Oak.

'I kept a hammer down by the side of the driving seat. I stuffed it into my jacket pocket, like, and ran down the alley parallel to where she were walking. I caught up wi' her and said summat about the weather. It'd been raining real heavy. She didn't answer. I knew she was one of them. I whacked her on't back of her head twice. Then, I slashed her with a hacksaw blade. Someone drove up with headlights on. I didn't have time to finish her off.'

Mrs Smelt was not 'one of them'. She was hurrying home, wondering if the local chip shop would still be open so that she could get a late supper for her husband and son. Instead, she woke up in hospital, where brain surgery mended the double fracture to her skull; time and nature healed the Y-shaped scar on the small of her back. She had been found slumped in the damp alleyway 400 yards from her home in Boothtown, Halifax. Nothing will ever heal the fear and dread that has disturbed her sleep ever since. She says she still fears all men and is a virtual prisoner in her own home once darkness falls. Like the first of Sutcliffe's victims, Anna Rogulski, she believes there is a stigma attached to having been attacked by the Ripper. She says she suffers continual depression that 'just seems to well up' in her, and remembers the happy-go-lucky person she was before.

Mrs Smelt remembers the words Sutcliffe used when he appeared out of the shadows just yards from her own home: 'Weather been playing us up, hasn't it' he said, as he walked past her, only to attack from behind moments later. She is a determined woman and has made the decision to stay in the three-bedroomed house where she has always lived since her marriage to her husband, Harry. She feels that local people are looking at her and pointing, and dreads the mention of the Ripper's name.

Nearly six years later, Birdsall told the Old Bailey jury the events of that night of 15 August 1975, which led up to Sutcliffe's second murder attempt. While he spoke, Mrs Smelt sat listening intently at the back of the court, dressed in a neat white suit and pink blouse. It was during Birdsall's outline of the attack that Sutcliffe left his seat in the dock for the first time and twice leaned over the brass rails to whisper urgently to his solicitor.

Trevor Birdsall recalled having read about the attack on Olive Smelt in the newspapers the next day, and remembered how Sutcliffe had come running back to the car and driven the remaining nine miles home to Bradford in silence. He had wondered if Mrs Smelt was the same woman they had seen that night, but did nothing. More than five years went by before Birdsall, prompted by the near hysteria surrounding the Ripper murders and attacks, told police what he remembered. By then, a further five attacks and thirteen murders had been carried out by the man he described as always a rather quiet person 'with a shy attitude to women generally'.

Birdsall told of the night when Sutcliffe attacked a woman in Bradford, using a stone wrapped in a sock. Birdsall said Sutcliffe walked up St Paul's Road, and out of sight. When he returned to

Birdsall's car, he got in 'fairly quickly'.

'He looked a bit excited and was not breathing normally. It looked as if he had possibly been running,' Birdsall told the court. Sir Michael Havers asked whether Sutcliffe had said anything, and Birdsall replied: 'He just told me to drive off. 'I asked him where he had been, and he said he had followed a woman to a house somewhere. He said he had hit her, I'm not too sure. He mentioned something about some money, but I can't remember too well.'

> *Sir Michael Havers:* 'Did you get any impression as to what sort of woman he had followed?'
> *Birdsall:* 'I would imagine the lady was a prostitute – but that was just my guess – because of the area.'
> *Sir Michael:* 'Had he got anything with him?'
> *Birdsall:* 'Yes. He pulled a sock from his pocket and there was a small brick or stone in it. I think he threw the stone out of the window.'

The trial judge, Mr Justice Boreham, interrupted at that point: 'Did he say whether he used it?'

> *Birdsall:* 'I think he did. Yes. I think he

107

hit her on the head. That's what he said.'

Mr Birdsall, bearded and pale, was visibly shaking as he gave his evidence. At one point Sir Michael Havers told him: 'If you don't feel well, say so. This is not a torture chamber.'

Mr Birdsall said that after the incident with the stone in the sock, Sutcliffe told him he had been questioned by police and had 'explained' everything, and everything was all right.

Birdsall also told of the time his suspicions were properly aroused. He had been out for a drink with Sutcliffe in November 1980, and shortly afterwards read about the killing of Jacqueline Hill in Leeds.

'The paper gave a description of the car thought to have been used by the murderer – a red Rover saloon. I thought it was possible it was the same as Sutcliffe's car. I sent an anonymous note to police on 26 November last year.

'I worried more about it, and very shortly after that I went to see the police myself.'

Cross-examined by James Chadwin QC, Sutcliffe's counsel, Birdsall said: 'I now know Sutcliffe has admitted what happened in the last five years, but I still find it difficult to fit that in with the man I have known for so long, a rather quiet, unaggressive person.'

It had taken Birdsall all of five years to realise his friend might not be so quiet and unaggressive.

It had also taken all his courage, and some persuasion from his girlfriend, to approach the police at all. When his note was ignored by them, he went in person to Bradford police station to repeat his suspicions. Tragically, both efforts failed. Two more months were to pass before Sutcliffe was arrested, almost by chance, by two officers on the beat.

When he was finally arrested and charged, Sutcliffe could recall the full details of each murderous attack – and still does today. Questioned about his state of mind when he attempted to murder Olive Smelt, he said with chilling calm: 'I saw this woman in a pub and she annoyed me, probably in some minor way. I took her to be a prostitute.'

Curiously, the way in which some of Sutcliffe's victims were described in court – in the abbreviated biographies which Sir Michael Havers sketched for the jury – was similarly casual. For example, Wilma McCann, the first murder victim, was described in this way: 'She drank too much, was noisy and sexually promiscuous – she distributed her favours widely.'

By autumn 1975, the police had failed to make any connection between the attacks on Anna Rogulski and Olive Smelt; there was no clue that Sutcliffe's attack on and murder of Wilma McCann was the third in a series.

Wilma was the mother of four small children, the eldest of whom stood hour by hour at a street corner early on the morning of 29 October, waiting and hoping that her mother would come home on a bus. Her crumpled body, blood streaming from horrendous head wounds and repeated stabbing, was found a little later by a milkman on the playing fields, just 150 yards away from her home in the rundown area of Chapeltown, Leeds.

Separated from her husband, she was in the habit of leaving her eldest daughter, Sonje, aged nine, in charge of the others while she went out with her friends to a number of pubs in Chapeltown, the innercity area of Leeds which was, much later, to become known as 'Ripper Country'. Once an elegant residential district where wealthy middle-class families lived with their servants, it has decayed over the years and has now reached rock bottom – a few square miles of squalid litter-strewn streets where neglected houses are rented room by room to an increasingly cosmopolitan population. Drug pushers, alcoholics and prostitutes with their pimps have all but taken over, their twilight world coming alive at night when they inhabit the many bars and clubs, and spill on to the streets.

This was home for Wilma McCann, who lived with her children in Scott Hall Avenue, no more than ten minutes' walk from the worst of it.

On the October night that Mrs McCann left

home in her navy jacket and white flared trousers to do the rounds of her favourite pubs, Peter Sutcliffe had also set out. By now he had taken to carrying with him a ball-peen hammer, a knife and a hacksaw blade, all hidden down beside the driver's seat of his car.

'I wanted to pick up a prostitute with the intention of killing her. I realised this one was a prostitute because she asked me if I wanted business. I may have given her the impression that I wanted to have sex, but this was not so.'

Wilma McCann, who had drunk a few too many Scotch whiskies that night, had been heading unsteadily for home at around 1 a.m. A couple of drivers had already slowed down to avoid striking her as she staggered into the road to thumb a lift. Sutcliffe drove past in his Ford Capri. He slowed down.

'I saw this woman thumbing a lift. She was wearing white trousers and a jacket. I stopped and asked her how far she was going and she said, "Not far, thanks for stopping" and jumped in. I was in quite a good mood and just before we set off she asked if I wanted to do business. I asked what she meant and, it seemed to me, a scornful tone came into her voice.

'She said: "Bloody hell, do I have to spell it out?" My reaction was to go with her. I parked near a field and we sat there for a minute. All of a

111

sudden, her tone changed and she said, "Well, what are we waiting for? Let's get on with it."

'Before we started, she said, "It costs a fiver."

'I was a bit surprised. I was expecting to be a bit romantic. I couldn't have intercourse at a moment's notice, I had to be aroused. She said, "I am going. It's going to take you all fucking day. You are fucking useless."

'I felt myself seething with rage. I wanted to hit her. I told her to hang on a minute and not to go off like that. She said, "Oh you can manage it now, can you?" It sounded as though she was taunting me. I said, "Can we do it on the grass?" This was my idea to start hitting her. She stormed off up the field.

'I had a hammer in the tool box and I followed her up the field. I had the hammer in my right hand and put my coat on the grass. She sat down on the coat and unfastened her trousers and said, "Come on, get it over with."

'I said, "Don't worry, I will." I then hit her with the hammer on the top of the head. I hit her once or twice and she started making a moaning noise. I felt, "God what have I done?" I knew I had gone too far.

"I sat in the car and could see her arm moving. I was in a numb panic. I half expected her to get up and realised I would be in serious trouble. I felt the best way to get out of the mess was to make sure she couldn't tell anyone. I thought to make sure she was dead I would stab her in places like her lungs and throat.'

Sutcliffe undid the woman's bra so that he could see where he was stabbing her. 'I was in a blind panic when I was stabbing her, just to make sure she would not tell anybody.'

He returned to his in-laws' house, where he and Sonia were living. 'I was very frightened and I can't remember driving back. I thought I was bound to get caught. I looked over my clothing before I went into the house, then I went straight upstairs to the bathroom, washed my hands and went to bed.'

The next day Sutcliffe saw the murder reported on the television news. He said he felt sick and still half expected a knock on the door.

'I carried on as normal, living with my wife. After that first time I developed and played up a hatred for prostitutes in order to justify within myself a reason why I had attacked and killed Wilma McCann.'

To his mind, the job had at last been done 'properly'. He had successfully baited and trapped a prostitute, remained outwardly calm long enough to reassure her, then carried out a methodical attack which, by now, had set a pattern – a pattern that was shortly to be recognised by police as his handiwork. Above all, he had murdered for the first time and got away with it.

The *modus operandi* Sutcliffe had developed, and was to stick to, was to entice women into his car and drive them to a suitably lonely spot. There he would ask the woman to get into the back seat with him, or to lie down on a patch of grass, waiting to strike the back of her head with a hammer as she bent down.

His victims all suffered multiple depressed fractures of the skull, which rendered them unconscious, and were stabbed repeatedly after Sutcliffe had disarranged their clothing. He used a knife or screwdriver to stab them, and had sharpened up a rusty Philips screwdriver specially for the purpose, using it on at least two victims to bore a hole through which he stabbed many times. After his arrest, Sutcliffe told the police he had thrown away the specially adapted screwdriver and where to look for it. It was retrieved from an embankment next to the M1 motorway. Sir Michael Havers was later to describe it to the jury as 'one of the most fiendish weapons you have ever seen'.

———— o ————

By the end of 1975, Sutcliffe was established in his chosen job as a lorry driver, making frequent journeys down the northern motorways and trunk roads. He was striking out further in his social life, too, and became familiar with pubs in cities and towns within the Manchester, Leeds and Bradford triangle. Yet he would still return, time after time, to the Chapeltown area of Leeds, sometimes with Trevor Birdsall or Ronald Barker, sometimes alone.

He was alone when he returned there on the night of 21 January, three months after the murder of Wilma McCann, and once more he had murder on his mind.

He described how he felt 'anguish' for several days leading up to each attack, and how the feeling melted away, to be replaced by a trembling, shivering calm immediately after the killings. Between them he was bland, secretive and watchful, and if indeed there was torment, no one was to remark on it at the time or later. Sutcliffe was, of course, spending hours each day alone at the wheel of his truck, and his behaviour at home was unlikely to be noticed as he slipped casually in and out while Sonia and her mother worked odd hours. His drinking companions had become accustomed to his outbursts against prostitutes and, drinking heavily themselves in a noisy pub, simply accepted that this was 'just part of Pete's normal behaviour'.

That behaviour was, in fact, becoming more bizarre than ever. 'I would get depressed and anxious for several days, and try to fight against what I felt I had to do. I even tried praying, but since I believed it was God who was speaking to me and telling me to kill, I became more confused.' Sutcliffe wants the world to understand that he 'had no choice'.

Even with hindsight, no one in his family can recall any odd behaviour by Sutcliffe during Christmas 1975. He was the same dutiful, thoughtful member of the family that he had always been, and, as at every other Christmas since he was a boy, he hand-delivered cards and presents to a number of elderly and housebound neighbours on the Ferncliffe estate.

Three weeks later, though, the dark side of his mind once again took over. His victim this time was forty-two-year-old Emily Jackson, whose description as a part-time prostitute in reports after her death was a source of astonishment to her friends and neighbours. The wife of a local roofing contractor, she had developed the extraordinary habit of setting out for an evening's drinking with her husband, then leaving him in a pub while she drove off in his van, with his full knowledge, in search of customers.

Deeply affected by the accidental death of her teenage son five years earlier, Mrs Jackson was no longer the same person she had been when bringing up her family of four as a loving wife and mother. Her husband, Sydney, fully accepted the new pattern of behaviour she had adopted. But that night, when he left the Gaiety pub in Roundhay Road at closing time, to meet her as arranged, he found no sign of his wife.

She had been picked up by Sutcliffe early in the evening and had allowed him to drive her in his car to a derelict site about half a mile away. Sutcliffe said: 'I felt an inner compulsion to kill a prostitute. I saw this woman and she said it would cost me £5. I remember there was an overpowering smell of cheap perfume and this served all the more for me to hate the woman, even though I did not know her.

'I could see how the first murder had unhinged me completely. I knew from the outset that I didn't want intercourse with her, I just wanted to get rid of her. I couldn't bear even to go through the motions of having sex with her. I wanted to do what I had got in mind as soon as possible. I pretended the car wouldn't start and told her I would have to look under the bonnet and asked her to help me. She held her light over the bonnet, I took a couple of steps back and hit her over the head with my hammer, I think a couple of times, and she fell down in the road.'

Sutcliffe then pulled the body into a yard. 'I made sure she was dead by taking my screwdriver and stabbing her repeatedly. 'I pulled her bra up and pulled down her pants. It gave me some sort of sexual revenge on her as, on reflection, it had done with Wilma McCann. I stabbed her frenziedly, without thought, all over the body. I was seething with hate for her.'

Having mutilated the body, Sutcliffe then searched the yard until he found a piece of wood between two and three feet long which he then pushed against her vagina.

As he left the scene of the crime, Sutcliffe was startled by a car which stopped a few yards away. 'It scared me so I put my hammer and screwdriver on the car floor and went straight home to my mother-in-law's house and had a feeling of satisfaction and justification. 'I didn't have any blood on my clothes so I didn't have to dispose of them.'

The similarity between Mrs Jackson's murder and that of Wilma McCann was unmistakable, and the man responsible, though five years away from arrest, was dubbed a modern-day Jack the Ripper. The label stuck and Sutcliffe has been called the Yorkshire Ripper, not only in newspaper headlines, but also in the formal surroundings of the Central Criminal Court. It is one of his main complaints.

Another of his complaints is that his next victim told the police that Sutcliffe had tried to have sex with her. In the early hours of Sunday, 9 May 1976 Marcella Claxton was left for dead by Sutcliffe, who believed he had perfected his murder technique.

While cruising through Chapeltown, he had stopped in his white Ford Corsair. West Indian-born Marcella, aged twenty, got into the car with him and they sat in virtual silence for the ten-minute drive to Soldiers' Field, a lonely and out of the way place that was perfect for Sutcliffe's purposes.

There, he ordered the girl out of the car and told her to strip, whereupon he struck the back of her head eight or nine times with his ball-peen hammer. He drove off at speed, but his victim regained consciousness. Staggering to a nearby phone box to call for help, she was panic-stricken to see his car returning. 'He got out and began searching the spot where he had left me. He must have come back to finish me off. Thank God he didn't see me.'

She said she was in fear of her life while the police continued to investigate the attack, frequently contacting them to offer further clues from her memory. She was always convinced that he would strike again. Despite appalling injuries, she was certain she could recall that her attacker wore a smart pinstripe suit, white shirt and a red tie. She said he was very well spoken, not more than 20 and had told her he didn't live in Leeds. 'He was like a salesman type, but at the same time the most terrifying person you can image. His eyes were glazed and he didn't seem to have any control of himself.'

It was not until after his arrest that the police

included this attack in Sutcliffe's dossier, but he remembers it well: 'I had to help them out, even after I were being held in't police station and charged. I remembered more than they did.' He was furious to hear that the police believed he had masturbated at the site of his attack on Marcella Claxton. 'I didn't want sex wi' any of them. And certainly not that one. Even t'police said she were like a gorilla.'

He was repeating a remark made privately by the police who had found that Marcella was educationally subnormal, with an IQ of only fifty. They were to claim later, at a Criminal Injuries Compensation Board hearing, that she had 'misled' them in their enquiries, for with her memory impaired, she had given a description of her attacker that was hopelessly inaccurate. On that basis, her original application for compensation was rejected in 1978, three years before Sutcliffe was named as the Ripper, but the decision was overturned in December 1981 when she was awarded an initial £3,000, to be increased by several thousand pounds after further tests.

She survived extensive brain surgery and some of the scarring from fifty-two stitches to her head is still visible today. She is also moody and withdrawn, quite different from the happy-go-lucky girl she was before Sutcliffe struck.

Initial police enquiries led nowhere, despite the

fact that Sutcliffe was by now on their files. He had been fined £25 by Bradford magistrates three months earlier for stealing lorry tyres from his employers, and had been sacked from his job. Yet although his personal life may have appeared to become unstable at this time, his killing method had developed a cool, psychotic and premeditated pattern.

The next murder in his increasing catalogue was the one later pinpointed by doctors as the point at which he totally succumbed to the evil compulsion that was driving him on. He had become controlled. Whereas after the earlier attacks he had run in panic from the scene of his crime, his actions immediately after the death of his third murder victim, Irene Richardson, were deliberate and calculated. This time he had stopped to rearrange her clothes, even her boots, after she died from his frenzied stabbing.

The murder took place more than a year after his previous killing, and nine months after his last attack, a period he claims he spent in turmoil: 'I was having a battle in my mind. My mind was in a turmoil as to whether I should kill people. I got into a morbid state.' The battle was over when the voices in their Quaker tone told him: 'God giveth, and God taketh life.'

He said he used to 'brood and blame everything on prostitutes', and he claims to have wrestled with these inner feelings in the last half of 1976. It was also during this time that he found the job that was to please him more than any other he had had since leaving school, being taken on as a long-distance lorry driver with the Bradford engineering firm of T. and W. H. Clark Holdings Ltd., and given a chance to drive their 32-ton articulated lorry, the biggest and best on the road at the time.

Sonia was persevering with her studies and also working regularly two nights a week with her mother as a nursing auxiliary, more often than not on a Saturday when she had no idea where her husband was, other than 'out for a drink wi' me mates'. The couple were well ahead with their plans for a home of their own, and were soon to start looking for a house to buy.

Despite these milestones of stability, Sutcliffe lost the 'battle going on in his mind', and set out on the night of Saturday, 5 February 1977 with his 'killing tackle' tucked under the driver's seat of his car. Police had been slow enough to see any link between his earlier killings and attacks, and to confuse them further he was now using three or more different cars for his night-time excursions. He always possessed at least two at any given time, converting them from cheap and shabby second-hand bangers to smart jobs that would never let him down, thanks to his obsession and skill with amateur mechanics.

He drove his white Ford Corsair – the one that Marcella Claxton had described to the police, remembering to mention its black roof – back into the Chapeltown suburb of Leeds. He spent most of his evening kerb-crawling, and had either been turned down by prostitutes or had turned down those who approached him. But then, on a street just yards from the scene of his encounter with Emily Jackson, he picked up a twenty-eight-year-old prostitute named Irene Richardson, who was on her way to a local drinking club. Mrs Richardson, who was separated from her husband, was dressed up for a night on the town. She wore a cheap, but smart, matching yellow skirt and jacket, and calf-length boots. She was down on her luck, and looking for business. Irene, the mother of two children, had run away from Blackpool with her lover, an escaped prisoner who later left her to go to London. She lived in a rented room in Chapeltown and had spent the last evening of her life in the Gaiety pub – Emily Jackson's favourite haunt – with several men who bought her drinks.

She agreed on sex with Sutcliffe, and he drove her determinedly towards the exact spot in Roundhay Park where he had left the lifeless, crumpled body of his previous victim Marcella Claxton. Sutcliffe already had a Stanley knife and a hammer in his pocket by the time Irene Richardson had clambered out of the passenger seat at

Roundhay Park; she turned her back to him for a moment, he struck her several heavy blows with his hammer, one of which drove her skull threequarters of an inch into her brain. He tore open her jacket and blouse and slashed at her abdomen with his knife. One wound on her trunk was six-and-threequarter inches long.

Then, controlled and unhurried, he carefully rearranged her clothing. He said later that her body had appeared 'luminous' to him, and that part of his so-called mission was to execute the attack successfully and calmly, leaving the body exactly where and how he planned, rather than fleeing the scene immediately after the murder.

At his trial, Sutcliffe said: 'I drove to Leeds to find a prostitute to make it one less. I saw this girl and she got in without a word. I told her that I may not have wanted her but she told me she would give me a good time. I drove her to a park and she wanted to go to the toilet. They were locked so she decided to urinate on the grass. As she was crouching down I hit her on the head at least two or three times. She fell down and I lifted up her clothes and slashed her lower abdomen and throat. I covered her up and put her knee boots on top and then drove off.'

He had been disturbed by nearby voices and then saw a car driving away from a block of flats where he later discovered the TV personality Jimmy

Savile lived. Ironically, the two men have struck up a sort of friendship in recent years after Savile, who has for many years carried out charity work as a hospital porter and prison visitor, met Sutcliffe in Parkhurst Prison after his trial. 'He used to come into my cell often, and joke about us both being a couple of Yorkie puds,' says Sutcliffe.

By the time Sutcliffe was transferred to Broadmoor Hospital, Savile was established there in the temporary post of Director of a Task Force set up to run the hospital while a new health authority was being formed. He still singles out Sutcliffe during visiting hours in Central Hall, and promised to help him with materials for painting and other hobbies.

Savile – an early-morning jogger – might have been destined to discover Sutcliffe's third murder victim on that frosty February morning in 1977. Instead, it was a neighbour, John Bolton, who saw her body lying under some trees while he was out jogging. The woman's body had been defiled, her skirt pulled up, and her boots placed over her legs, under her fur-trimmed jacket. She lay face down on the grass, her long dark hair temporarily hiding the stab wounds in her neck and throat.

The mark of a car tyre nearby gave police a clue that made them feel for the first time that they might be able to close the net. Their target, now positively identified as the killer of two previous victims, was not straying from his chosen area of Chapeltown, and must surely soon be caught.

However, the controlled cunning that had become Sutcliffe's key to success so far now led him away from Chapeltown and back to another familiar hunting-ground – the Manningham red-light area of Bradford, a few miles from the house in Clayton where he was still living with his wife and her parents. To confuse his pursuers further, he introduced another new tactic, killing his next victim indoors, in her own home.

Sutcliffe's delusions of 'being on a mission from God' appear to have been at their most vivid at this time. He was confident that he had been chosen to 'clean up the streets' and has spoken of 'saving the souls' of the prostitutes he butchered. 'It was my calling and I had no qualms about it.'

Late Saturday night, 23 April 1977, this misconceived self-righteousness asserted itself as Sutcliffe drove through the grim backstreets of Manningham. He saw thirty-three-year-old prostitute Patricia 'Tina' Atkinson, a divorcee with three children, threading her way unsteadily home to her bedsit in nearby Oak Avenue after an evening's drinking at local pubs. She was tall, slim and attractive. Sutcliffe watched her banging on the roof of a parked car, and shouting, drunkenly. 'It's obvious why I picked her. No decent woman would have been using language like that at the top of her voice.'

She jumped in his car, telling him she had a flat just round the corner; it took less than five minutes for them to arrive. 'I hung my coat up when I went inside because I didn't want her to see the hammer in the pocket.' This time Sutcliffe had selected a claw hammer for his purpose.

He saw Tina sit on the bed. 'I went up and hit her on the back of the head. She fell off the bed onto the floor. I saw lots of blood on the bedroom floor. I hit her again. I put her back on the bed by picking her up under the arms and hoisting her up. I pulled her clothes up and hit her several times more on her body with the hammer. I saw it marking her body. She made horrible gurgling noises when I hit her. She was still making gurgling noises when I left, but I knew she would not be in any state to tell anyone.'

Sonia was in bed when he got home to Tanton Crescent. He noticed bloodstains on his jeans, so he rinsed them in the kitchen sink and hung them up to dry, also wiping more blood off his boots before going to bed. 'Then I carried on as if nothing had happened.' He said that this was one of only two occasions when his clothes and footwear were bloodstained.

A boyfriend of Tina's called to see her early the next evening, and when she did not answer the door, he let himself in and found her. Sutcliffe had covered her body with bed linen; her sweater had been pulled up, her bra removed, her jeans and underwear pulled down. She had been hit with a claw hammer and on her lower abdomen there were oblong bruises that the police pathologist described as 'curious'. Tina's once-pretty face was unrecognisable, beaten mercilessly by hammer-blows.

On the bloodstained floor there was the imprint of a size-seven Dunlop boot. It matched a boot-print left on Emily Jackson's thigh. West Yorkshire police now had four murders on their books, and only two clues.

They did not even have the benefit of great public interest, for the murder of prositutes or 'good time' girls did not stir the minds of most families, who read of the killings with a shudder of relief that they themselves had no knowledge of that low-life world under the street lamps. There was sympathy, but no real communal fear, no sense yet of terror that a mass murderer was loose among them.

That was to come later, two months later, with the death of pretty teenager Jayne MacDonald, who was slain like all the others and found next morning with the tell-tale head injuries inflicted by a hammer, and many stab wounds in her neck and trunk. A knife had been thrust repeatedly into the same two wounds on the front and back of her body.

Jayne was sixteen, a shop assistant who had

recently left school, one of four children, and her father's great favourite. By the time her body was found at 9.45 a.m. in an adventure playground, her parents were frantic. Jayne was a sweet-natured and vivacious girl, who looked forward to her Saturday nights out.

On 5 June 1977, she had dressed in a blue and white checked skirt, striped halter top and a light summer jacket and gone out to meet some friends. She promised she would not be late home.

She enjoyed her evening at a Leeds city-centre *bierkeller*-style disco where she chatted to friends and danced with eighteen-year-old Mark Jones, whom she had met for the first time that evening. They dawdled around the city centre later, eating fish and chips. Mark said he lived nearby and that his sister would probably give Jayne a lift home.

His sister's car was not parked outside the house, so they lingered together a little longer, having 'a kiss and a cuddle', then Jayne said she would walk home alone. She set off into the night, happy and confident, unthinkingly taking a short cut through the red-light district of Chapeltown. At about 1.45 a.m. she was heading towards home at 77 Scott Hall Avenue, just six doors from the home of the Ripper's first murder victim, Wilma McCann, when her path crossed that of Peter Sutcliffe.

Increasingly, he had taken to spending Saturday

evening with his next-door neighbours in Tanton Crescent, Ronald Barker and his brother David. The three of them would pub-crawl their way around the district, and later Ronald Barker was to tell of these excursions, sinister in retrospect.

He remembered the three of them having a night out together a week before the murder of Jayne MacDonald. They went to a number of pubs in York. While the brothers played pool, however, Sutcliffe had disappeared. 'We were a bit annoyed because we didn't know how to get back, and at closing time we walked back to the car and Pete was standing near it. 'It was about threequarters of an hour since we saw him last, and he told us he had followed a lass out of the pub. I can't remember him saying anything else.' Barker expected them to drive straight home, but having fallen asleep in Sutcliffe's car, he woke up to find they were in Chapeltown, Leeds, and asked what they were doing there. 'Pete was driving and said something about this being Ripper country. The car stopped in Chapeltown and Pete got out. He didn't say where he was going and we didn't ask. He walked off and was away for about a quarter of an hour or twenty minutes.'

Barker said Sutcliffe sometimes spoke of girls he had been with. 'He said he went with a nurse at one time. He also said something about having two girls following him back to the car the previous night.

He said he had one of them in the back and one over the bonnet. Sometimes he would shout to girls from the car. He was fascinated by the red-light areas and always wanted to look at whores. Sometimes he got out of the car and followed them. I don't know why he resorted to them, because he had such a lovely wife sitting at home.'

Sonia, of course, was unlikely to be 'sitting at home' on a Saturday night, her husband's preferred night for his killings, and was often out working a night shift at the hospital.

It was after one of many nights out with the Barker brothers that Sutcliffe drove over to Chapeltown on his own and saw Jayne MacDonald hurrying home. After drinking in pubs around Bradford, he had dropped Ronald and David at the end of Tanton Crescent. As they went home he wheeled his car round and headed east for Leeds. He saw Jayne walking down Chapeltown Road. 'I were quite certain she were a prostitute, absolutely positive. She were walking along in the red-light area, for one thing, and then I saw her stop and chat to a couple of girls on a street corner. I felt sure she were one of them.'

Having watched for a few minutes from his car, he took a hammer and a kitchen knife from under the driver's seat and slipped them into his pocket. 'I walked behind her, following her a short distance. She never looked round. I hit her on the back of

131

the head and she fell down. I pulled her, face down, into the corner of a yard. Her shoes made a horrible scraping noise.'

He hit her again then pulled her clothes up and stabbed her several times in the chest, then in the back. Blood smears on her back showed that Sutcliffe had got blood all over his knife and had wiped it as clean as he could on her body.

When the police gently turned Jayne's body over, they found a broken bottle embedded in a gaping wound in her chest. Sutcliffe was later to claim that he had not deliberately pushed the bottle into the wound and that it must have happened as he pulled her across the rubble-strewn playground.

After his arrest, Sutcliffe told police he thought his wife had been working that night as she had a job in a private nursing home on Fridays and Saturdays. 'That is why I have done a lot of my attacks on a Saturday night. When I saw that the girl was so young and not a prostitute I felt I was inhuman and that the devil had got into me and I was a beast.'

The murder of Jayne MacDonald was to shock and sicken the whole of the local community and sent ripples of fear through every woman in West Yorkshire. This latest victim of the Ripper was a perfectly innocent young girl from a loving home; she was not a prostitute, and unlike his other victims she had not been drinking. A post-mortem examination showed she had taken only soft drinks that night.

Her father, former railwayman Wilf Mac-Donald, who adored his daughter, was to die within two years from a broken heart, having never recovered from the ordeal of identifying her body in the city mortuary. His world had been plunged into permanent darkness at that moment, and as he fell ill and faded, the feeling of mortal dread was growing in many other families like his. Overnight, there was a public clamour for the police to find the murderer.

Sutcliffe says he suffered shock himself when he saw the newspaper headlines. 'I still feel terrible about it. It was a young girl. I read of her father dying and it brought it all back to me. I realised what a monster I had become. I thought she was a prostitute. The urge to kill prostitutes was very strong and I had gone out of my mind.'

Two weeks after he murdered Jayne Mac-Donald, Sutcliffe struck again – but this time he experienced a shock of a different kind when he read the next day's newspaper headlines. His victim, left for dead, had survived and would soon have recovered sufficiently to talk to the police.

She was forty-two-year-old Maureen Long, who had enjoyed a night out in a Bradford club before wending her way home in the early hours of Sunday, 10 July 1977.

Sutcliffe spotted Maureen Long as she left the Mecca club and he stopped his car. 'Are you going far?' he asked her.

She said: 'Are you giving me a lift?'

Sutcliffe replied: 'Yes, if you want one.' She told him she had been to the club, and was living with an ex-boxer who was a 'spoilsport'. She directed Sutcliffe to her home but said he shouldn't stop outside. He drove past for a short distance and Maureen Long got out. She said if there was no one home they could go in.

'She asked me if I fancied her. I told her I did.'

Maureen returned to the car and told Sutcliffe she knew a place where they could go. They drove to nearby Bowling Back Lane.

'I had my hammer ready as she got out of the car. I also had a knife. I struck her on the head with the hammer while she was crouching, urinating.'

At Sutcliffe's trial, the Attorney General, Sir Michael Havers, said: 'There he is, from the moment of picking her up until all that happened, holding himself back, restraining himself, waiting for the right moment when she put herself in a position where he could use the hammer from behind.'

Maureen Long slumped to the ground after he hit her and he pulled her onto waste ground. He pulled up her clothes and stabbed her three or four times in the chest.

134

'I saw a light on in a caravan, but it didn't stop me. The next day I heard my victim was still alive. I got a nasty shock. I thought it was the end of the line there and then. I thought she would be able to identify me.'

Days later, though, Sutcliffe read that Maureen Long was suffering from amnesia. 'This made me less worried about getting caught. My desire to kill prostitutes was getting stronger than ever and took me over completely. I was in a dilemma.'

The last thing Maureen Long remembered was going to the cloakroom at the club at 2 a.m., and leaving to walk towards the city centre. When Sutcliffe drew up next to her in his white Ford Corsair, she was glad of the lift home. Several hours later her weak cries for help were heard coming from a piece of waste ground in Back Bowling Lane, where she lay with three broken ribs and stab wounds all over her body. Five years later she was still attending hospital as an out-patient, and also having fits.

The mother of three, Maureen was awarded £8,500 compensation by the High Court in 1982 after Mr Justice Balcombe heard that she was suffering from recurring nightmares and 'could no longer cope with life'. At Sutcliffe's trial, Sir Michael Havers had told the jury: 'You might think that Mrs Long is lucky to be alive at all.'

Mrs Long told the hearing that her youngest

daughter had been taken into care as she herself could no longer manage. Her nights were filled with horrible dreams. She suffered blackouts and headaches, and was terrified of going out. Mrs Long told the High Court she had been left heavily scarred by the attack and had lost all interest in sex. Her hair had turned grey and had fallen out around a two-inch-deep depression in her skull where Sutcliffe had hit her with a hammer.

Mrs Long said: 'If it was not for Sutcliffe I would be able to have my Jacqueline at home, but I cannot cope. The thought that he might one day get out terrifies me.'

The vague description she had eventually been able to give police of her attacker had not been a great deal of help, but she remembered the white Ford with the black roof. Unfortunately, Sutcliffe was soon to discard it and the trail went cold once more.

Later, when interviewed by the police, Sutcliffe said that he felt he had not achieved his purpose, which had been to kill her.

CHAPTER FIVE

Hunters

'I were totally detached, you see. I were looking down and thinking, "Oh somebody else had done it." You know.'

Today, at his most lucid, this is how Sutcliffe describes himself and his behaviour during the period when he was at the height of his murder campaign. In 1977 he carried out six homicidal attacks on women. Years later, he reasons that it wasn't 'badness' that was driving him on; it must have been temporary 'madness'. 'I had nothing against those women personally. I didn't know them at all before I done them in. I didn't even speak to most of them. Anyone with a grain of common sense can see that I believed God was telling me to do it. There was no other motive.'

By mid-1977, a tragic combination of events was making it possible for him to go on and on and on. He had settled into his lorry-driving job at Clark's and would often volunteer for long-distance runs that paid better. Each working day would see him behind the wheel of his 32-ton Ford Intercontinental, forging a solitary route down the motorways of the north, the Midlands and Scotland – occasionally crossing on the night ferry to northern France or the Netherlands. No one was close enough to note the deterioration taking place.

At home there was a flurry of excitement as he and Sonia – she with a great deal of enthusiasm – found the house they had been looking for ever since their savings had grown equal to the deposit they needed for a mortgage. Sonia and her mother were absorbed in the house-buying plans, and Sonia herself had come on so well that she was about to start a job as a supply teacher at a local primary school. Her earnings were taken into account when a mortgage was granted for the £16,000 house in Garden Lane, Heaton, a respectable – almost posh – area of Bradford.

It was literally the home of Sonia's dreams – a four-bedroomed, bow-fronted model of a suburban family residence, set back off the road and built on an incline so that the front and back doors were reached by a short, steep drive, with a neat patch of garden at the front and running round one side of the house. From the opposite side of the road, one looks up at the grey pebble-dashed silhouette of Number 6 Garden Lane, standing solidly alongside others with the same desirable qualities and finds it forbidding – but that may just be with the benefit of hindsight.

At the top of the concrete drive are the double doors of the garage. This was Sutcliffe's dream – his own mechanic's workshop, affording the means by which to tinker with his beloved second-hand cars, and the space to do it in. There were wall-racks for his tools – his hammers, knives, screwdrivers and hacksaws – the means by which to carry on his murderous mission, and a patch of garden nearby where a small bonfire would dispose of his bloodstained clothes whenever necessary. Just inside the back door, within a few yards of the garage, stood the washing-machine in which he could deal with any tell-tale stains not drastic enough to require burning.

Sonia enthused over this 'perfect' dwelling, endlessly planning the colours, the decor, the furnishings, the curtains and the lampshades. She simply couldn't wait to be part of that neighbourhood, to become one of the professional people who cared meticulously for their homes and their gardens, who guarded this little enclave against any overspill from nearby rundown Manningham, who had style and taste, just like her. To top the list of delights, Number 6 was the only detached house in the road. At the end of a row of similarly bow-fronted thirties jobs, it stood next to the neighbourhood's special amenity – a rough field sometimes used for football matches. A green open space. It were just like being in't countryside.

Sonia and Peter Sutcliffe moved into their ideal home in September 1977. Both had put the near-slum conditions of their council-house upbringing firmly behind them. They had made it to Heaton, to respectability.

There was no stopping Sonia now. Having spent every penny on the purchase of the house, she was determined that they would 'do it up' themselves. Everything would have to be done to her taste and her satisfaction and, because she didn't mind spending every spare moment working on the house, she didn't see why Peter shouldn't do the same.

Her mother, a daily visitor, remembers the excitement of it all. 'Sonia and Pete had saved hard for a house of their own. Sonia was a dedicated teacher and took pleasure in giving the children under her care a sound education to give them a good start in life. Pete also worked very hard at his job, which was physically and mentally demanding. He put in many extra hours of overtime and although he was tired he would always put the needs of others before himself. When they bought their own house it was in the best district of the whole of Bradford. Whatever spare time they had was put into the house, first redesigning, then plastering, tiling, decorating and painting, both inside and out, as well as tending the garden. We felt proud that my daughter's happiness and future were well assured...'

Sonia – intense, demanding and self-obsessed by nature – was now engrossed, her teaching job and her lovely new home filling her thoughts. Never a gossip or even a willing conversationalist, she was unaware of the thoughts filling her husband's mind and only vaguely aware of the increasing fuss going on around her over the Yorkshire Ripper murders.

'I had better things to do at that time than take any notice of the newspaper headlines, or sit chatting about something that was nothing to do with me. I've never liked that sort of thing,' she says.

When the West Yorkshire police became so desperate that they begged every woman in the country to ask herself, 'Is it my husband, my brother or my son?', what was Sonia Sutcliffe doing? 'I just didn't read it. I was busy marking my pupils' exercise books and planning things for the house. Pete was his normal self and there was nothing unusual for me to notice.' She sounds indignant and exasperated.

She was busy buying paint, rubbing down the woodwork, shinning up ladders, digging the garden, shifting the furniture round. She was perfecting her surroundings and fussing over every detail. There would be no greasy work-clothes worn in her house and staining the best chairs; no dirty footprints, even on the kitchen floor. Peter must learn the new rules and adapt to their new living standard. Acquiescent and considerate, Peter would take his work-clothes off in the garage or outside the back door and feed them into the washing-machine himself – 'it's all right luv, it's no trouble, I'll do it meself'.

'Sonia, bless her, seemed right happy now. Only a delicate little thing, but she worked as hard as any man, you know. She were exhausted by late evening, after a day's teaching and then painting the house, but she drove herself on. Everything had to be that perfect, wi' her.'

Pink floral wallpaper went on to bedroom walls, caramel and yellow paper in the sitting room; paintwork gleamed; the dining-room was pristine and formal; unexciting but solid furniture was installed. Dainty little covers protected the upholstery of armchairs and sofas from dirt, dust and people. His-and-hers wardrobes were fitted in the main bedroom, the attic was opened up to create a study-workroom for Sonia – her retreat – and a box-room on the first floor, the fourth bedroom, was earmarked for the child or children they were mercifully never to have. A teddy bear still sits on the little dressing-table.

The kitchen, the hub of all family life in childhood years for both of them, was little more than a utility room at 6 Garden Lane. Sonia was no cook and didn't even pack sandwiches for her husband's long day on the roads.

The whole house was a monument to Sonia's punishing hard work. She marked out her territory using pieces of her own hand-made pottery, with its curious abstract design. To congratulate herself on a job well done, she arranged a house-warming party at which she would remind the Sutcliffe family how superior her world was to theirs.

While she was tirelessly preparing her little palace for its grand opening, Sutcliffe had been busy too. On Saturday 1 October he drove over to Manchester and brutally murdered prostitute Jean Jordan at the start of a nine-day episode that was to see Sutcliffe at his most sick and depraved.

She was 'Scotch Jean', first killed by the hammer blows and frenzied stabbing, and then attacked again and disembowelled eight days later when Sutcliffe anxiously returned to her body in search of the £5 note he had paid her for sex.

The night on which he raced back to the still undiscovered dead girl, left on a patch of waste ground next to Manchester's Southern Cemetery, was the night of the house-warming party. Unable to find the £5 note, he deliberately and violently slashed at her body, then pulled it further into the open so that it would be found. To disguise his own trademark, he attempted to saw off her head. Pathologist Reuben Woodcock later told an inquest that Jean Jordan had been smashed about the head eleven times with a heavy weapon. She had knife wounds from the left shoulder to the right knee; there were eighteen wounds on her stomach and chest and another six on her right side.

Coroner Roderick Davies said: 'We can assume that he knocked her unconscious, whoever committed this crime ripped her up.' Sutcliffe says he intended to cut off her head and leave it somewhere else 'to make a big mystery of it. I were very frustrated not finding my £5 note and thinking my time was up. I remember I kicked her a few times. I was frustrated, and I thought I had been there long enough so I got back home and went to bed. I was surprised I did not have much blood on my clothes. I put my trousers into the garage to dispose of later. I later burned my trousers along with some garden rubbish.'

Sutcliffe was right to fear that 'his time was up', for it should have been. The next day an allotment-holder found the dead girl's body, along with her green plastic handbag containing the £5 note. It was one of a batch numbered AN51 121501 to AN51 121569 issued by a Bradford bank as part of a £25,000 payment going out on a Friday morning to thirty-five local firms for their wage packets. Thirty detectives from Greater Manchester joined thirty colleagues from West Yorkshire and moved into the Shipley area to question employees at local factories.

A couple of exhausting weeks later, their enquiries led them to 6 Garden Lane. 'Just routine enquiries, Mrs Sutcliffe, is your husband in? Right, nothing to worry about luv, just a few questions and that. We've got to do it, see. A house-warming party? Oh well, that's no bother then, is it?

Sutcliffe was polite, cool, relieved. Even with all that worrying and wondering, and practically *giving* them the clue that could have been the end of him, they couldn't work it out. He was too clever for them, that's what it was, the deadly clever combination of him and the 'voices'. Together they were invincible.

Six days later the detectives were back on the doorstep. 'Bloody 'ell, luv, what do they want this time? I'm getting right fed up wi' this.'

The police had been doing their homework and had checked on the housewarming party and Sutcliffe's parents. 'Just thought they'd come back, like, and note down his occupation and the name and address of his employers, and the registration number of his car. Just routine. Nice young couple, not long moved in. Both a bit worried-looking. Only to be expected. Nobody likes this sort o' thing.'

Perhaps the striking, black frizzy hair and neat beard that made Sutcliffe so distinctive-looking should have rung a bell with them two months later when they were able to interview a woman whom he had attacked and who described him accurately.

Marilyn Moore, aged twenty-five, was a prostitute 'doing business' in Chapeltown, Leeds, Sutcliffe's preferred hunting ground, on the night of 14

December 1977. An impoverished mother of four, she had left her flat in Bradford to drive over to Chapeltown, where she first saw Sutcliffe as she turned a corner into Leopold Street. He was standing on the kerbside, leaning on the door of his red Morris Oxford. She made a quick deal with him, told him her name was Carol, and climbed into the car beside him.

She sat beside him for nearly half an hour as he drove her over to Scott Hall Street where, he said confidently, he knew a secluded spot where they could have sex. She remembered later that he had looked at himself in the rear-view mirror several times during the journey, once smoothing down his black hair. He said his name was Dave and claimed to know a prostitute friend of hers, correctly naming her and her boyfriend.

After Sutcliffe had parked the car, he suggested they both got into the back seat and as Marilyn stooped down she felt a blinding pain on the back of her head. He shouted 'Dirty prostitute bitch' as he struck her again and again. Her screams were heard by a passer-by, and she was taken to Leeds Royal Infirmary for emergency surgery. She was able to tell police that her attacker had a neat beard and a moustache like Jason King, the secret agent hero of a popular TV series.

Police, certain that the murder attempt had been carried out by the Yorkshire Ripper, noted grimly that it had happened just 200 yards from the spot where he had struck his first victim, Wilma McCann, more than two years earlier. They put together a photofit picture of the man they wanted, but were never really confident that Marilyn had remembered him accurately, for her injuries were horrific. She had been struck eight blows to her head, and surgery was needed to relieve pressure on her brain at the place where her skull had caved in.

Years later, she said she still woke up at night, shaking and moaning. 'I can never forget what happened,' she said. 'I could see his face every time I closed my eyes. Sometimes I almost wish he had killed me – it might have been better than the nightmares.'

Chief Constable Ronald Gregory, heading the Ripper hunt, revealed later that he took Marilyn to Leeds University Hospital to be questioned under deep hypnosis, yet still he felt that her description might not be reliable. She telephoned three times to say she had just seen the Ripper in a public house, but each time it had proved a false alarm.

Little wonder that Marilyn was so nervous; she had come terrifyingly close to a brutal death and would never be able to erase the experience from her mind. A court later awarded her £10,500 in criminal injuries compensation.

The photofit picture she helped to compile

taunted detectives for three and a half more years, and when Sutcliffe was finally arrested they noticed the uncanny likeness. Yet there were no more unexpected knocks at the Sutcliffes' door and queries: ''Ello luv, sorry to disturb you, is your husband in?', to interrupt the relentless pattern of killing that characterised the first few months of 1978.

The intensity of the relationship between Sutcliffe and his wife had developed further amid the new privacy they enjoyed at Garden Lane. He would tell later of her determination to keep the house spotless, of her 'obsessive cleanliness', and that, despite his respect for the rules requiring him to remove his dirty work clothes and shoes before entering the house, Sonia would still spend hours cleaning the carpets. Their marriage 'had its ups and downs' he said, describing Sonia as 'over-excited, highly strung and unstable'.

Demanding his full attention, she would take the newspaper he was reading and 'swipe him round the head with it'. She would turn off the television while he was watching and insist he talked to her instead. Sonia indignantly denies that this was excessive behaviour: 'After we had both been at work all day I naturally liked him to come and talk to me in the kitchen while I got the evening meal ready. I don't see what's wrong with that.'

She hated the world to know that there were

rows between herself and her husband, and he told doctors openly that he sometimes worried the neighbours would hear their raised voices. 'I would always try and reason with her and I tried to be understanding, because I had seen her during her mental breakdown and I was concerned that that did not happen again. She couldn't help suffering with her nerves. She just had a lower threshold than other people. I didn't mind. I felt my duty was to be understanding, and it was something that came naturally to me. I enjoyed looking after her, even though her determination about some things was often very irritating.'

Sonia was doing well at her teaching job, and often brought work home. If Sutcliffe was away on a long-distance driving job and was going to be home late, she would curl up with her schoolbooks in the little attic room that was her retreat, and stay awake until he returned. 'I'd hear him come in, and walk upstairs to the bathroom. I'd be in my night clothes, and I'd talk to him while he washed. I'd tell him about my day and he'd tell me about his.'

As she talked to me of this, Sonia perched on the edge of the pale blue enamelled bath to demonstrate the cosiness of the scene. In front of her was the matching blue washbasin where she now knows that Sutcliffe was probably rinsing God knows what sort of dirt from his hands. Then they would go together to their his-and-hers wardrobes and double bed. While Sonia says primly that they had a 'normal' sex life, Peter describes it as 'great' although he does not dispute that he once suffered a mild form of venereal disease contracted from a source outside his marriage. Sutcliffe claims he caught the infection 'from a still-warm toilet seat'.

Sutcliffe would always be tolerant of his wife, seeing her as difficult, but at the same time vulnerable. He allowed her to dominate his home-life, giving in to petty demands on the grounds that the love they had was too important to put at risk over minor irritations. Besides, there were major traumas going on in areas of his life about which Sonia knew nothing. 'By then I were convinced I were being protected by an outside influence – something infinitely more powerful than the police, or anyone else. I believed I just couldn't be caught.'

Now living across town from his old mates, the Barker brothers and Trevor Birdsall, Sutcliffe was often out drinking alone. 'If I was late home it was easy to explain. I'd say I'd been on a long trip or been loading the wagon for the next morning.'

In reality, he was regularly scouring the red-light districts by night, though something of a model lorry-driver employee by day. After his arrest his boss, Tom Clark, said that he was a good driver. 'He never caused us any problems. He was never violent, and always quiet.' He would, however, become 'strangely upset' if people shouted at him or raised their voices. 'He was so sensitive, if he was told off his eyes would fill with tears. He appeared to be a very deep sensitive person.'

Sutcliffe, he said, was always clean and neatly dressed. 'he was very quiet – a bit of a loner. His lorry cab was like a palace compared with some. He had no pin-ups in his cab, just a lot of maps.' Mr Clark described Sutcliffe as 'a cut above the average lorry driver. He always spoke slowly, having thought out what he was going to say. He was very deliberate in all his actions,' he said.

Sutcliffe usually wore a leather bomber jacket, combat-style hat and fatigue trousers for work. It was not unusual for him to have been questioned about the Ripper murders. Many other employees of his and other local firms had been questioned by the police. As far as his employers were concerned, the only cloud hanging over him was the court case about to come up as a result of a breathalyser test in June 1980.

Mr Clark said Sutcliffe had told him all about the drink-driving charge. 'He said it had been a hot summer's day and he'd had a couple of pints to quench his thirst. Police noticed his wheels squealing as he took a corner in the lorry, and stopped him for routine questioning. He was due to appear in court and we would have had to sack him if he'd lost his licence. We'd have had no choice. Everyone was sorry about that.'

Sutcliffe was such a favoured employee that it was his profile Clark's chose to appear in a photograph they commissioned for an advertising poster. The poster hung in the entrance foyer to Clark's offices and was the first thing visitors to the premises would see. It went out in the company brochure, too, advertising the haulage facilities available. In the photograph, Sutcliffe was seen, unsmiling, at the wheel of his 32-ton articulated lorry. Sutcliffe himself boasts that he was the only really honest driver in the firm, the only one who refused to join in when the others were 'nicking stuff' wholesale. He was, consequently, the only one kept on by the company once the thefts were discovered. 'I didn't want to know about that sort o' thing. It weren't my style.'

Sutcliffe's style was something altogether different. In January 1978, a little more than a month after the attack on Marilyn Moore, he executed a homicidal assault on a Bradford prostitute, and once again appeared to have completely 'got away wi' it'.

That evening he had been helping his parents move to their new home, a modern maisonette near to Bingley town centre, which was more convenient for his mother whose health was now causing her severe problems. She was often breathless, suffering from chest pains. Her eldest son, Peter, was particularly concerned for her.

Later on that night he made a diversion through Manningham on his way home to Heaton. This was to become a text-book version of his murder technique. He had hardly sized up blonde young mum Yvonne Pearson before she was in the car beside him and agreeing to a £5 fee. 'On reflection, it was a very fateful moment for her. This was the one time when I was genuinely going home, but even so I still had my hammer under my seat.'

In a grimy, rubbish-strewn yard at the back of the mill where his father worked, Sutcliffe struck her heavily on the back of her head with a walling hammer, and pulled her body under an old discarded sofa among the debris.

He grabbed some of the horsehair stuffing from the sofa to thrust down her throat to stop her screaming as another car drove past, and held her nose. 'I let go after a while to see if she was still making a noise but she started again so I took hold of her nose again until the car drove away. It seemed like hours.' Yvonne's body was stripped, and then shoved crudely underneath the sofa, where it stayed undiscovered for two more months. The investigation was seriously hampered by the reluctance of those close to Yvonne to give detectives information about her background and movements. Police found a handbag belonging to the dead woman, but its contents revealed very little. Officers had questioned her during their enquiries into previous Ripper murders but she had been of little assistance. Yvonne herself was very uneasy about the killings, perhaps more so than detectives realised, though she was under pressure from her pimp and also needed money to bring up her two young children, three-year-old Colette and six-month-old Lorraine.

The twenty-two-year-old prostitute was finally found on Easter Sunday. By then, another girl had been killed and mutilated by Sutcliffe, and so far West Yorkshire police had spent £2 million on their unsuccessful hunt for him. Chief Constable Gregory announced plans for an élite murder squad to concentrate solely on catching the Yorkshire Ripper. 'His murders have reached epidemic proportions. So far this man has had the luck of the devil.'

After his arrest, it took Sutcliffe more than fifteen hours to relive, in meticulous detail, the crimes he had committed. Describing the walling hammer he used to kill Yvonne Pearson, he helpfully drew a picture of it for detectives.

Ten days after the cold-blooded attack on Yvonne, he was cruising around a red-light area away from his home territory. This was in Huddersfield, where teenage twins, Helen and Rita Rytka, made a miserable living from prostitution on the streets.

Even for twins, the girls were remarkably close, perhaps bonded more tightly than is usual by the sadness and suffering they shared as children. Their parents split up when the girls were small, abandoning Helen and Rita to a succession of institutions.

In May 1974, deeply unhappy but imaginative, the girls wrote to the *Yorkshire Post* looking for foster parents. They sent a poignant letter to the editor, saying that being fostered out together would be like winning £1,000 on the pools. They included a poem they'd written:

> Loneliness is to live in a world
> Where people do not care
> Loneliness is to go outside
> To find no one is there, and
> You fall down in despair,
> Falling on your knees in prayer.
> Asking God to rescue you
> From this cruel snare,
> But no one comes,
> No voice is heard,
> No one cares if I was lured,
> Lured into the deepest hole,
> Cast aside by those so cruel,
> And treated like a mule.

In common with other streetwalkers, all by now terrified of an encounter with the Ripper murderer, the eighteen-year-old girls had an arrangement.

Each would note down the make, model and registration number of a customer's car, as one of them went off for sex. Afterwards they would rendezvous under the railway viaduct in Great Northern Street, before accepting another offer.

The girls, both pretty with dark, glamorous looks inherited from their Italian mother and Jamaican father, had always stuck together. Abandoned at an early age, they had lived together in children's homes and with foster parents until leaving school, and now shared a seedy bedsitter in a Huddersfield back-street, earning their living from full-time prostitution.

Despite the arrangement they had, Helen climbed into the car that drew up beside her as she waited for Rita. The driver suggested they went across the road to a timber yard for sex, and it was so close by that she took the risk.

She was the only one of Sutcliffe's many victims with whom he had sexual intercourse. He went through with it 'because she had aroused me, and because I had to keep her quiet while she was moaning'. She was 'moaning' because Sutcliffe had come up behind her and struck her several heavy blows on the back of the head. She had fallen to the ground. 'She had got me aroused a moment previous, so I had no alternative but to go ahead with the act of sex as the only means of keeping her quiet.'

Helen was dying from her wounds, but Sutcliffe attacked her again. 'I took a knife from the car and stabbed her several times through the heart and lungs.' He pushed her slim body out of sight between some piles of timber, and threw a corrugated sheet of asbestos over her.

Her body was discovered a few days' later, and her distraught twin, Rita, appealed on television: 'For his own sake and the public's sake he should hand himself over. The public will appreciate he has done that. If anyone is holding information they should for their own sake come forward and give that information which is so vital to find him.'

She dressed in her sister's clothes to retrace her steps that night and was photographed for a police poster, her dead sister's face superimposed on her own, to help trap the killer.

Police kept watch as Rita patrolled the 'patch' she once walked with Helen, and official police protection was offered to prostitutes who would reveal regular customers' names and addresses to help in the hunt for clues. The offer was not taken up. The only clue gleaned from the Rytka killing was that her murderer drove a dark blue car.

Sutcliffe has always insisted there was no sexual motive for any of his killings. Although he admitted having intercourse with Helen Rytka, he said he had no choice. In court, when it was suggested that he had a sexual interest in his other victims, he became agitated and shook his head from side to side, mouthing, 'No no, no.'

Later still, he spoke to a fellow Broadmoor inmate about it, saying, 'Whenever any of them had no clothes on it was because they got undressed for sex.'

The other patient asked, 'But you were still humping them, weren't you?' Sutcliffe replied: 'No, I didn't hump any of them. Well, no. There was the Huddersfield one. That's the only one that had sex. But that was all she wanted to start with. I couldn't stop her, then I knew I had to get rid of her. I paid her a fiver. That's all they charge.'

Three and a half months after killing Helen Rytka, Sutcliffe struck again. His attack on forty-year-old prostitute Vera Millward was so violent, and her wounds so hideous, that court officials were ordered to remove photographs of her body from the files handed to the jury at Sutcliffe's trial. Prosecuting counsel Sir Michael Havers, having already warned them to 'steel themselves' before looking at any of the pictures, felt it was not fair for them to have to look at Vera Millward's photograph at all.

She was, in many ways, one of Sutcliffe's saddest victims, living in a run-down council flat in Hulme, Manchester, near to the Southern Cemetery where he had killed Jean Jordan. A Spanish immigrant, Vera had been widowed at a young age and the

The Sutcliffes' wedding day - summer 1974.

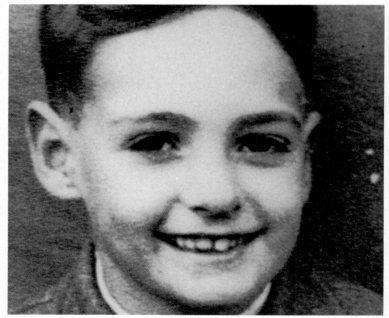

Above: A pint-sized Peter Sutcliffe (left), aged 6, peers at a world populated by giants.

Below: Sutcliffe's school photograph. His headmaster described him as "a very ordinary pupil".

Above: The Catholic Polish grave in Bingley cemetery where Sutcliffe claimed Jesus spoke to him.

Below: Sutcliffe, in pale coloured sweater, at work in the graveyard where he first heard his "voices".

Above: The Yorkshire Ripper arrives at Newport Crown Court, the victim of an assault by fellow prisoner, James Costello.

Below: Sutcliffe's strange watchful gaze, caught on film for the first time at his friend's wedding. The groom, Trevor Birdsall, later gave evidence at his trial.

Above: Gaunt and forbidding, the house in Garden Lane, Heaton, where Sonia still lives.

Below: The body of 19 year old Josephine Whitaker covered crudely by a blanket in the early morning mist at Savile Park, Halifax.

Patricia Atkinson

Josephine Whitaker

Jayne MacDonald

Wilma McCann

Helen Rytka

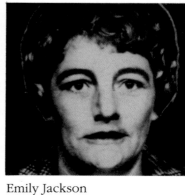

Emily Jackson

rene Richardson

Jacqueline Hill

Barbara Leach

Jean Jordan

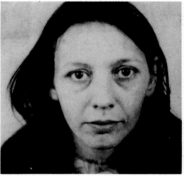

Vera Millward

Yvonne Pearson

Marguerite Walls

Sonia Sutciffe, alone and defiant as she fights her way through the courts.

five children of her marriage had been taken into council care.

Vera and her Jamaican boyfriend had 'an understanding' about her work on the streets, whereby he would stay at home with their two young children while Vera worked a patch nearby. On the night of 16 May 1978, she said casually that she was popping out to buy cigarettes and, knowing what that meant, he did not expect to see her for several hours. In fact, he never saw her again. For instead of her regular 'date' with an old and trusted client, Vera was picked up by a young man driving through the area.

They travelled in his car for about two and a half miles, to a quiet spot in the grounds of Manchester Royal Infirmary, where prostitutes and their clients were frequently seen. There, Vera – a frail and sickly woman who had chronic bad health and weighed just 8 stone – put up a brave fight when she was struck on the head by Sutcliffe. He killed her with three hammer blows and then stabbed her continuously in the abdomen. As she tried to fight him off, blood and brain tissue stained her clothes and body. Sutcliffe covered her corpse carefully with her overcoat.

A man collecting his son from the hospital's casualty ward heard three screams for help, which seemed to echo round the vast hospital grounds, but decided they were from a patient in pain on one of the wards.

Vera's body was found early the following morning by workmen. Police waited for Vera's regular client, a balding, bespectacled middle-aged man who usually parked outside her ground floor council flat, flashing his car headlights, each Tuesday and Thursday. Two days after she died, he turned up as usual, was questioned by police and eliminated from their enquiries. He hadn't been able to make it on the Tuesday, and Vera had hung around waiting for 'business' with passers-by instead. Sutcliffe had been the first to come along.

Ripper squad detectives from West Yorkshire drove over to Manchester to team up with the local crime squad. Within a few hours there were dozens of officers literally on their hands and knees, combing every inch of the area where Vera was found.

As police frantically stepped up their activity, Sutcliffe coolly wound down his. For almost an entire year, he lay low, watching and waiting. 'I believed they just couldn't catch me, and I were right. All they had were descriptions of several different cars – and they never seemed to work out that they were all owned by t'same person, me. They had a tyre mark from a car I scrapped. And they had two imprints of my boots, one from Emily Jackson and one from Tina Atkinson. That didn't get them far, and as far as I were concerned I were being totally protected from discovery.'

In his words, he was so 'detached' from the killings, that he successfully carried on an outwardly normal life for the next eleven months. Although there were one or two unnerving moments, they served only to reinforce Sutcliffe's belief that he was never going to be caught.

In August 1978, a police officer stood on the doorstep of 6 Garden Lane for the third time and asked some awkward questions. Sutcliffe's red Ford Corsair had been seen seven times on three nights in Bradford and Leeds. 'I told him I couldn't say exactly what I'd been doing, but that I had to drive that way to work and back.' Sonia agreed that her husband rarely went out alone in the evenings, and, questioned privately about whether he ever used prostitutes, Sutcliffe denied it.

Three months later the same constable, returning to ask Sutcliffe about his banking arrangements, obtained a statement in which Sutcliffe said he had been at home on the evening of the last murder – that of Vera Millward. The 'routine enquiries' petered out.

Sutcliffe's most active period as the Yorkshire Ripper was now behind him, but police had no notion of when he might strike again, or where, and they were under increasing pressure from the public to provide some answers to the attacks. By now there were two offers of £5,000 rewards for information leading to an arrest, and in February 1979

West Yorkshire County Council was encouraged to put up a further £10,000 despite Home Office disapproval of these 'bounties'.

It was not generally known at this stage that two letters had been sent, to the West Yorkshire police and to the *Daily Mirror* in Manchester, from someone signing himself 'Jack the Ripper'.

The letters were boastful and contemptuous, warning of further killings to come. Many hours of police time were to be wasted in laboratory tests for saliva on the envelopes and in the examination of the handwriting by a graphologist, for this was believed to be a significant breakthrough in the Ripper case. The scientists identified his blood group as B, which they believed would narrow their search. Psychiatrists examined the wording of the letters, and pronounced their target to be obsessive, cunning and mean, a severely disturbed psychotic who was enjoying his role as elusive prey almost as much as he was enjoying the sadistic killings.

The letters were posted from Sunderland, a factor which, police believed, narrowed the field even more. They were wrong and had been guilty of clutching at straws, for Sutcliffe did not write these letters, nor a third, which arrived in March of the following year on the desk of Assistant Chief Constable George Oldfield, a man who was by now obsessed with catching the Ripper.

Since Vera Millward's murder, Sutcliffe had

experienced a personal tragedy of his own. In his grief and pain, he had abandoned his 'mission' for a while. His mother, Kathleen, the long-suffering 'angel' whom Sutcliffe idolised, had died in the intensive care unit at Airedale General Hospital after a massive angina attack.

'I'd seen her deteriorate until she couldn't hardly get her breath, like. She were gasping, and forever needing to take her angina pills. We all knew she had a chronic illness, but when she died it were a terrible shock. She were only fifty-eight.'

It was Maureen, his sister, who had told Sutcliffe of his mother's collapse at home on 8 November 1978. She was taken straight to hospital and the family was called in. 'I'd been at home, and as soon as I heard I said I'd get straight over to hospital. Me Dad arranged to meet me there outside. But when I got there he hadn't arrived, so I went in and they told me she'd gone. I felt very lonely. And me Dad still hadn't come. He were nearly an hour late and I were just sat there, miserable and freezing cold, waiting, with no one to talk to. And I was still on my mission – not that night, but my mind was in terrible turmoil.

'Then I saw him. He came hurrying along the road and saw me waiting under the street lights. I couldn't believe it. He were with a woman, bold as brass, walking along together, chatting. I said to him, "Where the 'ell have you been? It's tekken you an hour to get here, and you were only a few minutes away. Where the 'ell have you been? You're too late, anyway. She's died, and all on her own."

Sutcliffe, outraged at his father's behaviour and distressed at not having reached his mother's bedside in time, went home to Sonia. Together, they both claim that they shared a 'spiritual experience'. 'Every clock in the house, including an electric clock and even a cuckoo clock, had stopped at 5.30 p.m., the time me Mam died.'

It was not an unnerving experience, they both insist, more comforting – a sign that Kathleen had been thinking of them. Later that day, Sutcliffe says he shared another experience in the unlikely company of his down-to-earth brother, Mick.

'Mick started to eat his tea off a tray on the table in front of him. Suddenly, the plate rose a few inches in the air, completely on its own. Nobody said owt for a while. Then his wife, Susan, said, "That's your Mam, that is. She's giving you a sign."' Sutcliffe, who says he was used to all sorts of phenomena, was not surprised by what had happened.

Sonia, never fond of any of her husband's family, other than his mother and his sister, Anne, had come to like them less and less during her married life. In an outburst after Sutcliffe's trial, she spoke of 'Sutcliffe senior' being 'hellbent on selfishly amusing himself for his entire life with small-town amateur dramatics, singing, cricket, football, boozing and womanising – anything but bearing the responsibilities of a man with half a dozen children to be brought up.

'He left all this work to his gentle-hearted and long-suffering wife and made a lifelong slave of the poor woman. Finally he even took to cruelly humiliating in person [a reference to the confrontation at the Bankfield Hotel] the poor soul who would never speak ill of anyone, which no doubt took her earlier to the grave.'

By November 1978, Sutcliffe had carried out fourteen homicidal attacks on women, and left many children motherless, yet while his own distress over the death of his mother was intense, he has never equated that with the distress he caused so many others. By the time he returned to his 'mission' in April 1979, the so-called Ripper killings had taken on a new, more sinister pattern.

———— o ————

His next six victims were to be perfectly respectable women who had no experience or knowledge of any kind of prostitution.

The death of Josephine Whitaker was deeply shocking to people in the middle-class community of Halifax where she lived, and sent ripples of disbelief and near-panic out to the rest of York-shire. The murderer who had terrorised them for nearly four years had been believed to be dead, perhaps from suicide, or in prison, perhaps for a crime unconnected with the killings, or married, settled down and now leading a normal life, never to strike again.

Those hopes were dashed when the body of the nineteen-year-old building society clerk, Josephine, was found in a park not 250 yards from her own front door.

She had been visiting her grandparents, excitedly showing them a silver watch she had just bought for £60. She stayed late and insisted on walking home on her own at about 11.40 p.m., heading across Savile Park in the respectable Halifax suburb of Bell Hall where her parents and younger brother lived. It was thirteen-year-old David Whitaker who first identified his sister's body the next morning when out on his paper round. He went over to where a small group of police officers were huddled over the grass and recognised Josephine's smart tan-coloured shoes.

Her grandparents, Tom and Mary Priestley, both in their seventies, were used to Josephine's weekend visits, but it was unusual for her to see them during the week. Mrs Priestley had been at a church party across the road from her home until very late in the evening, and Josephine had stayed on until she came back, to chat. She was pressed to stay the night, but had her contact lenses at home and had to work the next day. She took a route through the park known locally as the moor, a short-cut that she knew well.

Her stepfather, forty-seven-year-old bricklayer Mr Haydn Hiley, described Josephine as 'happy and confident'. He said: 'All I can ask is that if anyone can help the police then, please, I urge them to do so.'

He said he and his wife, Avril, a teacher, felt that if the murder led to the Ripper 'monster' being caught then the girl would not have died in vain. He said she was a tall fit girl, capable of looking after herself and not at all timid. 'I am quite sure that she would have put up a struggle if at all possible. We told her repeatedly never to cross the Moor, but she was a brave girl, loved horse-riding and was not afraid.'

Josephine had not taken her parents' repeated advice about sticking to the well-lit road at the perimeter of the park, but had taken a short cut straight across it.

'I'd been cruising around the town centre and seen nowt. So I drove towards home and saw this girl in the park. I believed she was a prostitute. What else would she be doing there at that time of night? I parked the car and ran softly up behind her to catch her up. I made some casual conversation. I knew the voices were protecting me. They inspired me to ask her the time, to get her to turn her head away from me. I wanted her to turn the back of her head to me for a moment. I had a watch on, myself, but the voices in my head told me she wouldn't notice that.'

Josephine was struck from behind by Sutcliffe's ball-peen hammer. She was dragged 30 yards across the grass, struck further with the hammer and mutilated with the weapon that was one of Sutcliffe's trademarks – the rusty Philips screwdriver which he had sharpened. Then Josephine was left to die in the mud. A man walking by the park said later that he had heard an unusual noise, 'the type of noise that makes your hair stand on end'.

One of the reasons put forward as contributing to the prosecution's decision to accept Sutcliffe's plea of diminished responsibility when he was first in the dock at the Old Bailey was that Josephine's family had, up until then, been spared all the details of her death, which included thirty stab wounds made by the sharpened screwdriver, several of them to her vagina. 'It was a giant Philips screwdriver which was badly worn,' said Sutcliffe. 'I used it on Josephine Whitaker and another girl.'

After his arrest Sutcliffe told police how he

had started talking to Josephine as he walked beside her across Savile Park.

'"You don't know who you can trust these days," I said to her. And there was I, walking along with my hammer and screwdriver in my pocket, ready to do the inevitable.'

Sutcliffe had driven to Halifax in his sporty Sunbeam Rapier. 'The mood was in me. No woman was safe while I was in this state of mind. I arrived at Savile Park without having any particular notion. I saw the girl wearing a three-quarter length skirt and jacket. I parked the car and followed her.

'I caught up with her after a couple of minutes. I realised then that she was not a prostitute but I did not bother – I just wanted to kill a woman.

'I asked her if she had far to go and she said she was walking home from her grandmother's. We were approaching an open grass area and she said she normally took a short cut across the fields.

'We started to walk across the fields and about 30 to 40 yards from the main road I asked the time and she told me. I said to her, "You must have good eyesight," and I lagged behind, pretending to look at a church clock nearby. I took my hammer out of my pocket and hit her on the back of the head twice. She gave a loud moaning sound and to my horror I saw a figure walking along the road.

'I dragged her further into the field and at a safe distance I stopped. I heard voices from somewhere behind me and saw at least two figures walking along a path towards the field.

'She was still moaning loudly. First I pulled some of her clothing off and then I turned her over and stabbed her numerous times in the chest and stomach with the screwdriver. I was in a frenzy.'

Inevitably, Josephine's murder led to a renewed and impassioned public call for police to find her attacker. Now at least they had an extra clue, for there were traces of mineral oil, of the type used in engineering workshops, in her wounds, and pinhead traces of metal particles.

George Oldfield warned all women that they could be at risk from the Yorkshire Ripper. 'The next victim could be your daughter, your girl-friend or your wife,' he said grimly.

Women took to arming themselves against the killer. They carried knives or scissors in their handbags, and several who were prosecuted for carrying offensive weapons claimed it was their only means of being able to go about their normal daily lives in safety. Others, more militant, organised street demonstrations calling for a curfew on men. They wanted violent films that depicted attacks on women to be banned from local cinemas, and picketed a Leeds cinema showing the film *Dressed to Kill*, claiming that it glamorised violence.

All over northern England, people were giving up their normal social lives. Evening classes closed down as attendances dwindled, while restaurants, theatres and clubs were all but deserted. Girl students were not signing on for university courses in northern cities, and others even dropped out to return to the safety of their family homes. Prostitutes moved further south to the Midland cities, rather than risk their usual beat in what was fast becoming known as 'Ripper country'.

George Oldfield and his squad were under more pressure than ever before.

The press and public were counting the cost, both in lives and in police manpower. An article in the *Evening News* took an appraising look at the police paperchase that was swamping the Ripper Squad. One officer was permanently occupied in sifting his way through a list of 17,500 names of men who had been in prison during the Ripper's 'quiet' period. It took him nearly a year to eliminate all but 500 names as he painstakingly traced each and every discharged prisoner from one address to another.

Another had been checking 13,500 cars

known to have been in the vicinity of just one murder, and Oldfield said he had a whole team checking engineering firms whose employees travelled regularly to the north-east. Thousands of men were being interviewed personally.

Typically, on the morning after Josephine Whitaker's death, there were 500 phone calls from the public. Nine new lines had to be installed at Halifax police station until the number gradually dwindled to thirty letters and calls a day.

Oldfield was the first to admit that the hunt for the Ripper was almost beyond him and his squad. He told how his men had missed Helen Rytka's murderer by just three minutes, and put it down to luck – the Ripper's good luck, Oldfield's bad luck. He and his senior officers had spent three days and two nights without sleep at one stage, when they believed time was the crucial factor. Then the trail went cold again.

Between them, police and the media went to unprecedented lengths to plumb the depths of the mind of the unknown killer.

Clairvoyant Simon Alexander, from Mansfield, Nottinghamshire, spent six hours with detectives, touring the areas where women had been murdered. As a result, he forecast that the police would soon make an arrest. He predicted that the killer would turn out to be about 5 ft

7 in tall, around thirty-three, broad and muscular. He went so far as to claim that, 'If this man were put in an identity parade, I would be able to pick him out.'

Mr Alexander, who had earlier worked with police hunting the notorious Cambridge rapist, ventured: 'I think the first killing was an accident, because he was being taunted, and the others just followed. Now he is pitting his wits against the police.' Wise words, as it transpired, but they did not really take the police any further at the time.

Psychiatrists consulted by the Ripper squad held a variety of opinions. One said he imagined the killer to be someone with a sexual hang-up, maybe with a hatred of prostitutes or women he thought to be prostitutes, because of his own sexual inabilities. He might be outwardly respectable, with friends and relatives who would never suspect him.

Another suggested he might lust after publicity and model himself on the original Jack the Ripper.

Handwriting expert Angela Dean, who had been consulted by Scotland Yard in cases where anonymous letters were important in evidence, studied a sample of the handwriting in one of the letters sent to George Oldfield and concluded that the writer was not well educated, although the handwriting was 'speedy and confident'. He was no introvert, she said, rather someone who liked to do things fast and in his own way. 'You can see the anger in the untidy yet obsessive slant of the lettering, the drive with which they have sped ahead of the writer's hand, though he has had to cramp some of them jaggedly together.' She said his unfinished 'a' and 'p' were a sign of arrogance or of strong self-indulgence.

When Jayne MacDonald was killed, Oldfield's men traced 257 people who had been to one party alone in a street of terraced houses. Between 1 a.m. and 4 a.m., 400 people had been up and down two nearby streets, and Oldfield's team had traced all but seventeen of them, urged on by the certain knowledge that one of that number must have been the killer.

Oldfield was still keeping secrets from the public, refusing to reveal the murder weapon or the details of injuries. He also felt a strong personal involvement, saying: 'I believe him to be a cunning crafty individual who watches every move I make very carefully.' He insisted, some thought weakly, that the 'Ripper's luck must surely run out one day'.

Meanwhile, the Revd. Michael Walker, vicar of St Jude's Church where Josephine Whitaker was christened, and now buried, was appealing for prayers. He said: 'There are people who dabble in evil and in devil possession. This man may be one of them. He is obviously possessed of an incredible evil when he does these killings. Something overwhelms him so completely that it shakes him out of a normal life to kill again and again... The Ripper is a man who is in need of our help. We must pray for him.'

However, the terrified public was in no mood for prayers. In letters, phone calls and in the clamour of dozens of newspaper headlines, they demanded that Scotland Yard be called in.

Behind the scenes, internal politics were rampant. Scotland Yard could not move in unless the Chief Constable asked them to, and Ronald Gregory agreed with his CID chief, George Old-field, that they should not. Gregory was adamant: 'There is no way I would call them in. That is not to decry the Metropolitan police in any way, because they are a very good force indeed. But a force of the size of West Yorkshire, 5,000, has as much and possibly more experience than Scotland Yard.' Privately, one senior officer remarked drily that 'Scotland Yard haven't caught their own bloody Ripper yet, have they?'

At a Press conference called to comment on the reluctance of West Yorkshire police to call in Scotland Yard, Detective Superintendent Dick Holland, at that time in day-to-day charge of the Ripper hunt, said: 'All they would do is send up a superintendent and a sergeant who wouldn't even know the area. There isn't anything they can do that we haven't already done.'

He admitted there had been discussions over a new strategy, but was at pains to stress that the case was still in the hands of the northern police forces. Meanwhile, morale among the officers permanently on the Ripper case was at its lowest. It was estimated that George Oldfield's men had seen 134,894 people and knocked on 23,051 front doors, taking statements from 20,295 people – some witnesses and others possible suspects. There had been 47,306 offers of information from the public.

Chief Constable Ronald Gregory denied that morale was low because of continuing failure. 'If I thought there was any man elsewhere in the country who could help this enquiry I would not hesitate to bring him in,' he said. But, he added, he had never considered asking for help from Scotland Yard, and they had not offered their help.

Filing cabinets bulged as every detail provided by the public was painstakingly indexed by hand, some of it cross-referring to incidents when car registration numbers cropped up several times, others where a description might repeat the mention of 'staring eyes' or a moustache or beard.

By June 1979 the Ripper Squad felt defeated and deflated. They had eleven murder investigations on their hands as they still believed the death of a Preston woman, Joan Harrison, was the Ripper's handiwork, but precious few clues; they could be certain about only six details. The man they sought was white, aged between twenty-five and forty, of scruffy appearance, wearing rubber-soled work boots, probably living in West Yorkshire and working for an engineering firm which took him regularly to the north-east.

The three letters Oldfield had received had added an unfortunate further dimension, because for a while potential suspects were being eliminated simply because their handwriting was not similar to that of the letter-writer. Then, in June 1979, two months after Josephine Whitaker's death, a new and dangerously false trail was laid. A cassette tape was sent to George Oldfield, and from that moment he nursed an urgent personal obsession against the man speaking to him on it.

'I'm Jack,' the voice said. 'I see you are having no luck catching me. I have the greatest respect for you, George, but Lord, you are no nearer catching me now than four years ago when I started. I reckon your boys are letting you down, George. They can't be much good, can they? The only time they came near catching me was a few months back in Chapeltown when I was disturbed. Even then it was a uniformed copper, not a detective.

'I warned you in March that I'd strike again. Sorry it wasn't Bradford. I did promise you that, but I couldn't get there. I'm not quite sure when I'll strike again but it will definitely be sometimes this year, maybe September, October or even sooner if I get the chance. I'm not sure where, maybe Manchester – I like it there, there's plenty of them knocking about. They never learn, do they George? I bet you've warned them, but they never listen.

'At the rate I'm going I should be in the *Book of Records*. I think it's eleven up to now, isn't it? Well I'll keep going for quite a while yet. I can't see myself being nicked just yet. Even if you do get near, I'll probably top myself first.

'Well it's been nice chatting to you, George. Yours, Jack the Ripper. No good looking for fingerprints. You should know by now it's as clean as a whistle. See you soon. Bye. Hope you like the catchy tune at the end. Ha, ha.' (Several seconds of the song 'Thank you for being a friend' were played.)

Handwriting on the envelope was identical to that on the letters from Sunderland. Saliva tests showed the sender had blood group B.

Oldfield was both shocked and elated. The mocking Geordie voice had been speaking to him personally, taunting him, and Oldfield was already at breaking point. His orders were to eliminate anyone who did not fall into the Geordie/blood group B category, and he sent all his men to the tiny pit village of Castletown, where local people still shudder at the memory. A white police caravan was parked conspicuously on waste ground just outside the village, where linguistic experts calculated that the Ripper was most likely to live, and the tape was played continuously on loud-speakers, accompanied by a plea for people to try to identify the voice – even if it was someone in their own family.

Dialect expert Stanley Ellis, a lecturer at Leeds University, had worked his way towards the area from the north bank of the River Wear which bisects Sunderland. He had arrived at Castletown, once no more than a hundred or so brick cottages, now a concrete jungle of 1,600 council houses straggling over four miles.

The police caravan spent two weeks parked by the shops on Chaffinch Road, booming out its sinister message. Then it moved on to the next area, Hylton Castle.

Conversation in every pub and club turned to the possible identity of the Ripper murderer. Detectives found that local people desperately wanted him caught, to the point where distraught parents would even ask police to check their sons.

Forty detectives went from door to door with

cassette recorders, to play the tape to each household. One of them said during the operation: 'It's a slog. But we'll keep going till we catch him.'

Whoever the hoaxer was – and police have never found him – 878,796 people listened to his voice on a Freephone recording, made available nationally.

Deep suspicion engulfed the 2,680 people living in Castletown. Marriages were threatened, friendships betrayed, causing extensive and permanent damage, which proved ultimately to be pointless. Meanwhile, Peter Sutcliffe was many miles away smiling to himself. 'It sent them all up north to Sunderland. I didn't send the tape. I'm not the type of person who would talk to anyone like that. Me? No. Some crackpot. Somebody says it were a copper.'

Dr Stephen Shaw studied the Ripper tape-recording and declared the speaker was an aggressive psychopath who failed to resist his impulses. He warned that threats on the tape to kill again should be taken extremely seriously. Prostitutes in Huddersfield, Bradford and Leeds came under pressure from police to tell on their customers. They were offered police protection and immunity from prosecution in exchange for their clients' names and addresses. But the police attempt at a 'truce' with the girls they frequently arrested in the past was a failure. The girls were terrified as detectives underlined the real threat to them by reminding them: 'Your next customer could be the Ripper. You might even know him as a regular. Next time it might be your turn to die.' Helen Rytka's sister Rita was given protection at a secret address in case the killer realised she had shared a beat with the dead girl and targeted her as his next victim.

Over all, the police failed in their attempts at a 'truce'. George Oldfield said he understood. 'Usually they are on the wrong side of the law and they just don't like police officers,' he said. 'But we want them to know that this time we share an objective – to catch this man.'

Prostitutes were just not willing to take what they saw as further risks by revealing their clients' details. They wanted to avoid the areas now called 'Ripper Country' but they were also determined to continue to make a living. They felt strongly that the police should be keeping the streets safe for them and everyone else. Many began to work in groups, each taking details of another's customers, and reporting back to an agreed spot within an agreed time. One girl, working out of her own home, claimed she had bought an axe and would not hestitate to use it if she was suspicious of a client. On the Jimmy Young radio show, Mr Oldfield tried a different tack. He told millions of listeners that he was sure the Ripper was suffering mental auguish and must need help and treatment. 'For his own sake and his family's sake, he should give himself up now.'

The American police officer, Captain James McDonald of the Boston Police Department, who had caught the Boston Strangler, came forward to offer British detectives his help. He told them: 'The Ripper is certain to be somewhere there in your files.' MacDonald saw similarities between the Yorkshire Ripper and the Boston Strangler. He said: 'The mistake we made at first was to believe we were looking for a violent sex attacker. We traced all offenders on our files in that category. But we were wrong. We realise now that sex attackers work through a number of different phases. At first they may not be violent or even commit major sex crimes. They often start with a lesser sex offence.'

Albert de Salvo, the Strangler, had been on police files throughout their investigation.

In an interview with the *Yorkshire Evening Post*, after Sutcliffe's trial and conviction, a senior police officer tried to limit the damage believed to have been caused by the hoaxer who sent the 'I'm Jack' tape and letters. The newspaper called him Public Enemy Number One. The police officer insisted: 'No, we didn't get it wrong. Those letters and the tape were received during the course of this inquiry and there was good reason to believe at that time that because of their contents the person *could* be the killer. Therefore we had to decide whether to keep the information to ourselves – which would have been a terrible thing if it had turned out that the killer was the author. We would have been severely criticised. The alternative was not to disclose the tape and letters to the public. Don't forget that throughout the inquiry we wanted to – and still want to – trace the author.

'At the time it seemed a strong clue. But on every death enquiry I have been associated with, something which appeared to be a strong pointer turned out to be fruitless. This is not unusual in any major inquiry.'

Chief Constable Ronald Gregory also said that he was convinced the correct course of action had been taken by publicising the letters and tape. 'We felt we had to alert everyone in the country,' he said. 'We said, "Whether this man is the Ripper or not we must find him." We would still dearly love to find the person responsible.'

Discussing the way in which the police were misled so thoroughly, he explained that forensic tests showed that the murderer of the Preston woman, Joan Harrison, had the B blood group. Around the same time, the first letter to the police from the hoaxer showed the writer to be a B-secretor. The first letter had warned that the killer would strike again – 'Old slut next time, I hope.'

The second letter, sent five days later, said: 'Might write again soon after another one's gone, maybe Liverpool or even Manchester again.'

On 16 May 1978 Vera Millward's body was found in Manchester. The predictions and boasts, said Mr Gregory, had come true to convince him beyond reasonable doubt that the Geordie speaking on the tape and the Ripper were the same man.

'George [Oldfield] and I discussed this and finally he reluctantly agreed we should go ahead and publish,' said Mr Gregory. 'Six days before our planned press conference, a meeting of senior officers from the six forces involved – West Yorkshire, South Yorkshire, Greater Manchester, Lancashire, Humberside and Northumbria – agreed that our public front would be to stress our total conviction that they were authentic.' An eighteen-page special notice was sent to every force in the UK saying that suspects could be eliminated if they did not have a Geordie accent or B blood grouping. When that notice went out I quickly became aware of strong dissenting voices in other forces.'

He said that one Detective Chief Inspector, David Zackrisson of Northumbria police, had methodically studied every newspaper article written about the Ripper inquiry and proved that everything in the two letters could have been gleaned from them. He believed that the Geordie was immersed in Jack the Ripper mythology and craved publicity like the original Victorian murderer. Mr Gregory said he realised his serious mistake when Sutcliffe was arrested. To his great annoyance, he said, the hoaxer had still not been found although 40,000 people were interviewed.

Mr Gregory concluded: 'I still however believe there is a possibility that the letters and tape were sent by the killer of Joan Harrison. Sutcliffe has not admitted that murder and the hoaxer may well have been trying to lead us off on a false trail, knowing he had alibis for the times of the real Ripper murders.'

One Detective Chief Inspector had listed phrases from tapes and letters sent in by the man claiming to be the Yorkshire Ripper, and compared them with phrases from the original Jack the Ripper letters of 1888:

Jack the Ripper letters 1888	*The Geordie tapes and letters 1978-79*
I am down on whores	My purpose is to rid the streets of them skirts.
The joke about Leather Apron gives me fits	The photo in the paper gave me fits.

I want to get to work right away if I get the chance

I will strike again if I get the chance

Beware, I shall be at work on the first and second inst in Minories at twelve midnight, and I give the authorities a good chance

Might write again after another one's gone, maybe Liverpool, Manchester again... I have given advance warning so it's yours and theirs fault.

The Lady (refers to victim Annie Chapman)

The Lady (refers to victim Vera Millward)

I was not codding dear old Boss when I gave you the top

I wasn't kidding last time I wrote saying the whore would be older.

But they won't fix me just yet.

Well I'll keep going for a while yet. I can't see myself being nicked just yet.

Ha! Ha!

Ha! Ha!

Yours, Jack the Ripper

Yours, Jack the Ripper

So, goodbye dear boss

Well, it's been nice
chatting to you,
George

A month after Oldfield had announced his 'breakthough' with the Ripper tape, he suffered a severe heart attack and was ordered to rest until further notice. At about the same time, Peter and Sonia Sutcliffe were being questioned for the fifth time by officers, who told Sutcliffe that his car had been seen in selected districts of Bradford thirty-six times, Leeds twice and Manchester once.

In the absence of a computer at West Yorkshire police headquarters, the many hundreds of thousands of files that had now built up were not adequately cross-referenced, so that the two policemen questioning him this time did not know that Sutcliffe had been seen previously. He was unable to account in any detail for his activities on any of the murder dates, but repeated that when he did go out in the evening it was always in the company of his wife. Sonia told them the same.

A note was made in the officer's book that Sutcliffe bore a resemblance to the photofit picture drawn up following Marilyn Moore's description. A sample of his handwriting was taken and, back at the Ripper Squad headquarters, this was compared with samples from the Sunderland letters. Sutcliffe was eliminated as a suspect.

'I were right. They didn't know owt.'

Sutcliffe had perfected a manner that continued to fool his family and work-mates so that, even in retrospect, they have not been able to recall an instance of serious suspicion.

By the time Sutcliffe killed Barbara Leach, he had been interviewed by the police five times. 'I were completely detached, you see. I was always dead calm. They couldn't get through to me. It just didn't fit, and I had no criminal record or anything. My wife hadn't got a clue. I didn't go out much, and when I did she thought I was at the yard preparing the wagon for the next day's work. Going out six times in one year isn't going out really.

'I never gave her any clues. That was part of it. I were on a vital mission and God was instructing me to clear the streets, and not to give any clues at all. I never came home covered in blood. I just stunned them unconscious, and I didn't get blood on me.'

Barbara Leach, his sixteenth victim, was heavily bloodstained when a policeman on his afternoon beat found her body squashed out of sight between dustbins in the back yard of a Bradford house. She had been struck with hammer blows from behind and stabbed with the sharpened screwdriver Sutcliffe carried with him.

She was a twenty-year-old university student, about to start her third and final year reading social psychology, an outgoing, fun-loving, attractive girl who shared lodgings with other students. On 1 September they had been enjoying a pre-term get-together at the Manville Arms pub in bedsitter land to the west of Bradford city centre – not Sutcliffe's usual hunting-ground at all. But Barbara's path crossed his that night when, after the late-night drinks, she went off on her own for a walk round the block, just to get some night air. Her friends had not wanted to walk in the light rain that was falling.

Minutes later, Barbara was attacked from behind and dragged out of sight. Sutcliffe, cruising the area, had drawn his car up at the kerbside when he saw her alone. She had no chance to fight him off.

A day after the discovery of Barbara's body, West Yorkshire CID issued a warning that no woman was safe out on her own in the early hours. Detective Chief Superintendent Peter Gilrain said: 'These are the most brutal and horrifying attacks on women and they are being picked off at random. He is certainly not concentrating on prostitutes any longer.'

Barbara, from Kettering in Northamptonshire, whose mother was a teacher and whose father worked in a bank, was an outgoing and popular student. She had many friends at the university riding club, and visited stables twice a week to ride.

Known as 'Babs', she mothered her flatmates and helped them with their studies. One of her friends, Paul Smith, said he believed he was the last one to speak to Barbara before the killer. He said she had a habit of walking alone now and again. Mr Smith added: 'She was a super girl, I just can't believe this.'

Women in Bradford, angered by the police warning not to go out alone at night because of the Ripper, marched through the city demanding better protection and more police action against rapists and prowlers. The 200 demonstrators marched past the Manville Arms pub – where Barbara Leach was last seen alive – and converged outside the city's police headquarters. There they read out the names of the Ripper's twelve victims. March organiser Anne Mason said: 'This is a protest to show our feelings about the Ripper, and a protest about the curfew the police have put on woman. They told us it wasn't safe to go out at night. But they have done nothing at all to make it safer.'

Police revealed that Barbara's wounds clearly showed she was a Ripper victim, but would say no more for fear of imitation or a false confession. One senior detective said: 'It's an animal we're after. Mind, I bet he looks like any ordinary bloke. That's just one of our problems.'

What prompted the detective's remarks was the way in which Sutcliffe had once again used his sharpened screwdriver to stab his victim repeatedly. At the time, police declined to publish details of the Ripper's butchery, for fear of copycat murders.

University staff were stunned at Barbara's death. Professor Sheila Atkin, in charge of her course, said she was conscientious and enthusiastic about her degree work.

Desperate to prompt a memory in a passer-by, the police organised a reconstruction of the last ten minutes of Barbara's life. WPC Barbara Terry copied the murder victim's mode of dress – she had been wearing blue jeans with a badge on the left side saying 'Best Rump', a beige long-sleeved blouse of cheesecloth material and red high-heeled boots. The policewoman set off from the pub and retraced the exact steps that the dead girl had taken round the block. The officer admitted that the exercise sent a shiver up her spine. Her ordeal ended part way down a cobbled back lane where Barbara's body had been found, and it brought some results – more than fifty people came forward to say they had been in the area at the time.

WPC Terry admitted afterwards that she found the experience 'eerie'. She said: 'I really felt for the girl. I felt as though eyes were upon me as I rounded each corner. I had a strange feeling that the Ripper himself might be lurking somewhere in the background, watching me.'

Some time later, fellow students at Bradford

University held a memorial service for Barbara. Her distraught parents had travelled to the city to plant a sycamore sapling in her memory, with a plaque bearing her name. Her father told the gathering: 'We miss her a great deal.' The girl's mother wept throughout the ceremony.

One month later a sharp-eyed detective, checking through a backlog of unprocessed actions in the Ripper Incident Room, singled out Sutcliffe for a further interview. He did not feel entirely happy about the alibis that had eliminated Sutcliffe in the past, so two detective constables saw him at home on 23 October 1979. They took a further sample of handwriting and, as before, Sutcliffe was eliminated as a suspect.

By now, public anxiety was intense. Mobile exhibitions were mounted in every part of West Yorkshire, posters were displayed on public buildings in every town and village, and the 'I'm Jack' tape recording was given maximum publicity. Police pleaded with women everywhere not to go out alone and not to come home unaccompanied after dark. They suggested a curfew, drawing furious protests from women demanding better police protection.

On two more occasions, both in January 1980, Sutcliffe was interviewed by the police. Once, while picking up a consignment of castings and engines at a depot north of Bradford, he was approached by two police officers, asking him about his work – 'Routine enquiries'. Showing Sutcliffe a photograph of a boot print, they asked if it was his. 'I stayed dead calm, and as I got into the wagon I realised I was standing on the steps, which were mesh, and they could look up and see for themselves that I was wearing those boots. But they didn't. They couldn't see what were in front of their own eyes.'

Later in January, the police saw him at home, and asked about the vehicles he had owned and whether he associated with prostitutes. Again Sutcliffe gave nothing away, and they left empty-handed for the eighth time.

In February, the police decided on a complete change of tactics in their murder hunt. They announced a media blackout. Work on the Ripper case had been brought to a standstill by the tide of paperwork, and there was a desperate sort of hope that the Ripper, deprived of the publicity he seemed to relish, might put his head above the parapet for the first time.

Sensing their mood, Sutcliffe also changed his tactics at the same point, giving himself another long rest. His job at Clark's was going well and he enjoyed the solitude and sense of being apart that he found at the wheel of his Ford Intercontinental. 'I suppose I were in a period of remission. My mind was still in turmoil, but I were working hard and coming home tired. Sonia had plans for us to sell up eventually and move further into the countryside where she could have a pottery of her own. I told her I'd try my hand at painting pictures, though she just laughed then. She'd never even thought of me as an artist.'

Sonia had not been present at Sutcliffe's ninth interview with the police, when a detective constable from Manchester joined a colleague from West Yorkshre to talk to Sutcliffe at the lorry depot in Bradford, Again, he offered good reasons why his vehicles had been seen in Leeds red-light areas. A report was filed during the following month, concluding that the officers felt suspicious of Sutcliffe but did not think he was the murderer.

Sutcliffe's apparent normality in the period between autumn 1979 and summer 1980 was so complete that he remembers an incident that presented him with the perfect circumstances for a Ripper-style murder, yet, instead, showed him as a responsible member of the public.

'I were driving up the M60 on a terrible foggy night. It were a blinder, impossible to see the traffic in front. I were in the big wagon, and suddenly there was a crunch at the rear. I stopped sharp, and went round back to find this little mini had run into me. It hadn't done any damage to the wagon at all, but the driver was a girl, squashed down by the roof of the car. She had nearly gone right under my truck and been killed. I talked to her and helped to pull her out of the wreckage when the police and ambulance came.

'Months later I went to magistrates' court as a witness. Poor girl was being done for careless driving and I'd been told to be there. Well, she came into the waiting-room before the case, and started talking to me. It turned out she thought I was her solicitor, and she'd been telling me all about what she was going to say in court. I suppose she didn't recognise me out of me working clothes. Anyway, she was dead worried she'd been talking to a witness. I tried to calm her down, but anyway she pleaded guilty so they didn't have to call any witnesses.'

All this, while the police hunt for the Yorkshire Ripper was at its most frantic! 'It didn't surprise me. I were quite certain they'd never get me. I'd proved it time after time.'

Even so, when the compulsion once again gripped him – and sent him driving towards Leeds with his mission again in mind – he decided to use a different method of killing. Before he reached Leeds city centre and the Chapeltown district he intended to scour, Sutcliffe saw and seized an opportunity that claimed his seventeenth victim.

She was Marguerite Walls, a forty-seven-year-old civil servant, who, on 18 August, had been working late at the Department of Education and Science office. She left shortly after 10 p.m. to walk the half mile to her home in Pudsey, moving with the brisk stride that had stayed with her since her days as a sergeant in the Woman's Royal Army Corps.

'My mind was already set on killing a prostitute. I saw this woman about 60 yards from me. I was already in some kind of rage. I couldn't do anything to stop myself. I were suffering inner torment and just wanted to get rid of all the prostitutes. It was just unfortunate for her she was there at that time.'

Having parked the car, Sutcliffe ran noiselessly up behind her, a length of cord in his inside pocket. He had temporarily abandoned the tell-tale screwdriver and knives. Catching up with Miss Walls over a distance of 400 yards, he stunned her with a hammer blow to the back of her head. 'A voice inside my head said "Kill, Kill, Kill."' As he struck further blows to Miss Walls's head, he shouted: 'You filthy prostitute.'

Then, producing the piece of cord, he half-carried, half-dragged her up the driveway of a nearby house, stripped her of all her clothes apart from her tights, and strangled her. She was left beneath a pile of grass cuttings near a garage at the house, with a trail of blood leading from the gateway, up the drive, across a rockery and into a wooded area to the left of the house. Her shoes were found the next day in the driveway; her skirt, shopping bag and cheque book near the rockery.

This was Sutcliffe's only killing by strangulation. 'I didn't like it. It took longer for her to die. She made terrible gurgling noises.'

Detectives investigating the murder ruled out any connection with the Yorkshire Ripper. The man leading the hunt for Miss Walls's killer, Detective Chief Superintendent Jim Hobson, said: 'This was a savage killing – a great deal of strength and violence was used to murder this innocent and respectable woman. It appears the motive for the attack was sexual. Miss Walls put up quite a struggle, but her clothes were torn from her. Her attacker must be of a heavy physique because he dragged her, this fit lady, or carried her, a fairly long way. I believe he may be injured and heavily bloodstained.

'My feelings are that it is a local man who did this murder. I have a team of detectives at Miss Walls's house, looking for addresses of male and female friends. She had boyfriends in the past but that was about twenty years ago. She was a very private person who would always go home after finishing work.'

While the police went up another blind alley, Sutcliffe had entered a period of activity. Five weeks later, on 24 September, he attacked a woman doctor from Singapore, visiting Leeds to attend a course at the Nuffield Centre. Dr Upadhya Bandara was walking home at night when she moved to one side to let someone overtake her. Instead, he put a rope around her neck and dragged her away. Although she lost consciousness, she later remembered that the man had a beard.

Sutcliffe said, 'Yes, I used the rope on that girl. She was walking slowly along like a prostitute, and I hit her on the head with a hammer. I had looped a rope round her neck. I didn't have any tools with me to finish her off so I used the rope.'

He dragged her down the road and when he realised her shoes were making a scraping noise, he pulled them off roughly and threw them over a wall with her handbag. 'I think my intentions were clear. I didn't really *want* to kill anyone. It was just something that had to be done.'

When Dr Bandara regained consciousness, she found a police officer standing over her. He had been patrolling the area in a white Ford Escort panda car, and had stopped just seconds after Sutcliffe had fled. 'I only just got away wi' that one. And I felt even more nervous next time – I were practically caught in the act.' Meanwhile, the police, confused by the garrotte attacks, now believed a new killer was on the loose and that this was his second victim.

Nothing but the luck of the devil could have been with Sutcliffe on Bonfire Night, 1980, when he struck again, for he had only just delivered two hammer blows to the head of teenager Theresa

Sykes, a few yards from her own front door, when her fitness fanatic boyfriend came running out on hearing her screams. The sixteen-year-old girl had bought cigarettes from a local corner shop in Willwood Avenue, Huddersfield, and was almost home when Sutcliffe emerged from the shadows and caught up with her. He was still huddled over her, about to strike her again, when Jim Furey – the father of Theresa's young baby – sprinted towards him. Sutcliffe disappeared into the night, seconds away from detection.

Theresa had bravely tried to grab the weapon Sutcliffe used, and was able to tell the police that it was metal. She also saw that his hair was black and that he had a beard and moustache. Sutcliffe says he ran out of sight and hid in a nearby garden when her boyfriend appeared, crouching there until the girl was helped home and the street was quiet again. 'I attacked her because she was the first person I saw that night. It didn't take me any time to decide which women were prostitutes. Something just clicked inside my head when I saw them.'

Neither this attack, nor the previous one – on Dr Bandara – nor the murder of Marguerite Walls, had been attributed to the Yorkshire Ripper. When he struck and killed for the thirteenth time, the public suffered the shock it had been dreading for nearly fifteen months. In Sutcliffe's own words, the killing of student Jacqueline Hill was somehow 'the straw that broke the camel's back'.

It sickened and terrified families everywhere, for the girl was twenty years old, a promising student with everything to live for. Her university career was a credit to her; her loving parents were proud of her success and her plans for the future; she was a Sunday School teacher, dedicated to children; and she planned a career with the probation service.

Jacqueline, in the third year of her English degree course, had attended a probation officers' seminar in Leeds city centre on 17 November, and was returning home to her students' hall of residence in Headingley at about 9.30 p.m. For the first time, Sutcliffe had come out into an area well lit by street lamps, to strike indiscriminately at the first woman who walked by.

Painstaking enquiries later revealed the exact moment when Jacqueline met her killer. She had caught the bus at 9 p.m., getting off at a stop along the main Leeds-Otley road. It was 9.23 p.m. and there was driving rain, so she decided to take the short cut across the back of the Arndale Shopping Centre.

The fact that the Ripper had come out of the shadows and struck in such a brightly lit place was worrying to the police. They saw the fear on the faces of women shoppers in Leeds the next day as they passed the canvas tent protecting the spot where Jacqueline's body was found. They saw children being held closer to their mothers, and families hurrying away from the place that held so much terror for them.

Girl students who lived in the same block of flats as Jacqueline described her as quiet and studious. She loved sewing, cooking and shopping. They told how they had all talked about protection from a Ripper killing, and how they had decided never to go out alone, always to travel in pairs. As the months passed since the last killing, their careful habits had slipped a little. One of Jacqueline's friends, Patti Hewstone, described her as 'hard-working, generous, intelligent and reliable'. She said, 'It's impossible to find a bad word to say about her. She was everything people want their daughters to be.'

Jacqueline's parents were devastated. So, too, was her boyfriend, Ian Tanfield, aged twenty-two, serving with the RAF at Leuchars in Fife. He was given compassionate leave to return home to Ornesby, Middlesbrough, three miles from the Hills' home. Six months later he would accompany Jacqueline's mother to Peter Sutcliffe's trial at the Old Bailey.

Sutcliffe had parked his car on the left-hand side of Alma Road, near to the Arndale Centre, and had eaten some Kentucky fried chicken and chips.

'I believed she was soliciting. They said there wasn't any prostitution round there, but there was.

There were a lot of them. I'm sure I saw her trying to stop two cars at the other side of the road. Then she crossed over and stood on the corner for a minute or two, then walked up this road. I just had my car parked there and she came right past me. I didn't say anything, I just got out and whacked her and that were it. I used a hammer. Then I just dragged her off, out of sight of the pavement.'

He says he saw Jacqueline turning round, as if to adjust her skirt or a stocking. 'This suggested to me the behaviour of a prostitute. God gave me the means of killing. He got me out of trouble time after time, and I was in His hands. He misled police and perhaps God was involved in the hoax tapes so that the police would be misled.'

After he had struck Jacqueline with a hammer, he dragged her onto a patch of waste land where he pulled her clothes off, and stabbed her with his yellow-handled screwdriver. 'I stabbed her in the lungs. Her eye was wide open and she seemed to me to be looking at me with an accusing stare. This shook me up a bit so I jabbed a screwdriver into her eye.'

At about 10 o'clock on the night of the murder, a student found Jacqueline's cream-coloured raffia bag just beyond the entrance to some waste-land. The student, an Iraqi, took the bag into the hall of residence and then noticed that there appeared to be spots of blood on it. After discussing his find with other students, the police were called and they went to where the bag had been found. Nearby was a large, detached, derelict house, which was searched. However, the officers did not discover Jacqueline's spectacles or a mitten until next morning. They did not find the body either. The following morning, Donald Court, the manager of a shop at the Arndale Centre, was walking along a ramp leading to a car park behind the building. Mr Court glanced over the wall, saw the body and ran to call the police.

The jury at Sutcliffe's trial was shown harrowing photographs of Jacqueline's body. They saw multiple head injuries and a severe wound in the region of her left breast. A post-mortem examination revealed five lacerations to the top and back of her head, and a stab wound in the right eye, penetrating an inch and a half.

Sutcliffe steadfastly refused to accept that Jacqueline Hill – along with several other victims – was not a prostitute. He still claims he saved their souls, and although he is now willing to admit that the Devil was the driving force in his madness, he does not feel remorse. 'I think if I felt guilty about anything like that, I couldn't live with it. I couldn't live with it.'

CHAPTER SIX

Arrest

Somehow the killing of Jacqueline Hill struck a chord with families all over Britain. There was renewed fear, despair even, that this murderer could not be caught – and at the same time a huge surge of public anger, unprecedented in a police manhunt.

Raw anxiety had been nagging West Yorkshire police chiefs for five years; now their nerves snapped. A week after Jacqueline's murder, they announced the setting up of a new 'think tank', bringing together the brightest and most experienced senior officers from forces outside the area, to be headed by George Oldfield's deputy, Jim Hobson. Later, Ronald Gregory was to describe his removal of Oldfield as 'the most difficult of many difficult decisions I had to make during the Ripper hunt'.

The new 'think tank' would bring together five police chiefs from all over the country, together with a leading forensic scientist, Mr Stewart Kind, director of the government's atomic weapons research centre at Aldermaston. Gregory had wanted to assemble the most powerful array of talent ever to work together on a murder inquiry.

This was his response to both Home Office pressure and also influences nearer home, the local police committee. He said local officers would return to their normal duties with his 'grateful thanks'.

His think tank was something of a compromise, however, for it did not bring in any officers from Scotland Yard. Jim Hobson had the authority to select his own team: Andrew Sloane, National Coordinator of regional crime squads; Thames Valley Deputy Chief Constable Leslie Emment; David Gerty, Assistant Chief Constable for the West Midlands; and Commander Ronald Harvey, Adviser to the Chief Inspector of Constabulary.

Gregory told a press conference: 'Their function will be to look critically at police action and to advise. They are probably the most experienced group of police officers who could be mustered to assist this investigation.' Public pressure had forced the change, he admitted. 'People want to know what we are going to do next, and I pray this will be of some help.'

Oldfield remained Assistant Chief Constable in overall charge of crime, but was no longer involved in the Ripper hunt. Gregory said he would be 'kept in touch with developments'.

The new think tank met in Leeds, then returned to their home bases, from where they would work. Jim Hobson was optimistic: 'I think we now have the best brains available to catch the Ripper and I am sure it can be done. I am quite happy with the way in which the inquiry has been going, but we will have to see what more can be done. It would be silly of me to think I can perform miracles. What we are looking for is new ideas.'

The change came at the right time. Three police officers were about to be disciplined over the delay in discovering the Ripper's latest victim, Jacqueline Hill, having carried out only a 'cursory' search of the area where her bloodstained handbag was found. Her body was not found until ten hours later, only yards from where the bag was picked up.

Some of the Ripper's victims, and the mothers of girls he had murdered, were to appear on television in a unique and harrowing attempt to draw the murderer into the open.

The first to speak out was the mother of Jacqueline Hill. For a week after her daughter's murder, Mrs Doreen Hill had been beseiged by the press, with reporters offering considerable sums for the family's story. Mrs Hill decided to give an interview to *BBC TV News*, which would then be picked up by the newspapers. She told how Jackie had left her flat on the outskirts of the city and moved to a hall of residence after her parents had voiced anxiety because of the Ripper murders. Mrs Hill appealed to whoever was shielding the murderer to come forward. Other anguished relatives were soon to follow Mrs Hill's example.

West Yorkshire police, desperate by now, encouraged them.

Speaking on the *Newsnight* programme, Olive Smelt, a survivor, said: 'Doesn't it bother you to think people hate you for doing this? It is nothing to be proud of, the things you do.'

Jayne MacDonald's mother, also interviewed on *Newsnight*, said: 'You are the Devil himself. You are a coward. You are not a man, you are a beast. I hate you and I believe the population hates you.'

Maureen Long, who had survived a murderous attack a fortnight after the killing of Jayne MacDonald, said: 'Someone wants to get hold of you and do some of the same things to you. If they come face to face with you, you had better kill yourself before somebody else does.'

Josephine Whitaker's stepfather appealed directly to whoever might be shielding the Ripper: 'I think the person harbouring the Ripper is as bad as he is. I can't understand the mentality of anybody who can cohabit with such a loathsome creature. He is an inadequate person, physically and mentally.'

Barbara Leach's mother said: 'Look over your shoulder, many people are looking for you. They hate you.' The dead girl's father said: 'You are an obscenity on the face of the earth. When they catch you, they should lock you up and throw away the key.'

A few days later, in a newspaper interview, Mrs MacDonald turned her anger on those protecting the Ripper. She said: 'This man is a coward but the biggest coward of them all is the person shielding him. If it is his mother, wife, sister or indeed a male, they should put themselves in the position of we women who have lost someone we loved. It makes my stomach churn to think that someone is saving his neck.'

Sutcliffe didn't watch the appeal, but his own nerve was going, anyway. 'Pressure on me was worse than ever,' he says. 'I were in a complete turmoil and I couldn't tell anyone. That was the worst thing. I couldn't tell Sonia and I'd never kept anything secret from her.'

Due to appear in court on a drink-driving charge, which he knew would mean the end of his job, he was also beginning to show outward signs of the inner madness that he had been able to conceal for so long. One day at work, when the boss told him off for being late, he was astonished to see that Sutcliffe had tears in his eyes. In retrospect, his family – who were seeing more of him and Sonia than usual, at Christmas and New Year get-togethers – remember that he was edgy and anxious, sometimes seeming close to tears.

On 2 January 1981, he was arrested in Sheffield

while sitting in his car with a prostitute whom he intended to kill. Sutcliffe still boasts that he would have been 'done' for a driving offence and nothing more, had he not handed police 'everything on a plate'.

'I told them everything. They didn't have a clue. All they wanted to know was why I had false number plates on the car. I suppose I could have told them it were for a robbery, but I had that woman with me. Still they didn't realise I was the one they'd been looking for.' Deep contempt for the police is a recurring theme in all conversations with Sutcliffe about his arrest.

On that Friday afternoon, he had left the house in Garden Lane at about four o'clock, giving Sonia the impression he was going to Bingley to see his family. Instead, he headed for Leeds in his brown Rover saloon car, stopping at a scrapyard on the city outskirts, where he picked up a couple of number plates and stuck them over his own car plates. 'The insurance had just run out, and I knew I were about to lose my licence in court, so it weren't worth renewing it.'

Feeling depressed and anxious, he cruised the red-light district of Sheffield, and was turned down by a girl who said later she just 'didn't like the look of him'. But West Indian Olivia Reivers, already serving a suspended sentence for soliciting, got into the car beside him.

ARREST

It was to be the last time Peter Sutcliffe picked up a prostitute, and it was almost Olivia Reivers' last night alive. During his trial, Sutcliffe said he had the sharpened screwdriver and the hammer with him that day, and he'd sought out Miss Reivers with the object of killing her because she was a prostitute. He told the court that the murder was to be part of his mission.

While chatting to the girl in his car, Sutcliffe was approached by two police officers. He was asked by his counsel, James Chadwin, if he had wanted to run away.

Sutcliffe replied: 'I had an opportunity to drive away.'

> *Mr Chadwin:* 'That is not the answer to the question. Did you want to get away at that stage?'
> *Sutcliffe:* 'No. I could have done. I could have literally driven away before the police knew I had false number plates.'
> *Mr Chadwin:* 'Did you want her to try and make a run for it?'
> *Sutcliffe:* 'Yes.'
> *Mr Chadwin:* 'Were you intending to get away at that stage?'
> *Sutcliffe:* 'I thought so.'
> *Mr Chadwin:* 'Why did you want to get away?'

Sutcliffe: 'I am not entirely sure that I did.'

Mr Chadwin: 'You said you had thought of it, why didn't you make any attempt?'

Sutcliffe: 'Because, by the time the police had arrived, I didn't feel the vengeance. I felt very little animosity at all towards Miss Reivers.'

Sutcliffe and Reivers had spent twenty minutes together in his car before the arrival of the police – Sergeant Bob Ring and PC Bob Hydes.

Olivia remembers being surprised that Sutcliffe, who said his name was Dave, had headed directly for a suitably out of the way spot, for them to have sex in the car. He talked to her about 'problems at home', and she thought that might be why he was going with a prostitute. When it came to it, though, he could not perform, and as they sat talking, a police patrol car appeared and parked up in front of them, bumper to bumper, so that Sutcliffe could not drive off.

The officers did not fall for 'Dave's' story that the woman was his girlfriend, and on checking with headquarters they established that she was a prostitute and also that the car number plates were false.

As they led the girl to the patrol car for further questioning, Sutcliffe grabbed the ball-peen hammer and long-bladed knife hidden under his seat, and slipped away to a building set back in the trees and shrubbery behind him. He hid his murder weapons behind an oil tank and then reappeared, telling the officers he had left the car to urinate.

Routinely, they took him to a nearby police station where he gave his correct name and address, and was inwardly amused to find that they were interested only in his driving offences. The number plates had been stolen from the West Yorkshire police patch, so an officer was sent from there to collect him in the morning. 'I just went to sleep, I did. I felt, like always, that I'd get out of this one if I wanted to. I could convince them it were just theft. I were still being fed instructions as to how I could go on with my mission, although I'd been prevented from killing that girl in the car.'

Next morning he was taken across to Dewsbury police station. Sutcliffe insists that he would never have told the police who he really was, had he not received a message from his 'voices'. It came after lunch on Sunday, during a second long bout of questioning. He had already been interviewed by Detective Sergeant Desmond O'Boyle, who had come over to Dewsbury from the 'Ripper Room' at Leeds police headquarters on hearing of an arrest in a red-light area, involving a prostitute. Sutcliffe was calm, pleasant and altogether 'normal' throughout the interview, and O'Boyle was by no means convinced that the Yorkshire Ripper was facing him across the table in the interview room.

'I had an answer for everything,' says Sutcliffe. 'I told him the police had seen me before; I told him why my car had been logged by police in red-light areas as I was driving through. I stayed cool as a cucumber. He didn't know a thing.' Police called briefly on Sonia, telling her only that her husband had been detained for questioning.

While the prolonged questioning of Sutcliffe was going on, Sergeant Bob Ring, one of the arresting officers back in Sheffield, became intrigued by the case and popped back to Melbourne Avenue where he had first seen Sutcliffe and Olivia Reivers in the Rover. He made a close inspection of the immediate area where the car had been parked, and near the oil tank, among dead leaves on the ground, he found Sutcliffe's hammer and his knife.

The police operation was swift, smooth and well timed. They kept Sutcliffe in overnight at Dewsbury and, first thing on Sunday morning, they called on Sonia again. Officers searched the house and garage, finding a hacksaw and a screwdriver to add to the hammer and knife, and to other tools in the glove compartment of Sutcliffe's car.

Sonia, who believed her husband to be in trouble over his cars, agreed to go with them to Bradford police station, where she was questioned for several hours about her life with Sutcliffe. Years later, she still complains that it was the police who 'prevented her from learning German' – her little joke about the way they interrupted her as she watched a German language course on television that Sunday morning.

It was not until Sunday afternoon, still at Dewsbury, and following a line of general questions about his movements on certain dates, this time from the Ripper Squad's Detective Inspector John Boyle, that Sutcliffe claims he received a 'signal' that this was the moment to tell the truth.

Boyle had been hinting that Sutcliffe had slipped out of his car on the night of his arrest for a sinister purpose. Suddenly Sutcliffe said: 'I think you have been leading up to it.'

> *Boyle:* 'Leading up to what?'
> *Sutcliffe:* 'The Yorkshire Ripper.'
> *Boyle:* 'What about the Yorkshire Ripper?'
> *Sutcliffe:* 'Well, it's me.'

'I realised that this was the time to tell them, because they were saying, in other words, that they had found the weapons I had hidden. I had been given the signal from God, through the police, that now was the time to tell them.'

He had no solicitor with him, despite offers from the police for him to be legally represented, and he did not ask for one now. 'I had guidance from God, for my mission. I didn't need a solicitor. God was aware of everything that was happening and it was in His hands.' Sutcliffe immediately began a confession statement that was to take more than fifteen hours.

He said he was glad it was all over 'after all my suffering', and insisted on telling Sonia himself. She was driven over to Dewsbury police station from Bradford and arrived at 10.30 p.m. She came face to face with her husband for the first time for two days. He was calm and composed as he told her bluntly: 'It's me, luv. I'm the Yorkshire Ripper.'

While Sonia dealt with her own numb shock, and faced the ordeal of telling her parents, Sutcliffe was recalling with ease each of the killings he had carried out, together with every detail. He took police to locations where they could recover more of his murder weapons.

However, his 'full and frank confession' began with the killing of Wilma McCann, and it would be some time before he admitted the two homicidal attacks he had carried out before his first murder.

He also omitted the murder of Marguerite Walls, hoping that because it was by strangulation it might never be recognised as his handiwork. He said later that he thought it might 'open lots of new lines of enquiry that were nothing to do whatsoever with me', preferring just to 'deal with the ones that had been attributed to me'.

As he sat in the police interview room admitting that he was 'a beast' for having killed, Sutcliffe still felt his 'mission' was unfinished and therefore did not mention his compulsion, his hallucinations or his 'voices'.

His arrest, and the charges against him, were by now a cause of public celebration. Police officers were almost indecently delighted to have the Ripper locked up in their cells at last, although there was later to be criticism of their enthusiastic announcement to the Press and other media that the hunt for the Yorkshire Ripper was over, when the man they were holding had not yet appeared before a court.

Criticism of a stronger kind came much later, after Sutcliffe's trial, when an official enquiry accused the Ripper police squad of 'mistakes, errors of judgement and professional conduct that did not always measure up to that expected'. Colin Sampson, the West Yorkshire Chief Constable who headed the official review, said the 'exact science of hindsight' had shown up serious errors. He said it had been right to call into question the way the search for the Ripper had been handled. The inquiry, he said, raised a very definite need to look at serial killers and say: 'Well in this case the horse has gone, but for goodness sake can we ever allow it to escape again?'

Giving a lecture on serial murders to the International Police Exhibition and Conference, Mr Sampson said that the introduction of computer technology would in future greatly assist police investigations. He said critics had demanded to know why the police had not had access to computers during the hunt for the Yorkshire Ripper.

'The answer is, simply, there wasn't one. There was nothing at that time which could have handled the sort of volume of information,' he said. The Yorkshire police were swamped by paperwork, very little of it co-ordinated. He said the card-index system, which took up a whole floor of police headquarters, contained *nine references* to Sutcliffe, but the system had 'just not been able to cope'.

Mr Sampson's 30,000-word summary of his findings described how some of the police interviewing of Sutcliffe during the Ripper hunt had demonstrated 'a lack of depth', although he softened his criticism by saying that officers had been hampered by the need to be discreet during sensitive questioning of men who used prostitutes. He also said that the police were saturated with information coming in from the public and often simply could not cope. Detectives had on occasion been sent out on enquiries without knowing that the same suspect had already been interviewed.

During the six-year span of the Ripper murders, West Yorkshire police also had to use their resources on coal miners' strikes and disputes in the steel and water industries. And Mr Sampson admitted that one glaring error was the failure to link attacks. Police were monitoring the sighting of vehicles in known red-light areas in northern towns and cities, but the number of double area sightings quickly swamped them. More than 21,000 vehicles were recorded in two cities. As a result, interviewing of suspects was then restricted to triple area sightings, involving nearly 2,000 vehicles. Sutcliffe had been interviewed about both double and triple area sightings.

But for now, the West Yorkshire police indulged in a great deal of public back-slapping, and the two officers who had arrested Sutcliffe were fêted as heroes.

The trial was prepared with unprecedented haste, so that it took just four months for the case to come to court. Because it was considered to be of such public importance, local Crown Courts were ruled out and the Number One Court at the Old Bailey was named as the appropriate place for the trial sensation of the century.

From the start, the Yorkshire Ripper case was seething with controversy. There were complaints against the Press, for everything from possible contempt of court for showing photographs of Sutcliffe before his trial, to making payments to Sutcliffe's family and friends for their stories. Sonia and her family were to complain to the Press Council of undue harassment by the media as they tried to carry on with their lives.

On the opening day of the case itself, there were the first, faint rumblings of unease at the deal struck between defence and prosecution, to accept Sutcliffe's plea of manslaughter due to diminished responsibility, then astonishment when the judge himself stepped in to say he would not accept the plea.

It was known that the Attorney General, Sir Michael Havers, prosecuting for the Crown, had agreed to accept the lesser plea, rather than insisting on murder charges. He had studied reports from three eminent psychiatrists, each of whom had diagnosed Sutcliffe a paranoid schizophrenic. Now Mr Justice Boreham declared that murder charges must be put, and that a jury must be brought in. The case was adjourned for just one week and both prosecution and defence prepared themselves for an unexpected trial.

Sutcliffe was most unhappy with both sides. 'I couldn't get my lawyers to do what I wanted,' he says. 'They were supposed to be acting for me, but I had my own legal arguments. I didn't see why I should have to stand there and listen to them putting forward this theory and that theory. I was the only one who knew the facts, and I knew they should let me plead guilty to manslaughter on theological grounds.'

He reasoned that he was not insane, but was suffering from some sort of 'temporary aberration', which meant he believed that God had been telling him what to do. The way he saw it, he therefore had had no choice in the matter; he was neither mad, nor bad, but simply 'acting under orders'. Apparently unable to accept that there is no place in law for this argument, he remains angry and bitter at the way things proceeded. At one stage he wanted to sack his lawyers because he discovered they were not Catholics, and he felt the same way about the psychiatrists speaking for the defence.

On 5 May, the Crown's case against the Yorkshire Ripper re-opened in Court One, where Sutcliffe pleaded not guilty to murder in each of the thirteen charges put to him but guilty to manslaughter due to diminished responsibility. He pleaded guilty to each of the seven attempted murders.

It took Sir Michael Havers a day and a half to outline the prosecution case. Occasionally he would refer to the murder weapons, laid out on a table directly in front of Sutcliffe, a few feet from the dock. There were seven ball-peen hammers, a claw hammer, a hacksaw, a long, thin, pointed kitchen knife, several carving knives, eight screwdrivers, a wooden-handled cobbler's knife and a piece of rope. Sutcliffe edged his way past the collection as he went into the witness box.

If the true purpose of the murder trial in front of a jury had been to put the whole story of the Ripper hunt in front of a vengeful public, the crowning moment was when Sutcliffe agreed to give evidence himself.

Dressed in the same grey suit he wore each day, with an open-necked blue shirt, he crossed the courtroom swiftly, flanked by prison officers, and took the oath confidently in a surprisingly soft, high-pitched voice with a pronounced Yorkshire accent. He was taken, step by step, through his evidence by his defence counsel, Mr James Chadwin QC. He never betrayed an emotion, never registered either shame or remorse.

He spent his first full day in the witness box describing his hallucinations in Bingley Cemetery, when he heard 'voices' coming from a Catholic gravestone. He told of his relationship with Sonia, and how he became upset when he discovered she was seeing another man. He talked of his 'deep depression' before and during that time, and linked the onset of the depression to his motor-bike accident up on the moors.

On the second day of his evidence, Sutcliffe told the court that at no time since his arrest had he ever

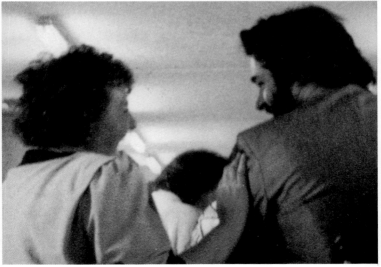

A laugh, a joke and the hand of friendship from a female visitor in Broadmoor Hospital.

A brilliant likeness of the author, drawn free-hand by Peter Sutcliffe in ballpoint pen on a piece of card. But the watchful eyes are his own invention.

Inset: The original passport photo he worked from.

Above: Peter Sutcliffe's version of the Mona Lisa - note the watchful eyes he has given her.
© *S & G Press Agency Limited*

Left: An intriuging portrait of Sonia Sutcliffe, painted by her husband.
© *S & G Press Agency Limited*

Peter Sutcliffe, bloated and unhealthy-looking, has a special smile

for one of his one of his favourite girlfriends, Marion Hope - a patient in Broadmoor's women's wing.

Above: A holiday snap of the author, taken by Sonia on a Greek hillside.

Right: Sonia Sutcliffe in holiday mood in the Greek islands with author Barbara Jones, May 1988.

Left: Sonia poses in a busy Athens street.

Below: Together in the sunshine at Piraeus harbour. Sonia Sutcliffe and Barbara Jones photographed by tour operator, George Papoutsis.

The maximum security hospital that is now home to Sutcliffe.

thought about pretending to be mad in order to gain a lesser sentence. When asked by Mr Chadwin if he thought there was anything wrong with him mentally, he replied, 'Nothing serious at all, no.'

When asked if he believed he would spend less time in custody if he could convince people he was mentally disturbed, he insisted, 'No, there would be something wrong with me mentally if I thought that.'

He denied knowledge of the symptoms of paranoid schizophrenia, saying to Mr Chadwin that he would not know how to pretend he was suffering from that condition. He claimed to have been advised 'by God' how to carry out each attack and murder, except for one, having received no instructions with regard to killing Yvonne Pearson. Mr Chadwin asked him why he had murdered her.

> *Sutcliffe:* 'Because of the directness of what she said and the way everything happened.'
> *Mr Chadwin:* 'What did that convey to you?'
> *Sutcliffe:* 'That it was all arranged.'
> *Mr Chadwin:* 'By whom?'
> *Sutcliffe:* 'By God.'
> *Mr Chadwin:* 'If that incident, so far as you were concerned, and all the other incidents, had not been arranged by God, would you have committed any of these attacks?'

Sutcliffe: 'No.'

Cross-examined by Sir Michael Havers, Sutcliffe claimed at one point that it had been 'a great ordeal' for him to go through with his confession to the police, and admitted that he had not at first told them of his strangulation of Miss Walls, or of his attempted strangulation of Dr Bandara. Sir Michael picked up the piece of rope from among the other exhibits and asked him if it was the same rope he had used on both victims. Sutcliffe confirmed that it was, and also admitted that he had had the rope with him as he sat in his Rover with Olivia Reivers. Sir Michael pointed out that he also had a hammer and a knife with him. 'You were keeping your options open.'

Earlier in his trial, questioned by his own counsel, Sutcliffe had explained that he could not go through with his attack on Dr Bandara: 'At the time I was having messages. I simply heard the word "Stop" and I felt that way about it myself so I left the scene. I was having a conflict and found it extremely horrible, the act of strangling her. That is when I heard the word "Stop".'

He said he hadn't wanted to kill any of the women. It was just 'something that had to be done'. It was his 'mission'. 'I tried on every occasion to prevent myself from killing but I had a terrible conflict and I lost practically every time.'

When asked if he had seen the Yorkshire Ripper described in the media, and what sort of man he thought they were making the Ripper out to be, Sutcliffe replied that 'they made him out to be a monster. Oh, a terrible thing'.

On his second day in the witness box, Sutcliffe was asked about his use of the sharpened Philips screwdriver. 'How did you use this rusted old screwdriver, sharpened to a hideous point, to stab Josephine Whitaker through the same wound three times?' asked Sir Michael. 'By moving it about,' was the reply.

He added that when he read in the newspapers that Josephine was not a prostitute he 'got a nasty shock', for the 'voices' in his head had insisted she was a prostitute. And he had told police later: 'There was I with my hammer and big Philips screwdriver in my pocket ready to do the inevitable.'

He was asked about stabbing Jacqueline Hill's eye with his screwdriver, and his explanation to police that she had been 'staring at him accusingly'.

> *Sir Michael:* 'You are not going to tell the jury she was not entitled to look accusingly at you?'
> *Sutcliffe:* 'I don't know. I think she was already dead but her eyes were open.'
> *Sir Michael:* 'Do you have any regrets about what you did to her eyes?' There

was a long pause, prompting Sir Michael
to ask: 'Do you find that a difficult
question to answer?'
Sutcliffe: 'Yes.'
Sir Michael: 'Is it difficult because you
are not quite sure which is the right
answer to give for the jury and the
doctors?'

Sutcliffe came back: 'You are much quicker
than I am, Sir. I have not considered this at all.'

Mr Justice Boreham intervened during questioning about individual murders to ask him why
he had tried to cut off Jean Jordan's head with
a hacksaw, to which Sutcliffe replied, 'Because
she was in league with the Devil and between
them they had hidden the £5 note and I was
going to do the same thing with her head.' The
judge continued, 'I don't want to get into a
theological argument, but she and her colleague
the Devil had beaten you and your God?'

'Yes,' said Sutcliffe 'It seemed so.'

When asked by Sir Michael if he had thought
about what might happen to him, Sutcliffe said
he realised he would be in prison for the rest
of his life, and said he had had no idea about
the special defence of diminished responsibility.
Referring to a remark he had made to Sonia –
overheard by a prison officer at Armley jail –

he said he told her he might get 'ten years in the loony bin' if he could persuade people he was mad, just to cheer her up. She had been visiting him on remand, and Sutcliffe had seen her in tears, in a distressed state that was rare for her. 'I tried to comfort her, to tell her things weren't that bad. I didn't like to see her crying.'

Hospital prison officer John Leach, who had observed Sutcliffe during his remand period at Armley, had told the court how Sutcliffe was put in a room on his own in the hospital wing, supervised round the clock. He had his own shower in the room, and was escorted on each outing from the ward. Officers kept a logbook to note down anything they considered relevant about the prisoner. This would include signs of illness.

Mr Leach said that on 8 January he had been present when Sonia had visited Sutcliffe, in the company of Sutcliffe's solicitor, Kerry McGill. Mr Leach said Sutcliffe and his wife were left together for a short time and, as usual, Mrs Sutcliffe 'ran' the visit.

'She brought pieces of paper with itemised things on them because of the limited time of visits,' he said. 'They were mostly personal matters.' He said he noted that Sutcliffe said on this occasion that he would not feel any animosity if his wife started a life of her own.

'He said, "I am going to do a long time in

prison, thirty years or more, unless I can convince people in here I am mad and maybe then ten years in the loony bin.'''

Mr Leach said Sutcliffe often spoke to Sonia about her starting a new life.

Under cross-examination, he said the following day he made a new entry in the logbook after a visit by Sutcliffe's wife: 'A little less frantic than previous visits from his wife but she completely overwhelms him and dominates him and the situation.'

Reports from other prison officers were read to the court. One read: 'He has need to talk at times and boasts about his near-misses with the police. E.g. having blood all over his hands and being chased by police. Says he does not go out intending to kill, but gets into compulsion. Very confused. Seems to lose track of time. Seems to think he has been here longer than he has.'

Another report said: 'Something said by his wife during visit. She kept asking why he had not informed her of his compulsive thoughts so he could have got medical advice. He told her to leave it to the medical people here to find out.'

Prison officer Fred Edwards told the court that Sutcliffe talked to him about his case being heard at the Old Bailey. 'He was smiling broadly and rocking back in his chair at the time,' said Mr Edwards. 'He said he was going to the Old Bailey and he was very pleased with that news. He was saying to me that the doctors considered him disturbed and he was much amused by this. He was not protesting that the doctors were wrong about him; he appeared amused.'

Another officer, Anthony Fitzpatrick, said Sutcliffe had told him about an agreement between lawyers in the case. Sutcliffe was discussing with him the possibility of spending time in a long-term prison. 'He told me he wasn't going to a long-term prison. He said he was going to Park Lane mental hospital near Liverpool. He said: "A bed has been reserved for me there." 'The officer said his solicitor had told him an agreement had been reached between the defence and the prosecution, and a psychiatrist had said he would do no more than ten years to satisfy the public.

'He was quite cocky about it,' said Mr Fitzpatrick. 'It was unusual for him to be so. He seemed quite adamant.'

Later, in his final speech, Sir Michael Havers was to add a great deal more to the debate over whether Sutcliffe was mad or 'just plain evil'. He was scornful of both Sutcliffe's insistence that he was on a 'divine mission' and of the three psychiatrists' assertions that Sutcliffe was mentally ill. Sir Michael told the jury to remember that Sutcliffe had been 'quick to inflict pain' and had been willing to prolong death.

'He was willing to take the unexpected opportunity and willing, in the end, to kill any woman. Is that an unfair catalogue of this man's vices?' he asked. If all the facts were true, he said, then Sutcliffe was 'a sadistic, calculated, cold-blooded murderer who loved his job. His crimes are horrible and sadistic beyond our ordinary comprehension.'

Sir Michael said that if it was possible to put the doctors' reports to music they could be compared to a symphony: there had been a quiet opening with little of great interest happening, a pianissimo passage where things needed to be stirred up and then Sutcliffe's so-called primary schizophrenic experience in Bingley cemetery. Sir Michael ridiculed this version of events, saying that when Sutcliffe claimed to have heard God's voice 'it must have been something worth treasuring. This was a very moving experience and he wasn't going to tell anyone. Another explanation is that he simply hadn't thought of it before.'

Sonia did not attend the Old Bailey hearing every day. 'I desperately wanted to go into the witness box to speak up for Pete. I stayed in the witness room on several occasions, waiting to be called, but in the end the defence decided it would be best not to put me in the box.' At the end of the first week in court, her house in Garden Lane, Bradford was attacked by a firebomb, causing damage of around £1,000.

Immediately after Sutcliffe's evidence, the court heard the views of three psychiatrists, who followed one another into the witness box to try to explain in layman's language how they had come to diagnose him as a paranoid schizophrenic.

Headed by eminent forensic psychiatrist Dr Hugo Milne, from Bradford, they appeared to be almost on trial themselves as they were subjected to aggressive cross-examination by the prosecution. Mr Harry Ognall, for the prosecution, asked Dr Milne about the sequence of interviews that led to Sutcliffe's revelations about voices from God. All the differing explanations Sutcliffe had given could not be reconciled, he suggested.

Dr Milne disagreed and said they could all 'hang together'. He said they described a picture of long-standing paranoid schizophrenia and gradual loss of insight. 'It is an eventual admission of the full symptoms of long-standing paranoid schizophrenia,' he said. Mr Ognall referred to the pattern of attacks and the gaps between. Sutcliffe had spoken of morbid depression and hallucinations and described them as attacks, telling police that sometimes he had two a month and sometimes he thought he was all right, but the attacks always returned. They did not fit into any regular pattern. He asked whether any pattern could be discerned in Sutcliffe's crimes.

Dr Milne said: 'This has been one thing which has occupied my thoughts before he came to trial. The only pattern that I can see that eventually makes clinical sense is that towards the end there were an increasing number of attacks. Earlier on they seemed to be much more sporadic and then a cluster. It was only in the last few months one seemed to follow another, when he became much madder.'

Ten of Sutcliffe's twenty attacks had taken place on either Friday or Saturday nights when his wife was working.

Mr Ognall: 'This is a man who is prompted by God, the hapless and hopeless victim of God's will. This is a man who believed he was God's instrument. Why did God direct him only on Friday and Saturday nights?'

Dr Milne: 'Paranoid schizophrenics are extraordinarily cunning, extremely involved in premeditation and determined not to be found.'

Mr Ognall: 'A very great proportion of normal criminals are also cunning, clever and anxious not to be found. That isn't the hallmark of a schizophrenic. It is the hallmark of the normal criminal. I suggest that this pattern is a badge of

a premeditated killer.'
Dr Milne: 'I don't accept that.'

He was asked if Sutcliffe had told him how he had been caught with a hammer in his car by police in 1969, and been charged with going equipped for theft. Dr Milne agreed that Sutcliffe had withheld that from him.

> *Mr Ognall:* 'How can you possibly say that he has not withheld information from you and has satisfied you that he has told the whole truth?'

Mr Ognall asked if Dr Milne would have found it significant that Sutcliffe had been found with a hammer in a red-light district.

Dr Milne agreed that it showed Sutcliffe had told him lies. He explained that there might have been some remission in Sutcliffe's schizophrenia during the period between 1969, when he first claimed to have heard 'voices', and 1975, when he first killed. He may also have been closely involved with his wife and this might have diverted his underlying desire.

Mr Ognall commented on Sutcliffe's lack of criminal activity when he was in London for a year. 'This appears to be a very local God – speaking to him in Yorkshire but not in London.'

Dr Milne said that he could have been in a period of remission.

It was suggested that Sutcliffe had 'pulled the wool over the eyes of the doctors' by pretending to be schizophrenic in the hope of a lighter sentence; that he might have mimicked some of his wife's symptoms from the time she had suffered from schizophrenia; that the lorry driver from Bradford had 'made monkeys' out of the doctors. This they have never forgiven.

Pressure on the three doctors was so great that Mr Justice Boreham felt obliged to remark to the jury, during his lengthy summing-up at the end of the case, 'The doctors, whichever side they are instructed by, are here as professional men giving their professional opinions and they would not be biased, whichever side they are on. What is challenged is the factual basis which they have all accepted, namely that this man was deluded into thinking that he had a divine mission to kill prostitutes. The fact that the doctors have accepted that is a matter of considerable significance. It is substantial but it is not conclusive, but this is a matter for you all.

'The emphasis I am going to place on it is whether or not there is really a solid basis for the belief and how confident they are about it. The doctors, for their part, have accepted that if the factual basis is not reliable then their opinions fall to the ground and their diagnoses go. It is the defendant's evidence which is crucial in this case.'

The judge said that the jury must take a 'quiet, calm and objective look at the evidence'. He said it would be 'humbug' for him to pretend that he had not got his own views. 'I have been sitting here as long as you and of course I have my own views.'

However, he said, the jurors must make up their own minds. They must come to a just verdict. The most important witness was the defendant – 'the only one who could tell them what was in his mind'. He said the jury would have to ask themselves three questions before deciding whether Sutcliffe was guilty of murder or manslaughter.

The first question was: 'At the time of each of the killings was Sutcliffe suffering from abnormality of mind?' If the answer to that was 'Yes' then they had to ask if that abnormality arose from inherent causes such as mental illness. The third question was: 'Was the abnormality such as to substantially impair his mental responsibility for his acts?'

Mr Justice Boreham said there was nothing very troublesome about the words used in the first question. Abnormality of mind meant that Sutcliffe's state of mind was so different from that of an ordinary being that the jury would describe it as abnormal. 'In this case it is said that his will was overborne, directed by, influenced by what he believed to be a divine outside source and therefore his mind was abnormal by reason of that influence so that he could not exercise his own will to control his acts.'

If the jury decided that Sutcliffe did not have an abnormality of mind, that was the end of the matter. If they decided he did, they must move on to the second question about whether that abnormality arose from mental illness. 'You and I are not capable of deciding whether this mental illness gives rise to the abnormality, so you may feel you should take the advice of the doctors, particularly as there is a consensus among the three of them,' the judge advised.

The third question meant they must decide the extent to which Sutcliffe's own mind and will were overtaken by his divine experience. 'It is sometimes a good test to ask oneself, on ordinary layman's terms, was this man on the borderlines of insanity, partially insane?'

The medical evidence, the judge said, was important but not conclusive. The touchstone to the whole case could be Sutcliffe's assertion that he believed at the time of each killing that each of his victims was a prostitute. 'If that was not established – if, as the prosecution says, he knew jolly well in the case of the last six that they were not prostitutes – the diagnosis goes and the defence fails.'

The judge sympathised with the jury who, he said, might be asking themselves how they were going to judge whether Sutcliffe had told them the truth as to what moved him to kill and to kill again. 'That, in the end, is going to be the fundamental question,' he said.

'Ladies and gentlemen, the answer to that is very simple. There is no magic or mystique about it. It is your collective good sense and knowledge of the world which you will apply to the issue. If I may venture one belief – I think you will find if you keep your feet on the ground it will stop you getting your head in the clouds.'

As the six men and six women of the jury rose to consider their verdict, Sutcliffe prepared for a long wait in the oak-panelled dock, flanked by five prison officers.

Sitting at the back of the court were the parents of murder victim Barbara Leach, the mother of Jayne MacDonald and survivor Olive Smelt. Mrs Doreen Hill, mother of Sutcliffe's final murder victim, nineteen-year-old Jacqueline, arrived after the jury had retired. It would have been her daughter's twenty-first birthday that day. Relatives of several of the victims shared speculation over coffee in the Old Bailey canteen.

The public gallery was packed, as it had been

throughout Sutcliffe's trial. Some people had queued all night for a place. Others were offering to sell their places for up to £20, and there were plenty of takers.

The jury were out for a matter of a few hours before returning their majority verdict 10-2, that Sutcliffe was guilty of thirteen murders and seven attempted murders.

The judge recommended that Sutcliffe should serve at least thirty years – 'An unusually long period, but I believe you are an unusually dangerous man. I express the hope that when I have said life imprisonment it will mean precisely that.' He imposed life sentences for each of the murders, and each of the attempted murders.

CHAPTER SEVEN

Confessor

It was a cold damp Monday morning in January 1981 when psychiatrist Hugo Milne arrived at his office, in the centre of Bradford, to face a week routinely busy with appointments and consultations with the familiar mix of neurotics, depressives, drug abusers and offenders referred to him by the courts. Before he had a chance to get to grips with his caseload, Dr Milne took a telephone call from one of his secretaries. 'Do you remember Sonia Szurma? The girl who had a breakdown in London and came to us for three weeks? The one who thought she was Christ, and had to be restrained. You might be needing her notes now.'

Dr Milne was mystified. Why should he need the case notes on a former patient who had been back in the community for seven years? Until that moment he had made no connection between the arrest of the Yorkshire Ripper and the deeply disturbed girl he had examined in 1974 when she sought to return to teaching after suffering a schizophrenic episode. Now he was to find that they were man and wife, and that he had been appointed by the Home Office to examine Sutcliffe and describe his mental state. His evidence would be crucial in the case of mass murder.

The first thing that had struck Dr Milne, as he entered Sutcliffe's cell at Armley jail, was the power of the killer's staring eyes. 'I remember very markedly his piercing eyes, which tended to follow you round the place. Subsequently he has painted some self portraits in which those eyes are incredible. He's quite skilled as a painter and some of the stuff he did – mainly about his delusional experiences and his own impression of himself – is extraordinary. And what always struck me was the eyes.'

Sutcliffe once asked for a photograph of me, and later produced a portrait from it. At first glance, the picture is an extremely good likeness, drawn with professional skill, but on closer examination there is something wrong. It's the eyes. The killer has reproduced his own watchful expression on my face, in my eyes, and the result is uncannily close to the look on his face in his favourite photograph of himself. He had asked me for a close-up picture, and I provided the one used in my passport. In it, I was wearing a V-neck cord jacket, my hair was short with blonde highlights, and I was looking straight into the camera, smiling slightly.

Sutcliffe's reproduction was uncannily accurate. The slight smile was there and the slight inclination of the head. The hair style and cut of my jacket were perfect. But the eyes no longer looked frankly at the camera lens. The gaze was off-centre. giving me a wary and suspicious watchfulness.

I studied a colour photograph he had given me of himself. Taken in a photo-booth – the kind found on any railway station – it was well-focused and rather striking. Sutcliffe looked nothing less than Christlike. He had posed carefully for the automatic lens. His features were much leaner than they are today, with none of the pallor brought about by ten years of incarceration. His complexion was a healthy pink; the black hair and beard were reminiscent of many a statue of the Sacred Heart – the kind that adorns many Catholic homes – but the eyes, as always, were Sutcliffe's giveaway. The look was one of wary and suspicious watchfulness. I am convinced that this has never struck Sutcliffe himself and that he incorporated it into the picture of me without thinking.

He drew the sketch in Biro, on a crude piece of card, and apologised to me in an accompanying note about the unsophisticated drawing materials. It was all he could find to use on the ward, where he continually complained about official refusals to let him have paint and artpaper. The work was, nevertheless, remarkably good.

Sutcliffe asked me to have the colour photograph of himself copied twelve times so that he could send prints to his many women friends, with a personal message on the back of each.

In Broadmoor, every patient is photographed annually for official records, and can ask for copies to send to family and friends. Sutcliffe didn't care for the official photograph of himself. He preferred the younger, leaner version in the ten-year-old snap from the photo booth.

Dr Milne commented that throughout the time he saw him in custody, he was 'very pleasant, neat and meticulous, never anything but polite, very, very well controlled'. By 'controlled', the psychiatrist means that, as a paranoid schizophrenic, Sutcliffe was doing his level best to hide his inner self, for the secret at the heart of his mission was not to be given up easily, and Milne needed to call on all the skills of his twenty-four years as a forensic psychiatrist. His particular skill lies in the interviewing of homicidal psychotics.

He has a kind, avuncular manner, a soft voice with a cultured Scottish accent and a razor-sharp intelligence that enabled him to peel back the layers of Sutcliffe's defences. Even with these advantages at his disposal, it was not until several interviews had taken place that Sutcliffe revealed the great secret that he had never confided to anyone before. He told Dr Milne about the 'voices' he had heard in the graveyard at Bingley in 1967, eight years before the killing began.

Milne identified this as Sutcliffe's primary delusion, a time-bomb looking for a target. That

target presented itself when he was humiliated
by the prostitute who cheated him out of £5 on
the night following his row with Sonia over her
friendship with another man.

———— o ————

Today, Hugo Milne probably knows Peter Sutcliffe
better than any other man alive. He has interviewed
him in depth at least a dozen times, and the
coincidence which brought him into professional
contact with both the Ripper and his wife has given
him a unique insight. He knows the man, the nature
of his crimes and the intensity of the relationship
between Sutcliffe and Sonia.

He said that Sutcliffe was initially 'somewhat
suspicious' of him, but adds: 'You can't blame him
for that.'

He soon found out that Sutcliffe and his wife
were very close, and that both resented any
intrusion on their relationship. Dr Milne recalls a
rift between them when Sutcliffe's brother was
allowed to visit him instead of Sonia. Sutcliffe
thought she had failed to come – 'maybe it was a
game on the part of the prison officers' – and it
caused a misunderstanding that lasted for three or
four days until the doctor himself got to the bottom
of it. He says Sutcliffe was extremely upset about
it, and that was the only time he saw any kind of

split between the couple while Sutcliffe was on remand.

Dr Milne said Sonia was 'perfectly properly angry' when her medical records were produced during her husband's trial. It had been pure coincidence that he had assessed Sonia years earlier after her schizophrenic attack, and now it was being suggested that Sutcliffe was mimicking her symptoms.

'He had seen Sonia throughout her illness, though they were not then married, and the prosecution tried to establish its hypothesis that he used this knowledge to mimic the symptoms.

'One of her delusions was that she was the reincarnated Christ, and that was one of the aspects Sutcliffe was accused of mimicking. What the prosecution did not use, which was in the case notes, and this was annoying to me, was that Sonia was so disturbed that she was running around in a state of virtual nakedness. Sutcliffe wasn't mimicking that.'

Dr Milne said his professional opinion was that Sonia had always been the dominant personality in their relationship, 'because Sonia can't be anything else'. He added: 'I say that in all fairness. I get on perfectly well with Sonia but there have been times when she has been anti-me. Then that goes and she simmers down. I wouldn't say that she made Sutcliffe bend to her will in their domestic life.

I guess many women make their husbands do things. It's not necessarily bending the will, it's the husband taking the easy way out.'

Dr Milne said he became certain at their second or third meeting that Sutcliffe was not bad, pretending to be mad, but was an out and out schizophrenic. 'There were some snide references to the length of time my colleagues took to realise Sutcliffe was schizophrenic, when we took the witness stand one after the other. The court found it hard to realise that, because Sutcliffe had spent a long time with me, he had become florid – in other words he was willing to open up and talk about himself – and that made it a relatively simple diagnosis for the doctors who followed me.

'There was innuendo during cross-examination that other doctors had been influenced by me because of my comparative seniority. One of my colleagues was asked how long he took to diagnose Sutcliffe and he replied 'twenty minutes'. Of course, by then Sutcliffe had been talking to me about his delusions, and as soon as he was ready to do that with me of course he would do it with other people. They were, if you like, going in on the tail-end of interviews I'd done. It was nothing whatever to do with me putting pressure on them for a diagnosis.'

He said Sutcliffe had been talking openly to him about his mission, his messages from God, his actual offences and what he'd done, and wasn't withholding any information. 'To begin with he was very, very resistant to questioning, and in fairness I didn't blame him because he was seeing me for the first time and he was charged with thirteen murders.'

Dr Milne said he sat with Sutcliffe in a room 'about the size of my office'. Sutcliffe had a bed in one corner and a hospital officer sat in the other corner. 'It wasn't exactly the ideal situation in which to interview someone charged with thirteen murders and seven murder attempts.'

Dr Milne was very concerned at one stage about Sutcliffe's insistence that he had seen little blood on his clothes, and his wife had never seen blood on them. 'Being a cynic and a sceptic,' said Dr Milne, 'I went along to see the professor who did all the pathology and told him frankly I was finding it hard to believe. We went together to the university pathology department and he explained to me that the nature of the wounds was such that the amount of blood would be minimal.' The doctor knew of Sutcliffe having compared his killings to the slaughter of pigs. 'Yes, pigs are stunned first and the pathologist explained that to me.'

Dr Milne has unlocked the door to the secret world that Sutcliffe inhabited when he changed his role from unremarkable workmate and neighbour to devious and sadistic killer. The psychiatrist was the first to share the revelation that Sutcliffe believed came from God – the 'voices' speaking in Old Testament language, telling him prostitutes were scum and must die; the divinely inspired mission to cleanse the streets.

Milne said: 'Sutcliffe and Sonia fell out when he believed she had stood him up over another man. He went out to get his own back by going with a prostitute, and the girl made a fool of him. That was the incident that started the delusions about prostitutes. That selected the delusion for him, and he acted accordingly. He had been ripped off by a prostitute, so they were an evil upon the world. You can see the original connection with reality, but ultimately it became completely and utterly detached from the real world, and that was the onset of the full-blown paranoid schizophrenic illness. He was getting back at Sonia at first, but then that motive was overtaken.'

Although Sutcliffe himself has said repeatedly that he came under the total control of his 'voices', an outside influence that he identified as God, he had no insight whatsoever into his worsening mental condition – and still hasn't.

Instead, he rationalises. 'It could have happened to anyone like me. Anyone who had been brought up a Catholic with an unshakeable belief in God. People should try and put themselves in my position. I was working in the cemetery, thinking about my dead grandmother lying there in the earth, and about my friend's mother who had committed suicide. I was susceptible to a spiritual experience, and it happened there and then. Once I was certain it was God who was speaking to me, I had no hesitation in accepting everything that was said. And one of the most important aspects was that it must be secret.'

His refusal, even today, to admit responsibility and guilt is, according to Milne and others, altogether typical of his paranoid schizophrenia. He acknowledges the blood on his hands, and will readily furnish details of each homicidal attack, but he believes he was acting as an instrument for the 'voices', for God. 'I were detached. I were thinking somebody else had done it. It couldn't have been me. I wouldn't have wanted to hurt any of those people. I didn't even know them.'

Dr Milne said there was an 'odd sort of remorse' in Sutcliffe. As he opened up about his crimes, he said he realised that he should not have done what he had done, but that related only to those women he had misidentified as prostitutes. They had not belonged in his mission, and he was distressed about that. 'He believed he had been entitled to do what he had done. It was like someone with delusions who shoplifts and then protests that he or she is really the owner of the store.

'I had a patient like that once. She said she was related to the President of America and therefore

Woolworths belonged to her, so she could not be said to have stolen her own property.' He said Sutcliffe thought what he was doing would rid the world of prostitutes and therefore he could not see that he was doing wrong.

Throughout the many interviews that took place, he added, 'Sutcliffe was always very considered in his replies to questions. He would never blurt something out. He would always stop and think, and if he thought he'd got it wrong he'd go back and change it. He has an enormous degree of control.'

As Sutcliffe's condition worsened, he was still able to present a totally normal, if sometimes bland, face to the world. There was no external evidence of the inner turmoil; even in the immediate aftermath of a killing, Sutcliffe was able to mask his feelings, doubtless helped by his IQ level, which is around twenty-five intelligence points above the average.

Hugo Milne offers this explanation. 'It is difficult to understand that a paranoid schizophrenic could behave normally, like you or me, and continue his work and be able to control his behaviour. 'Those who don't work with madness don't understand that mad people are not always the picture of shambling oddity, strangely dressed, speaking to themselves, generally bizarre. Obviously, full-blown disorganised, deteriorated schizophrenics – the madmen of literature – do present like that. But paranoid schizophrenics who gradually deteriorate, and who are in themselves neat, tidy and methodical, as Sutcliffe was, will hide their madness from normal society but play out that madness in their delusional system.'

The medical definition of schizophrenia is a group of illnesses having characteristic mental symptoms leading to fragmentation of personality. The patient undergoes experiences which are unfamiliar and which cannot be understood as exaggerations or prolongations of familiar sensations. Thought, emotion, drive and movement may be disordered. The illness often recurs, each recurrence increasing a chronic disability until a plateau is reached. The final result, oddity, social incapacity or chronic invalidism requiring prolonged hospitalisation, may be modified by treatment and its social effects mitigated by professional guidance.

Early adult life is the most frequent period of onset, but the illness often begins in adolescence and sometimes at later periods of life. A characteristic insidious onset is often preceded by introversion, subdued behaviour or suspicious secretiveness. Males are a little more frequently affected than females and single subjects more than married ones.

First admission rates for schizophrenics are about fifteen per 100,000 of the whole population in Britain. About 80 per cent of the patients under sixty-five who have been in hospital continuously for two years or more are schizophrenics. The disease is characterised by a change of personality with uncoordinated thought, emotion and impulses occurring in a setting of clear consciousness, memory and orientation.

The patient may feel that his thoughts are controlled and ideas are being put into his mind. Delusions – false beliefs unassailable by fact or reason – occur frequently; their content is varied and may be persecutory, grandiose, hypochondriacal, nihilistic, etc. Primary delusions arise *per se*; secondary delusions are the patient's attempt to account for his strange sensations and may seem clear and logical if the primary premises are granted.

Dr Malcolm MacCulloch, medical director of Park Lane special hospital in Liverpool, was one of the three psychiatrists to examine Sutcliffe and give evidence at his trial. On the eighth day of the hearing, he was asked by Sutcliffe's counsel, James Chadwin QC, 'What in your opinion was his mental condition at the time of the killings in this case?'

To which Dr MacCulloch replied: 'He was suffering from paranoid schizophrenia.'

He had made that diagnosis in a short time, but had continued to check it and still had the same opinion. In some cases there were external signs of the illness – certain kinds of movement or expression – but in other cases no external signs would appear, even during examinations lasting ten hours. 'As far as I am concerned there were no external signs on Peter Sutcliffe when I saw him on three occasions in Armley prison.'

However, he said that he had been watching Sutcliffe in the dock at the Old Bailey, and had noticed certain signs that were immediately consistent with his schizophrenia. One of them was a persistent and repeated looking up by Sutcliffe (on about thirty-eight occasions) to the same spot – a light cluster about ten feet above the judge's head.

He had also noted Sutcliffe's abnormal lack of emotion, especially during heated exchanges about the weapons he used and the wounds he had inflicted. 'I think he has appeared unduly passive in his expression. I don't put that forward as a diagnostic sign, but it is consistent with someone suffering paranoid schizophrenia.'

If a patient showed just one of eight 'first rank' diagnostic signs, he said, it would be fair to diagnose him as paranoid schizophrenic. Sutcliffe demonstrated four of the eight signs:

(1) he had bodily hallucinations, which involved a sensation of being touched or an electrical sensation, feelings deep in the chest or abdomen;

(2) he had influence of thought, believing his thoughts were being influenced or that he could read other people's thoughts. He might also feel his

thoughts were being tampered with by an outside influence.

(3) He also had delusional perception. 'If a person was having a schizophrenic experience and he saw a piece of screwed-up paper, he would see it and know it was a piece of screwed-up paper, but the delusion was the instant and certain knowledge that he himself was "all screwed up". The point is that there is an instant knowledge which is unshakable, which cannot be deduced logically from the perception. He would think it had a meaning special to him and would not be shaken from that conviction.'

(4) Sutcliffe's fourth sign, said Dr MacCulloch, was his passivity – a feeling of being driven, in the sense of being able to do things under the influence of an outside force.

By the time Dr MacCulloch was giving his evidence, Hugo Milne had already spent nearly four days in the witness box. He and the other psychiatrists were to say afterwards that they felt it was almost as though they were on trial as well as Sutcliffe. Dr Milne, in particular, was grilled remorselessly by the prosecution, and he describes himself now as having been 'caught in the crossfire'.

He said: 'The law found the case very difficult, in practical terms. At first they accepted Sutcliffe's plea of mental illness. Then, because the judge, Mr Justice Boreham, declined to accept that plea, they had no choice but to say, "If he's not mentally ill, then he must be acting. If he's acting, then he's malingering, and if he's malingering then he's taking the mickey out of the medical profession."'

It was against this background that exchanges like the following took place in court. Mr Harry Ognall QC, for the prosecution, asked Dr Milne why Sutcliffe's last six victims were not prostitutes and were not lured into cars in the same way as earlier killings.

'It was a change of behaviour,' replied Dr Milne, 'a sign of Sutcliffe's increasing madness.'

> *Mr Ognall:* 'I would put this to you, as he said himself to the police: "Each time my feelings were more random and indiscriminate. I now understand I had the urge to kill any woman." This is what the circumstances of those six killings show, isn't it?'
>
> *Dr Milne:* 'I do not agree.'

Later, Mr Ognall said he wanted the jury to recognise the distinction between, on the one hand, a man driven by the delusion of a divine mission to kill prostitutes, in which he is merely the helpless vehicle for God's will, and on the other hand a cool, calculating and controlled killer of women who killed because it afforded him a cruel satisfaction.

'That man,' he said, 'is one who has set out deliberately to deceive the doctors as to his mental state, because rightly or wrongly he confidently believes that it may be to his enormous advantage to be convicted of manslaughter on the grounds of diminished responsibility.'

Dr Milne agreed with him that because a man killed repeatedly on a succession of separate occasions, it did not necessarily mean he was suffering from diminished responsibility, and that many men who had killed repeatedly were not necessarily suffering mental abnormality. However, having diagnosed him as a paranoid schizophrenic, he believed that Sutcliffe fell into the category of diminished responsibility. He described Sutcliffe as 'alert, astute, articulate and extremely cool, calm and collected'.

These exchanges were part of the prosecution's determination to prove to the jury that Sutcliffe was not mad, simply bad. In Milne's words, 'They didn't want a lunatic in the dock. They wanted someone they could punish.'

He said they found it very difficult to understand that Sutcliffe could lie and manipulate those around him, and still be schizophrenic, for to them, lying was simply evil and not a facet of mental illness. This was exasperating to Dr Milne and his colleagues, as was the verdict, which found Sutcliffe sane and guilty of murder and sent him to

Parkhurst prison.

'It was an emotional thing; people were demanding their pound of flesh. None of us, neither I nor my colleagues, was saying anything other than that he had killed, he was extremely dangerous, and that he would remain dangerous for many, many, many years.'

The doctors have now been vindicated, for in 1984 the then Home Secretary, Leon Brittan, agreed that Sutcliffe must be transferred from the prison system to a maximum security psychiatric hospital. This followed a request by the principal medical officer at Parkhurst, Dr David Cooper, for Home Office doctors to examine Sutcliffe and reassess his condition. At that time, says Dr Milne, Sutcliffe was 'very much more florid', talking of people coming into his cell and saying he felt the presence of one of his victims, Emily Jackson. Apparently the two doctors were 'quite horrified' to find he was such an obvious paranoid schizophrenic. One told Dr Milne that he was so concerned about the case that he had written to the Lord Chancellor, but 'it was blocked, nothing happened'. Some time afterwards, Sutcliffe was transferred.

However, his right of appeal was turned down by the Court of Appeal. He had made his submission on the grounds of fresh evidence that would show he had not been malingering and was now showing obvious signs of schizophrenia. It would

have made no difference to his term of imprisonment or incarceration in hospital, but Sutcliffe and
the doctors were keen to have the original plea
of diminished responsibility finally accepted. 'The
right of appeal was dismissed without any evidence
from the one man who could really say whether
Sutcliffe had been malingering or not, Dr David
Cooper.

'I did the assessment myself because I felt
Sutcliffe had changed not only qualitatively but
quantitively, in that he was more mad in practical
terms. I was angry and sadly disillusioned when the
Court of Appeal refused leave for Dr Cooper – a
very experienced man who had had Sutcliffe under
close observation for a year or more – to produce
even a written report, or to give evidence.'

The sexual aspect of Sutcliffe's series of murders
was another cause of controversy between the
doctors and the law, the prosecution being determined to show that Sutcliffe was a sadistic sex killer.
This was at the centre of their argument that he
was bad, rather than mad. Milne, on the other
hand, argues powerfully that although there was
undoubtedly a sexual element in some of the killings – not seen in the fact that some of the victims
were prostitutes, but in the method by which he
killed them – it was his schizophrenia that was
driving him on.

This argument, supported by other psychiatrists

in the witness box, recurred throughout the trial and is typified in this exchange between Mr Ognall, for the prosecution, and Dr Milne, when the murder of Josephine Whitaker was discussed. Mr Ognall asked, 'If we can discern here a sexual element, that tends markedly to go against the divine mission theory, do you agree?'

Dr Milne agreed.

Mr Ognall then referred to remarks in Dr Milne's report which suggested that injuries to Josephine Whitaker's vagina could be accidental rather than deliberate. 'How on earth are we to reconcile the pathologist's evidence of three stab wounds deep into the vagina with what you said? I suggest that indicates most fiendish cruelty, deliberately done for sexual satisfaction. Do you agree?'

Dr Milne replied: 'It may be the most vicious cruel thing to do, but not necessarily for sexual satisfaction.' He said Sutcliffe told him he never wanted to be seen as a sexual killer.

> *Mr Ognall:* 'I accept he has never wanted to be seen as a sexual killer because if he puts himself forward as that his divine mission goes out of the window – that is why, isn't it?'
>
> *Dr Milne:* 'It could be.'
>
> *Mr Ognall:* 'If we were to find a number of these sexual molestations, the more

instances we find the more it would erode
the validity of your diagnosis?'
Dr Milne: 'It would lead to erosion, yes.'

He was asked about the killing of Jacqueline
Hill, and the way in which Sutcliffe had exposed her
breasts and stabbed her. Sutcliffe had told police it
was just 'something which came over me'.

Mr Ognall: 'Am I naive if I suggest that
betrays a clear explicit [sexual] element in
this killing?'

Dr Milne agreed it might be interpreted as a
sexual motive.

Mr Ognall asked why Sutcliffe should have tried
to scratch Olive Smelt on the buttocks. Dr Milne
said he saw no particular significance in that. Sutcliffe had told police, in connection with Emily
Jackson's killing, that he pulled her clothes up 'in
order to satisfy some kind of sexual revenge as, on
reflection, I had done with Wilma McCann'.

The fact that he placed a piece of wood against
the dead woman's vagina could, agreed Dr Milne,
suggest an underlying sexual component.

Mr Ognall: 'Helen Rytka – he had sexual
intercourse with her?'

Dr Milne said that was a sexual component but not an abnormal act.

Mr Ognall reminded him of Sutcliffe's own description of killing Helen Rytka, by hitting her with a hammer, having sex with her, stabbing her and taking her clothes off. 'Normal?' he asked Dr Milne.

Dr Milne: 'Not normal, no.'

Mr Ognall: 'Can you think of anything more obscene or abnormal than his behaviour to that girl?'

Dr Milne agreed it was obscene but he said: 'I still think it was a case of sexual behaviour for entirely the wrong purpose – to avoid detection, to quieten her and get away.'

Mr Ognall: 'Why did he have to have intercourse with her to keep her quiet?'

Dr Milne: 'As he himself said, this was what the girl expected.'

Mr Ognall: 'Look Dr Milne, he is having intercourse with a woman who has been cruelly attacked and is near death. I ask you again – no underlying sexual component?'

Dr Milne: 'A sexual component, yes.'

He agreed there was also a sexual element in the attack on Marguerite Walls. Dr Milne was pressed to agree that the injuries in those cases militated against the divine mission theory. He said he could not accept that Sutcliffe was a man who got sexual pleasure from killing.

Sutcliffe's own counsel, James Chadwin, tackled the debate over a possible sexual motive when making his final speech to the jury. He referred to the scratch on the small of Olive Smelt's back and said: 'Isn't that really stretching things too far? It is for you to say. Are you impressed either by the suggestion made at one stage that a series of wounds near the tummy button are some indication of sexual gratification? Surely not.'

Emily Jackson's death had been cited as another example of Sutcliffe's alleged sexual motive, said Mr Chadwin. 'Bear in mind this man was obsessed with prostitutes, paranoid, and is likely to have had a special interest in a particular part of a prostitute's body. But is there any evidence that he was deriving sexual enjoyment?'

Sutcliffe had left Marguerite Walls's body in a humiliating position, but surely this fitted in with Sutcliffe's consistent explanation in cases where clothing was disarranged: to show them for what they were, to make them disgusting. This was a desire that fitted better.

Mr Chadwin said the sexual intercourse with Helen Rytka could not be brushed aside, and the prosecution was entitled to claim a sexual element there. The Crown was also entitled to suggest the same in Josephine Whitaker's murder, but it was for the jury to say whether they attached any sexual significance, for instance, to the way in which the weapon had been inserted more than once. They might feel this was more in keeping with Sutcliffe's loathing of prostitutes. The prosecution, he said, had drawn attention to the six cases with some hint of sexual gratification but had ignored the fourteen cases where injuries did not point to sexual enjoyment.

The Attorney General turned to the theme in the cross-examination of consultant forensic psychiatrist Dr Terence Kay, who agreed that to insert a weapon through the same hole a number of times had a sexual meaning.

'Much more like a sadist killer than someone on a mission?' suggested Sir Michael. Dr Kay had stated that multiple stabbings were a common method of killing, but stabbing through the same hole as a deliberate thing was very rare.

He added: 'I have to balance whether this is done for sexual excitement or pleasure, or whether it is the act of a man whose feelings for human beings are blunted by schizophrenia.'

Asked what his reactions were to the injuries inflicted on sixteen-year-old Jayne MacDonald, Dr Kay said: 'Like everyone else – horror. I tried to detach myself to make a clinical decision. I tried to balance for and against, very savage and brutal,

I searched for a motive.'

He told the court that Sutcliffe believed Josephine Whitaker was 'in league with the Devil', and that it was the Devil who made her cunning, prompting her to say she had been to visit her grandmother. It would be more evidence of Sutcliffe's schizophrenic thinking, that he would consider it made her look cunning in her attempt to appear innocent. He agreed there could be a sexual motive but did not claim to know what went through a schizophrenic's mind all the time. 'I do not know what particular thoughts they have in regard to sex or anything else under every condition.'

Would Sutcliffe's schizophrenia ever have run its course, had he not been caught? Would the 'mission' ever have been completed? For Dr Milne, it is 'one of the only things I couldn't be certain about in the case'. Untreated, the delusions would have persisted; and Sutcliffe has never sought, nor accepted, treatment. He told doctors that it would be wrong to say he wouldn't kill again if he was 'out'. He said: 'I know it's wrong to kill but when you've got a reason, it's justified and all right. If there were women around me now, it wouldn't take long to get those thoughts again. The prostitutes are still there, even more now I gather, and my mission is only partially fulfilled.'

It is a frightening hypothesis that had he been arrested after his first attack, or even after the first murder, he might have been diagnosed a paranoid schizophrenic, sent to a secure hospital, given medication and been put up for discharge into the community.

Since his conviction, Sutcliffe has been treated as a lethal weapon by both the prison system and the authorities at Broadmoor, a situation which Dr Milne considers to be perfectly proper. 'But the strange thing is that, as opposed to many killers I've seen, he is one of the least lethal – to men, anyway. He was never any threat to me. I think of other individuals whom I have met and whom I would not want to be anywhere near again, because I would be in fear of my life.

'I can think of several men like that, but Sutcliffe isn't frightening to me. His eyes are disconcerting, yes. But many people have disconcerting eyes.

'Maybe some people think I, too, have disconcerting eyes but that's because I might be putting pressure on them if I'm doing a medical or legal assessment of them. I have worked with someone who you might describe as disconcerting because he never looks at you, even when he's talking to you. Some so-called experts write about eye-to-eye contact but I think that's rubbish. Some people are shifty. Sutcliffe was not.

'I think he was relatively honest with me. I don't believe he was completely and utterly honest with me about his entire behaviour but in general terms I was sufficiently convinced to get up and say he was a schizophrenic. That resulted in me being taken to the cleaners in the courtroom. That doesn't bother me because it is my clinical opinion. If people don't like it, well that's tough.

'As a result of what they were reading about the court case, and the evidence I was giving, some of my patients actually rang my secretary and said it was dreadful for me to come down on that side and say Sutcliffe was mad instead of bad. Extraordinary, isn't it?'

Dr Milne is at all times indignant that his professional integrity was questioned over the Sutcliffe case. He said his attitude to the Donald Neilson case was quite different to Sutcliffe's, because of the man's state of mind. Like the Ripper, Neilson was a serial killer. Dr Milne told the defence: 'I've examined him and he is the classic psychopath of all time.'

The doctor said: 'Even I can get mixed up with the concept of evil and psychopathy. Evil and mental illness are entirely different phenomena. So, although Sutcliffe had done all those dreadful things, I was perfectly satisfied to give evidence that he was mentally ill. I would do the same thing again.' He said he would not be surprised if Sutcliffe was one day sent back to Parkhurst prison. It depended on the quirk of who was looking after him at the time. They might feel: 'We can't do anything for him, he can go back to prison.'

Dr Milne said it could become a political thing, 'playing games with people, giving them labels. What would be easier for me to say is that I don't think he'll ever come out again full stop, and I have suggested, right from the beginning, that this fellow was going to have to be kept in maximum security for forty to fifty years. I can't imagine any Home Secretary letting him out.'

The doctor delivers his final assessment: 'I don't think there was anything clinically interesting in his childhood, or in his teenage years. The only important point for me is that Sutcliffe was, and is, a schizophrenic. In every other respect, I'm afraid to say that he's really rather boring.'

CHAPTER EIGHT

A Complicated Woman

Sonia Sutcliffe is pale and thin and anxious. She looks sad and careworn, weighed down in every way by the package she is carrying. As she walks up the steep drive to her house she looks straight ahead at the double garage doors, painted black. Inside, her husband once stored the weapons he used for murder and hid the bloodstained clothes he had not wanted her to see.

However, this is not on her mind. Sonia, who appears weak – almost frail – is, in fact, a particularly strong and determined woman. Today, she has decided on a course of action that is quite drastic, but simply must be carried through.

She enters the house through the kitchen door and goes straight to the stairs leading to bedrooms and bathroom. Opening a window on the first floor, she lifts a rifle to her shoulder, takes aim with an unpractised but accurate eye, and fires one shot. The target immediately slumps lifeless and falls to the ground.

Even more upset than she thought she would be, Sonia hurries downstairs and directly over to the small warm body, picking it up and carrying it back home, feeling shocked.

She has killed a grey squirrel which had been proving a nuisance for many weeks by burrowing into the loft insulation under the eaves and building a nest there. Pest control officers from the local council had been unable to dispose of it, so Sonia felt she had no choice. The animal was appealing, but it was destroying her home. She worked out that a .22 air rifle would do the job, and the problem was eliminated with a single shot – except that she felt so terrible about it. So terrible that she took the dead squirrel to a taxidermist to be stuffed, so that she would always be able to keep it and stroke it, to comfort it and herself.

——— o ———

Sonia is an intensely, aggressively, private person. Ironically, it was in order to protect that privacy that she came out of the shadows and faced the public for the first time, in the summer of 1989.

Furious at the image of herself as portrayed by newspapers and magazines, Sonia Sutcliffe wanted to claim compensation once and for all. She painstakingly prepared herself over a period of years for a series of legal battles that would establish her as an impressive litigant, and would win her more than £300,000 in damages to date.

Immediately after her husband's arrest, she had been seen as one of his victims – in many ways one of the most pathetic and distraught. Eight years later, she was to emerge as a strong, articulate, determined and intelligent woman, more than able to cope with the unfairness life had handed her.

The Sonia Sutcliffe I know is a combination of these two, and much more besides. She is a complicated woman, by turns self-righteous and stubborn, disapproving, superior and utterly unyielding, then apologetic, becoming withdrawn and ultimately vulnerable. It is difficult to tolerate her outbursts of moral indignation, her censorship of normal, everyday behaviour, yet at the same time impossible to turn on her as she quietens and looks distressed.

She cares deeply for her elderly parents but has at times insisted they move out of her house for lengthy periods so that she can have the solitude she needs to concentrate on her legal cases. She cares deeply for Sutcliffe, but is a source of anguish to him when she books a visit to Broadmoor, then cancels at the last minute because she is 'under pressure' with her litigation.

It would be easy to sympathise with her if she had appeared from the start to be sensitive to the monstrosity of her husband's crimes; if she were a pitiful victim of those crimes herself – in short, the lonely, betrayed wife utterly distraught at the discovery of her husband's true identity.

Even taking into account her own periods of illness since her mental breakdown in 1974, it is not possible to sympathise with Sonia's attitudes since the Ripper's arrest and trial.

It is no secret that she has fought against claims of compensation brought by Sutcliffe's victims and their families. She organised a legal separation from her husband in order to protect herself during his bankruptcy proceedings, and from the compensation claims which followed. And she was outraged when the victims' families won the right to Sutcliffe's half of the marital home, forcing her to put the house on the market. Later she and her mother involved me in a plan that would enable them to keep the house, but Sonia remained bitter about the need to do this. In an outburst against the victims' families, she said: 'It is more than the limit that on top of everything I should even be having to fight to try to keep my own roof over my head. Forever and always the public only hears people screaming about one side of this story. There has been scant regard, if any, given to the thought that there could possibly be another side.

'For instance, if one takes a clinical look at these persons who instigated the ensuing legal tussle, a particularly clear picture emerges. In the first place there is Mrs MacDonald wanting £6,722 to be compensating her for a dead daughter. This mother, who has plenty to say, noticeably makes no reference to the fact that she lost her sixteen-year-old daughter in the small hours of the morning.

Why the mother let her child be out and about at 1.30 a.m., I wouldn't know. But what I do know is that I am more than grateful that neither my mother nor father permitted myself to be out and about at that time of night, especially not at the tender age of sixteen.

'As far as Maureen Long and Marilyn Moore are concerned, in chasing after what they would hope was the financial bandwagon, and trying to grasp £8,500 and £10,500, respectively, a closer examination of the string of reasons given why they could consider themselves to be entitled to the money shows that Marilyn Moore justifies attempting to collect £10,500 for herself under a pretext that she is no longer able to do her work (if you can call prostitution work), when within the year she gets convicted of being a prostitute again, in the same vicinity where she was attacked. Whereas I truly am not being allowed to continue in my profession – and the difference is that the vocation I had chosen in life is worthwhile, and not what can be termed merely as a laidback job, which doesn't require that a person be possessed of a single brain in their head.

'These people graspingly trying to get these monies have not only received injurious compensation already, but most probably press payment, and still they want more. How many times over do they want to be paid? And how many times should a person be expected to be punished, when he is already paying by having had his freedom taken away? What these would-be money grabbers are trying to do is based on nothing more than blind consuming vengeance, as they know quite well that the person in question is incapable of meeting their unjust demands.

'If it was just a question of the cash, there would be some logic in them going after those members of the Sutcliffe family who have merely used the case as an excuse to attain effortless wealth for themselves. Clocking up to the tune of at least £31,000 between them and then instantly purchasing property, when people can spend an entire lifetime slaving away, trying to buy their own homes. By comparison, my home has been honestly acquired and it has been worked on extremely hard to make it into the place it is.

'So, for people to come along with misplaced motives against myself, aiming to throw me out of my own house, that has already been legally made over, it is nothing more than vicious persecution of an entirely blameless person, especially when I don't even owe these people a single thing.'

There is no hint of compassion. More an outright contempt for people whom she considers to be of such lower intelligence than herself that they are incapable of any real understanding or emotion. Extraordinarily, she believes they should 'learn by what has happened to them. All human experience, good or bad, can teach us valuable lessons'.

On my first meeting with Sonia, six years ago, she was astonished to be asked if she now hated her husband. 'Why should I hate him?' she said. 'He has done nothing to me.'

Asked how she could bear to live in the same house she shared with him during eight of the Ripper murders she replied: 'Nothing bad has ever happened to me there.'

The way she sees it, the bad thing that has happened is that she and her family are permanently deprived of the presence among them of genial, easy-going Pete, so tragically mentally ill, without them knowing, that he earned himself a life sentence. The ineptitude of the police force combined with the evil of prostitution to prey on that mental illness and drag poor Pete into a hellish whirlpool from which he had no escape.

In spring 1984, Sonia had wanted to talk to a journalist, to put forward some strong views she held about a book soon to be published. It was *Somebody's Husband, Somebody's Son* by Gordon Burn.

She hated the book and wanted to gain an injunction against it. She gave me a copy of it, marked in red where she felt most strongly about the wording. Her notes in the margin on several pages are illuminating.

Burn has quoted Sutcliffe's brother Mick, as he describes an evening with Peter and Sonia at the Horse and Hounds pub near Garden Lane. Mick complains that he had nothing in common with Sonia's teacher friends, and says it 'wasn't my bloody idea of a good night', being introduced to one after another. He called them 'long-haired bastards all talkin' down to us as if we know nowt'. Sonia marked this passage 'TRUE', in the margin.

In Burn's account of the trial, he mentions Mr Harry Ognall's cross-examination of Dr Hugo Milne, on whether Sutcliffe derived sexual excitement from the killings. Dr Milne had said in his report that Sutcliffe consistently denied this, and also denied that he had used the incidents afterwards 'to help in the sexual situation' at home. Sonia marked this: 'vile man'.

Where Mrs Doreen Hill, grief-stricken mother of Sutcliffe's last murder victim, Jacqueline, is quoted as saying that perhaps the best thing would be locking him in a room with thirty prostitutes and letting them loose', Sonia had written the word 'sadist' in the margin.

Talking to me about reports of her husband's killings and his arrest and trial in the press, Sonia said he had been continually 'misinterpreted'. She claimed that it was not true that he had intercourse with Helen Rytka. She said he had been tricked into admitting this during police interrogation. Her

274

attack was all the more astonishing as Sutcliffe himself has always admitted having sex with Helen Rytka, and his semen was found in her body.

Sonia was also forthright in her denials that 'Pete entertained himself by going to see seedy immoral slags contorting themselves into total naked exposure', as the *Daily Mirror* claimed in an article in May 1981, at the time of the trial.

She claimed that Burn's book, written with the co-operation of Sutcliffe's father and brothers, tried to make her a scapegoat. She said Sutcliffe's family background was the worst possible start in life, claiming that her husband 'missed out on a father's love' and told her he wished he could have had parents like hers. Despite his obvious intellectual potential, she says, he was pushed into a well-paid job to supplement the family that was always short because the father preferred to 'squander his wages on himself'.

The well-paid job was grave digging. 'I ask you, what sort of job is that for any poor innocent boy straight out of school at fifteen, with an incomplete education?'

If Sutcliffe had been remotely like his father, she wouldn't have married him, she says. 'He isn't a drunken fornicator. He is sensitive and gentle. Everyone who knew him liked him. He was too good-natured to even say no to his boss when he asked him to do extra work. I got fed up sometimes on my own. Sometimes I thought he would be home, then he would ring and say he had to do overtime.'

She told me they had the perfect marriage. 'He never changed, and he hasn't changed now.'

She showed me proudly round their home in Heaton, the respectable suburb of Bradford where they moved after spending the first three years of their marriage with Sonia's parents. The house had come under attack since Sutcliffe's arrest. Damaged by a vandal's firebomb during the trial, it also needed complete redecoration after police moved in to search every inch of it as they built up a case for the prosecution.

The house is an immensely important symbol. It is the middle-class home where Sonia feels she really belongs, after working her way out of the grim council estate where she was born and brought up. Her mood visibly lightened as she opened one door after another, pointing out her odd-shaped pieces of pottery – 'I prefer to call them sculpture, actually.'

She took me to the attic room at the top of the house where she would spend solitary hours in the evenings, marking exercise books or day-dreaming about future plans to open her own craft centre. She explained how she would hear Sutcliffe come home at night and would sit on the edge of the bath, chatting to him while he washed at the handbasin.

In their bedroom, she still sleeps in their double bed. The clothes in her wardrobe are pin-neat. The silver wedding dress her mother made is hanging there. Sutcliffe's wardrobe is empty. 'I gave the clothes to Oxfam,' she said with a sudden giggle. 'Otherwise they would have been sold to raise money for those people.' She uses the same language as he does to describe the murder victims and their families. 'Just imagine, there are men walking around Bradford wearing the Yorkshire Ripper's clothes!'

The house was cold. Furniture was hidden under dust sheets as redecoration was about to begin, and Sonia had been staying at her parents' home in Tanton Crescent again. She planned to move back. 'Sometimes I've had to call the police, when I've heard someone trying to break in. But I've never felt really frightened. I'm not going to be forced out of my own home by anybody.'

On subsequent visits, after she had moved back in and her parents were living there with her, the house was still cold. I found it formal and unfriendly. Sonia was greatly exercised over in-accuracies printed about it. 'Some newspaper said the house was semi-detached. Can't they see it's detached – the only one in the road?'

There is a bus stop round the corner of Garden Lane, about 200 yards away. On dark evenings, with the news of another Ripper murder fresh in their minds, women stepping down from a bus would walk quickly, nervously, to their front doors. Sonia says she did not do that. 'I didn't go in fear of my life. I didn't gossip about the Yorkshire Ripper. I just don't gossip about things. I just wasn't involved in all the speculation about who it could be. I had other things on my mind – my schoolwork, for example. The whole of Yorkshire and the north were talking about him, but not me. I knew about it, but I wasn't mesmerised by it like some people.

'Even if I had followed all the Yorkshire Ripper rumours, I would never have known it was Pete. You must remember that it was only twenty nights in five years. And there was no blood for me to see. He often did his own washing. He was very considerate like that. They say I should have seen him coming home covered from head to foot in blood. It wasn't like that. The police even did tests afterwards in an abattoir, and agreed with pathologists that there was not a lot of blood. People think I must have been naive or stupid not to know. But the victims were not cut up. They were stunned, and little blood ran.'

Sonia says her first question to her husband, when he told her he was the murderer, was: 'Why? Why did you do it?'

'He told me about the voices in his head, the

voices he believed were from God. I can't judge his mental state but obviously he is seriously ill. I feel compassion for him.'

With a hint of the same complaining tone that is also his hallmark, she says: 'Too many people are ready to pass judgement. How many of them are paragons of virtue? I am a deep-thinking person, but others have a very limited mentality. They have shown a great lack of compassion. At the trial they wouldn't let him plead diminished responsibility. They made a political decision to give the public what it wanted.'

She is convinced that the police would have charged her as an accessory if they could. 'If they could have nailed me, they would have. They tried hard enough.'

Even before she began to feel 'persecuted' by the victims and their families in the pursuit of compensation, Sonia admits she did not feel compassion for them. 'All my emotions were taken up with my own family. I was going through mental torture over them and trying to help Pete when he most needed me. I didn't have any feelings towards those people. I didn't know any of them. They just weren't in the same circle as me.' She means that they were not her social equals. She has described some of the women victims as 'base' and complained that suffering can be an experience from which one should 'emotionally grow', rather than allowing it to take over. 'They have claimed thousands of pounds from me, knowing it could break me financially. Yet I had done nothing. They had their criminal compensation, some of them. My house is all I had when this happened. I made up my mind to fight for what is mine. I don't believe in running away from trouble.'

For several years her fighting came to nothing. There was a damages claim against a local newspaper which brought her a few thousand pounds, but her first substantial success was a copyright action against the *Yorkshire Post*, which made two settlements of £25,000 in 1988.

Until then, Sonia had become increasingly desperate in her fight against claims from the victims and their families. However, she says her desperation never reached the point where she felt like giving up – or committing suicide. 'It's not in my nature to give in. I'm a fighter.'

She was outraged when a county court judge ruled that despite her husband's bankruptcy, she must make over half of the value of her house to a trust set up by the claimants. It was then that her mother, always close to breaking point, told me that she felt suicidal herself. She had been bewildered and distraught when Sutcliffe was arrested, telling herself and the rest of the world that it was impossible that her son-in-law could be the murderer who had made them all feel threatened for years. She remembers every detail of the Monday morning in January 1981 when the news was brought to her.

'I had been a bit concerned when Sonia and Pete didn't turn up for their usual Sunday afternoon visit, but I thought they might come in the evening. Later I rang their home, and when there was no answer I thought perhaps they might have gone to visit his family in Bingley. In the early hours of the next morning my husband and I were awakened by loud hammering on the door. It was half past one and dark outside. I looked through an upstairs window and called down – "What do you want?" They said they had some news about my son-in-law. I was worried and dialled 999 for the police. They arrived within fifteen minutes and told me the men outside were all right. They were from the Press and I should let them in.'

Mrs Szurma let the men crowd into her kitchen, and the police left, not having told her the news that was to devastate her. The journalists told her: 'They've caught the man who has done all those killings. The Yorkshire Ripper. It's Peter Sutcliffe, and he was found in a car with a girl.'

Confused, Mrs Szurma thought the girl must be Sonia. She was persuaded to hand over photographs of her daughter. The journalists left, and as the night wore on a crowd gathered outside 44 Tanton Crescent. Reporters were knocking at doors and windows, and Mrs Szurma was still uncertain about what had happened. She rang her elder daughter, Marianne, in London, but she had heard nothing either.

'I couldn't believe what was happening. I couldn't think of anything more terrible that could possibly happen to us. There must have been a terrible mistake. I felt sick inside. I couldn't even leave the house to buy food. The press had set up their own refreshments caravan outside. My husband and I were trapped.'

Mrs Szurma became ill, and took lengthy sick leave from her job as a nurse. When she returned, her workmates were hostile towards her, believing that she must have known, or should have known, that it was Sutcliffe who had committed the Ripper murders.

Despite Mrs Szurma's own suffering, it was overtaken by her torment on Sonia's behalf. 'What happened to her was in many ways worse than death. At least if one is dead one feels no pain, but no human being should have to endure what she was going through.'

The education authority had posted Sonia her employment documents immediately after Sutcliffe's arrest. Her teaching job was withdrawn. There was no covering letter.

'I was forced to see my daughter lose not only her husband but her source of income and employment. And there was worse to come as

Sonia became virtually an outcast of society, reviled and hated as Pete's wife.'

Mrs Szurma desribed how she became afraid for Sonia's life when her house in Garden Lane came under attack, and she and her husband finally moved in to help protect her. During Sutcliffe's trial, she said, it became obvious to her that he was ill. 'No person in his right mind could do the things he had done. When he was later moved to Broadmoor Hospital it was final proof that the verdict was wrong. He should have been allowed to plead diminished responsibility.'

The Sutcliffe she knew was kind and considerate. 'I became very fond of him. I cannot say a wrong word about him. I am a nurse and when someone is sick he cannot help himself. He was really the most considerate person I have ever known. I cannot judge him for what he did in sick moments. It was his illness. I feel just the same about him now as I always did. I love him like a son.'

Mrs Szurma still writes regularly to Sutcliffe, and visits him at Broadmoor when she can. For six years, she fought off her own ill health in order to care for her husband and for Sonia. When the court order came in 1986, forcing Sonia to put the house on the market, she broke down. 'We will be homeless, out on the streets with no help or sympathy from anyone. The legal system has let us down, and it seems so unfair that we should be made to suffer further when Pete has already been sentenced and is paying the price for what he has done.'

At the end of the first day's court hearing, when Sonia was contesting claims against her husband's half of the house, her father collapsed and was taken to hospital. He had suffered a stroke, and would be seriously ill for some time. Sonia and her mother – now in her sixties and retired from her job – contacted me.

Mrs Szurma said: 'There is no future for any of us. I don't think I can go on. I can't even help my husband or my daughter any more. Sometimes I look back to the war we lived through when we were younger, and I honestly believe that these last six years have been worse – the only difference is that there is no end to our present suffering.'

She did not want to deprive the trust set up by Sutcliffe's victims, but she did not have a penny piece to offer them. I saw a woman completely broken by what had happened. She had grieved for years over the loss of her rights as a Czech national. Her own elderly mother was very frail and living alone in a tenement building in Prague. Now her husband was very sick and had partially lost his sight. Her daughter, Sonia, nursed by her family through a mental breakdown years earlier, was driving herself further and further into a state of numbness, so withdrawn that she would often stay in her room all day, unwilling to talk, unable to cry.

I sat down with the family, in the cold, rarely used dining-room of Sonia's house in Garden Lane, and we talked for four hours. I felt sure that funds could be raised for the victims if the family was prepared to talk to me fully over a period of time, and give me access to information – and to Sutcliffe himself – which would truthfully and accurately portray, in a serious book, the circumstances of their lives during the period when Sutcliffe was carrying out the series of murders, and later when he was arrested and tried. Several publishers were keen to offer a substantial advance. The funds were to go to the victims' trust. I spent ten days with the family, and agreed to help them find a publisher who would put up an initial £15,000 for a book project. Sonia claimed, for a period of weeks, to be too tired to co-operate but still desperately needed the money. In the end, believing in the book as I did, I took out a personal bank loan for £15,000 and gave it to them. A few months later Sonia and I went on a fortnight's holiday to Greece. Later still, in August 1988, I was to visit Sutcliffe in Broadmoor for the first time, accompanied by Sonia.

Mrs Szurma is a warm, talkative, bustling woman, physically small and neat, emotionally big-hearted and easily reduced to tears. She is forced to be the strongest member of her household, bringing some sort of order to daily life despite the ever-present anguish felt by all of them. Yet she finds time for small kindnesses that are typical of her generous spirit. She occasionally visits a Czech patient at Broadmoor, and contacted his mother for him when she was in Prague. Gifts from her often take the form of hand-knitted sweaters which she completes quickly and expertly, using wool bought directly from the mills in Bradford.

Sonia, who is introverted sometimes to the point of complete silence, is often irritated with her mother. She told me: 'Ma seems to talk everything through, even the shopping list, all the time. When she returns from shopping, she will go on for half an hour about what happened, who she saw, what she bought. I find it hard to tolerate. I need to concentrate on documents I'm preparing for my court cases. I want to empty my mind of everything but the task in hand, and all the time I can hear my mother chatting away in the background. Sometimes I lose my temper and we have a row. I say sorry later, and she's ready to forgive straightaway. I just can't help myself.'

She said her mother wanted to do the housework: 'But it just doesn't come up to my standards. I often do it all again.'

Her father, on the other hand, is a kindred spirit. 'We don't have any problems at all. I respect his wishes if he wants to be quiet and alone, and he does the same for me. We can live very happily side by side.'

Sonia's dream is to buy her own home elsewhere, leaving her parents at Garden Lane. She would like to live in or near London where so much of her time is spent. There is easy access to Broadmoor and to her lawyers, still preparing new cases at her request.

When preparing her libel claim against *Private Eye* magazine in 1989, she insisted that her parents move out to Harrow, Middlesex, to stay with their elder daughter. They were there for several months, in the terraced house where Marianne and her Indian husband, Haleem, live with their four children. Mrs Szurma told me: 'We can't go home until Sonia says so. She says she needs to be alone. We are really overcrowded at Marianne's house. Sometimes we feel like homeless children.' She told Sutcliffe, during a visit to Broadmoor, that she and her husband were buying their own food while they lived there.

They spent Christmas there while Sonia worked on alone in Garden Lane, heating up frozen food while she produced a 30,000-word statement for the High Court case. 'I couldn't have Marianne and the family here for Christmas anyway, I just couldn't face the preparations I would have to make, and the mess I would have to clear up.'

Sonia, who had turned down offers totalling

many hundreds of thousands of pounds to 'tell her story' at the time of Sutcliffe's trial, has dedicated herself instead to a long and bitter war of attrition against the media. There are still a number of cases she intends to pursue, and in the process of preparing them herself she has become something of an expert litigant. Her obsessional nature is turned to advantage in the examination of every detail, the checking and double-checking of facts. She has told me many times that she thinks she would make a good lawyer. She refuses to discuss her breakdown in 1974, except to say that Sutcliffe was kind to her. However, she has said that she does not accept the diagnosis of schizophrenia, at the same time often complaining of stress and tiredness. She has three-monthly checks with her doctor, and takes Valium. She has also experimented with homeopathy, encouraged by her sister who studies radionics and iridology and has taken an Open University degree in pure and applied science. Marianne once visited Sutcliffe at Broadmoor and insisted on examining the iris of his eyes to develop her studies further. He said he felt a fool in Central Hall, with other patients wondering what his visitor was doing. Sonia, on the other hand, is an admirer of her sister's pursuit of knowledge, and of her plans to treat others once she has qualified.

Sonia was furious at suggestions that she was suffering a further mental breakdown when Sutcliffe was arrested. She says that she once came to the door to speak to a journalist, solely to dispel the rumours that she was 'going out of her mind'. Yet, she can hide behind her illness when she feels it necessary. She sent me a terse letter once, and claimed later that she 'hadn't known what she was doing' when she wrote it. On another occasion, she claimed she could not remember signing some legal papers.

She admits that her emotions are often repressed, for example her memory of hiding her disappointment as a five-year-old when she was not given the Christmas present she longed for. She finds it difficult to cry. She had been sitting at home watching a Geman language lesson on television when police first called to tell her they had arrested her husband. It was a Sunday morning, at about 11 o'clock.

Sutcliffe had insisted he should be the first to tell Sonia, so she was taken to Dewsbury police station without knowing what had happened. 'I thought he might be in trouble over one of his cars, perhaps the insurance or tax disc. I thought I might have to bail him out.'

Instead, she was shown into a room where she waited quietly for a few minutes. Then Peter was brought in, flanked by police officers. 'It's me, luv,' he said. 'I'm the Yorkshire Ripper.' There was shock and disbelief, then numbness. It was hours before Sonia broke down sobbing on the shoulder of a woman police officer. She was allowed to recover before being subjected to many hours of intense questioning.

She has never cried in public since that day. I have seen her angry, livid, desperate, anxious, helpless, unhappy to the point of heartbreak, all extremes of emotion, but I've never seen her in tears. As the unhappiness intensifies, the drawbridge goes up and she retreats into an unnatural silence, all her feelings trapped inside.

Once she spent an entire two-hour visit in Broadmoor with her head resting wearily on Sutcliffe's shoulder, staring fixedly at the floor, not speaking one word. 'It's her nerves,' Sutcliffe says. 'She can't help it. I knew she were nervy long before I married her. But I've got the patience to deal with it. I never minded, even when she were going on at me at the end of a long day.'

He told psychiatrist Dr Hugo Milne of Sonia's demanding ways and her incessant nagging, her obsessive cleanliness about the house, but he told him only because he was pressed to do so. 'I never wanted to criticise Sonia,' he told me. 'But they explained it could be part of my mitigation that I might have been under stress at home.'

I have experienced Sonia's 'demanding ways' myself. On our two-week holiday I sometimes found it hard to tolerate her continual criticism. She would virtually reprimand me for reading a book that had nothing to do with the marvels of Greek mythology that we had come to see. 'I just don't know how you could,' she'd say. 'I'd never do a thing like that. I mean, it's a waste of time coming here if you're just going to read a paperback.' The fact that it was a paperback – Thomas Hardy – seemed only to inflame her sense of outrage.

She would 'never do a thing like listening to a Walkman' either, even if it was playing Beethoven. It was clear that what she actually did not like was the attention of her companion wandering from her. To understand that led to some degree of sympathy on my part, but it did produce continual tension and irritation.

Sonia had travelled separately to Athens, as her holiday was to continue beyond mine. She would go on to Cyprus for a fortnight with a teacher friend who had been writing to her. She arrived at the Western Airport carrying one small piece of hand-luggage – her wardrobe for the entire month's holiday. She was dressed in a cream cotton suit and the wooden-soled clog shoes she always wore.

She looked pale and thin, as always. Her striking black curly hair, worn down to her shoulders, turned heads, as always. Despite the journey, she was keen to get on with some sightseeing, so we drove up to Lycabettus, a beauty spot overlooking Athens. She was the most animated I have ever seen her, completely taken with the sight of Athens at night and thrilled to spot the Acropolis, floodlit in the dusk.

Over supper at an outdoor restaurant, she announced that she was calling herself Oksana – the Czech name she was christened with – for the next two weeks. Her mother had cried as she left that morning, so Sonia had already bought postcards at the airport and was keen to post them as soon as possible. She talked about how she and her sister, on their many holidays together as teenagers, had always spoken Czech to each other to be different from other British holidaymakers.

On the drive back to our city centre hotel, we saw groups of smartly dressed – and legal – prostitutes. Sonia did not comment. Our tour guide joined us for supper and, in conversation, mentioned a German girlfriend of his. Her grandfather had been a prominent Nazi and the family were still very involved in the 'Fatherland', and had insisted that the girl stayed with them instead of coming to Greece. We talked of how the whole family had suffered because of her grandfather's reputation, and Sonia became quite agitated as she stressed that nobody should have to pay for the sins of their relatives.

Some days later she brought the subject up once more, and we had a violent argument as she attempted to defend Hitler, saying that one must

292

understand his motives were good, although he had 'gone too far' with his methods. The row centred for a while on her refusal to accept that Hitler and Nazism were evil: 'I don't like that word. It's open to misinterpretation.' She said it was important to remember the originally good motives which inspired Hitler – his dream of a master race to make Germany all-powerful.

His despotism came from an early life that was bitterly disappointing, she said. 'He was prevented from expressing his creativity, prevented from studying art. Only an artist could understand his profound frustration, the permanent chip on his shoulder. It is essential for artists to express themselves.'

His ambition was to keep Germany pure. Surely we should sympathise with that? The Jews were an intruding race. Once his plans were set in motion, she said, the men carrying out his orders had no choice. They were terrified for their own lives. Even high-ranking Nazi officials had a compulsion to carry out orders. 'It was a hunger – a need.' The doctors who experimented with mothers and babies, she said, were doing what they believed was legitimate research.

Long after we had started raising our voices, I realised that this must be part of her rationalisation of the terrible things her husband had done. She was not happy about using the word evil to describe him, and she said that she had come to understand what her husband had done, 'spiritually and intellectually'.

I asked her if she was equating her husband's madness with Hitler's madness. No, she said, that had been said by others; she was not comfortable with that, and added that if I, too, felt that way about him then she would not be willing to let me meet Sutcliffe.

She wrote postcards to him daily, and explained to me that she was his lifeline, his main point of contact with the world outside Broadmoor. It was a cruel place, she said, where some of the warders had a bullying attitude to patients. Sonia felt that Sutcliffe was a target for 'bullying and meanness'. Portraying herself as forgiving and perceptive, however, she said she understood how some of the warders had been caught up in the system and had to conform. They needed their jobs for security for their families, so probably had to do things they didn't really agree with. Others were hungry for promotion. She thought journalists were like this, too. Pursuing stories by methods they might not feel happy about, but committed to their careers – 'just following orders'. I stopped it there, not wanting to become involved in a further heated argument.

My diary for the two-week holiday is a vivid reminder of how maddening Sonia could be, and of how well I came to know her.

TUESDAY 10 MAY

On our first full day in Athens, she had got up
early and insisted we went out without
breakfast. We walked up to the Acropolis,
stopping at the post office to send off
postcards. Sonia had learnt some Greek in
1974, when she and Sutcliffe planned to
honeymoon in the country, and had recently
brushed it up. She used it for the first time to
a surprised assistant behind the post office
counter.

At the Acropolis, under an increasingly hot
sun, she examined every exhibit minutely, and
spent a further hour in the museum there.

Over lunch at a pretty hillside café, she told
me of the friends in Cyprus whom she was
going to visit. A headmistress and her husband
had been writing to Sonia since Sutcliffe's trial,
wanting to get to know her. Sonia did not find
this odd. She had had hundreds of letters,
some addressed simply to 'Sonia, England'.
Some reviled her, others were accusing. Others
extended friendship, and she particularly
appreciated those which were not only
sympathetic to her, but to Sutcliffe too.

She recalled those early days when it was
so hard for her and her family. She said she
and her sister, Marianne, had coped in
different ways with the stress of Sutcliffe's

arrest. They had been very close as children, Sonia said. They had travelled all over Europe together. Soon after her marriage in 1974, Sonia went to India with her sister and brother-in-law. There had been a few problems from time to time between her mother and her sister's husband, Haleem. 'He is British-educated, and arrogant. He rather looks down on my mother,' she said.

Sonia was sharing her Greek island holiday with Marianne by sending postcards almost daily, cramming her tiny writing into the confined space in a teacher-like essay on whichever monument or historic site she had visited. 'Once we were like twins,' she said. 'But when the family came under pressure it was I who had to be the strong one. We both had the chance to be strong, with our good background and education. But I also had the strength of an intense relationship behind me.'

She said things might have been more difficult had she only known Sutcliffe for a few months. 'If you knew him you would see how sensitive and intelligent he is. He is a brilliant artist, too, completely self-taught, no thanks to his family or education.'

Sonia said her own life was taken up almost entirely with legal wrangles – libel and copyright cases against newspapers and *Private*

Eye, and Sutcliffe's bankruptcy case.

She fussed a great deal over travel arrangements, yet neglected details and could be off-hand with waiters and cab-drivers. We spent an evening at a *son-et-lumière* performance at the Acropolis, surrounded by American tourists. The script was in pedantic English, actors hamming their way through it in a declamatory style that soon became tedious. At the end, I turned to Sonia and said: 'Well, what did you think of that?'

She was utterly spellbound. 'It was absolutely marvellous,' she breathed.

WEDNESDAY 11 MAY

Coach to Delphi, 7.30 a.m. Sonia in a sundress and home-knitted cardigan, hair tied back.

She stayed close to our woman guide at Delphi, negotiating the temple of Apollo in her wooden-soled Dr Scholl clogs. She complained that she would have stayed for hours if we hadn't been tied to the coach timetable. I felt relieved. To my embarrassment, she went up to the guide and congratulated her on her teacher-like approach. 'I'm a teacher myself and I use the same methods. Of course it's easy to be a good guide for others when you really know what you're talking about, isn't it?'

She had not yet relaxed into a holiday mood. Over lunch, I noticed she was still pale and haunted-looking. She told me how she had had to take up Sutcliffe's legal battles. 'I couldn't have lived with myself otherwise.' She launched into an attack on her husband's victims and their families who had had criminal compensation, '. . . but that's not enough. They want me to suffer. Take my house, everything. If they succeeded, they'd probably have to repay the compensation they've had. They haven't got the intelligence to work it out.' She was convinced that a newspaper had 'put them up to it'.

Sonia talked of Greek mythology. She seemed knowledgeable, but I didn't know if she was trying to impress or was simply enthralled by it. She was very much the artist, the teacher, the classical scholar.

Back in Athens, over dinner, she told me of her 'ultimate humiliation' when newspapers had claimed she was a victim of Sutcliffe's crimes, too, and she longed to be understood by his other victims and wanted their sympathy. She became very agitated and covered her face with a table napkin as she said it was the worst possible portrayal of her. 'I'd never beg them to understand me. I don't care if they do or they don't. I don't care what they think of me.'

I reminded her that what happened in 1981, when Sutcliffe was arrested, must have been worse. 'It was different. I've had time to absorb it and deal with it.'

Sutcliffe had explained what he did, and she had come to understand how it happened. Naturally, she had immersed herself in his case and had been certain he would get a manslaughter verdict. 'He *should* have got a manslaughter verdict.'

THURSDAY 12 MAY

Sonia looking more relaxed, suntanned. We took a boat trip to three small islands. She loved Hydra, the artists' colony. Told me she longed to be a sculptress once more, once her legal battles were over. The next two years were crucial, she said. After that she might learn to drive, and start a new life.

She was still wearing the cream cotton suit she had arrived in. In the evening she retired to her room at 8 p.m., saying she had private things to do, but next morning said she had not gone to bed till 2 a.m.

FRIDAY 13 MAY

I spent most of the morning at an Athens cemetery, where I had promised a friend I would leave flowers at his father's grave. Sonia spent four hours at the archaeological museum. She talked me right through the museum guide, over lunch.

We sat outside a little cafe at Piraeus, the port of Athens. Even in trivial conversation, I noticed her language was pedantic: 'I see the sun is trying to come through, but I'm not absolutely sure it will win that particular battle.'

She was sometimes puzzled by phrases that seemed everyday to me. We talked about swimming. What did I mean by saying I was a fairweather swimmer? What is swimming out of your depth? I found it heavy going. We travelled by boat to Porto Heli, and moved into a pretty apartment overlooking a secluded bay. Sonia simply loved it. I cooked a simple supper. She produced the decaffeinated coffee which she always carries with her. She gave up ordinary coffee when she realised it could be addictive. She had tried homoeopathic pills prescribed by the doctor who was treating her young niece for epilepsy but she couldn't tolerate the pills. They made her feel disorientated, she said. They didn't help her to deal with stress, and she couldn't get on with her legal work, so stopped taking them.

She said she always slept well, six or seven

hours a night.

SATURDAY 14 MAY

Set off for Olympia, at 8.45 a.m. She had been up and about for some time, fussing and fidgeting. I drove a hired car over the bumpy primitive roads. Sonia told me how Sutcliffe spent patient weeks teaching her mother to drive. She had passed her test, but Sonia hadn't got that far. 'Pete had great patience, always.'

Sonia admitted she was not so patient. She found her mother irritating – fussy and overexcitable. When her parents moved in with her it was so that three could live as cheaply as one, she said, and because they worried about her safety when the house was under attack. She said she was 'kind enough to let them move in all of their things' but then she set about getting rid of 'rubbish' they'd accumulated over thirty years.

'I didn't really want my house full of shabby furniture. I spent weeks rubbing the stuff down and varnishing it. I showed Mother how to do it and encouraged her to help. I wanted her to feel better about it.'

She said she needed peace and quiet to concentrate on her cases. She felt a victim of Sutcliffe's victims and their families. 'They

want the roof over my head. Pete is suffering,
serving his sentence. What more do they want?
It was me who redeemed the mortgage, not
Pete. The house is mine.'

Some of these people, she said, were
'base'. Of course, they had suffered and
grieved, but suffering could enhance an
intelligent person, who would turn it into
compassion – like she had. It was not
intelligent of them to harbour bitterness and
hate. It was ruining their lives. I suggested they
had suffered more than her, and that might be
why they wanted her punished; that, and her
continuing support for Sutcliffe. 'What would
they expect their wives and families to do if
something went wrong with them mentally?
Desert them?'

She talked of her own suffering. 'I am
physically very strong. I may not look it, but I
don't really feel physical pain. If I was asked
which I would prefer – a broken leg, or mental
anguish – I'd choose the broken leg.' Physical
pain had never been a problem. 'I'm sure I
could have a baby and feel no pain at all.'

At the great temple of Zeus, at Olympia,
she claimed to feel the spirit of the gods. I
asked if she believed in God. 'That's a very
personal question,' she said. I learnt later that
she had recently taken instruction in the

Roman Catholic faith and been baptised at the Church of the Holy Spirit, near Broadmoor Hospital.

Hair tied back in a bun, guide book in hand, she drifted around the museum looking serious, bookish.

We drove home late, missing signposts, and arrived at the apartment at 1 a.m. Sonia had locked her bedroom door – she didn't say why – and now could not find the key. She had to go through my room and in by a balcony door.

SUNDAY 15 MAY

Sonia spending hours in the bathroom. I can hear water running. She says it's cold water and she has no towel. She won't use mine, even though it's perfectly clean. 'I'll dry naturally, on the beach.' She went off alone for a swim. She likes to be alone – and laughs at the idea of being lonely. I asked what books she read. She said she was much too preoccupied with legal problems to read anything else. Her voice is soft and breathy, hesitant. I never heard her swear, although she wasn't shocked when I shouted rudely at a road-hog driver on one occasion. She described a journalist she knew as a 'damned liar' and that seems to be as far as she will go.

She talked about her husband's trial. 'I had

to support Pete. I was fully prepared to go into the witness box. I *wanted* to. But they wouldn't let me, and now I think they were probably right.' She was learning that it might not be good for her to appear too obviously sympathetic towards him. She had stayed at her sister's house during the trial, until her mother and brother-in-law had a major row. Mrs Szurma had wanted to come to the Old Bailey each time Sonia attended but Sonia told her she would ruin everything if she made a fuss. 'She couldn't promise me that, so I wouldn't let her come with me every time.'

She said her mother had a very loving nature. She had wanted to work as a nurse because her own sister had become ill and died at the age of nineteen, and it was a terrible unhappy time for the family in Prague.

Sonia said Sutcliffe's trial had been a sham. His plea of diminished responsibility had not been accepted because of political and economic reasons only. None of his 'very reasonable' legal arguments had been reported.

She ate supper incredibly slowly, picking over the food. She said she had given up salt for health reasons, but missed it sometimes.

MONDAY 16 MAY

Left early for Epidaurus. Sonia apologising for her inefficient map-reading. We talked about Sutcliffe's paintings. 'We planned to sell up and buy a place in the country. I was going to do pottery and he wanted to paint. I said to him: "You, an artist?" I had no idea then of his incredible talent.'

In Parkhurst prison he produced *Ominous*, his painting of a rugged cliff face with the heads of men and women superimposed on it.

'He painted madonnas, too, and angels. The madonna's face is full of sweetness. He could never do that if he was not a sweet person himself.'

He could not paint in Broadmoor. 'It's all part of their bullying. They are supposed to be nurses but sometimes they seem to have no compassion.'

Sonia had made official complaints and had written to the Home Office pleading his case for a move to Park Lane. She had preferred the visits to Parkhurst to the Broadmoor trips. Going across the water on a ferryboat to the Isle of Wight was 'soothing'. She remembered some old times with Sutcliffe, smiled at the memory of him once putting on a favourite shirt while still wet – and it starting steaming on him. Talked of their visit to the

305

Tutankhamun Exhibition in London, and of
their closeness.

They had shared the 'spiritual experience'
of the clocks in their house stopping when his
mother died. Sonia said she had had many
major spiritual experiences herself. They were
not frightening; rather, they were reassuring.
You got these experiences when you were
ready for them – not everyone was ready for
them, ever.

She said that Sutcliffe was very distressed
at his mother's death, but 'dealt with it
himself'. She said 'I didn't have to baby him.'

TUESDAY 17 MAY
Took an island-hopping flight to Paros. Over
lunch on the sea front she wrote postcards to
her nieces and nephew – 'giving them a little
history lesson'. She said she and her sister
sometimes wore Indian-style saris when they
attended social functions with her brother-in-
law, who is a Muslim. She enjoyed doing that.

I got a telling-off for writing one-line 'trite'
messages on my postcards. 'I would never
waste a postcard by doing that.' I got another
one for drinking a glass of wine. 'I noticed you
had a gin and tonic last night. You should be
very careful about alcoholism, you know.'

There were rather tedious arguments about

the need to eat before going sightseeing. 'You should store energy, even if you don't really feel like eating.' She showed real concern for my wellbeing, but it just went on too long.

Sonia accused me of wanting to 'run away' from her on the coming Sunday because I had to return to England and could not accompany her to Cyprus for a further fortnight.

She constantly referred to tiredness, her own and mine, and to how much sleep one needed. She would insist on rising early, but would then spend half an hour in the bathroom, making us both late.

Our tour guide joined us for dinner and they got on so well that I left them chatting and went for a walk.

WEDNESDAY 18 MAY
A lazy day on the beach, but I got another telling off for listening to my Walkman. Sonia rather irritable, I offered to lend her my straw sunhat when she went on to Cyprus, but she said I just didn't want the bother of carrying it home.

THURSDAY 19 MAY
A trip to Mycenae, the ruined city. I'd packed a picnic, but had thrown out some limp lettuce from the day before. Sonia absolutely furious,

flying into a real tantrum as she told me:
'But I really wanted that. I was looking
forward to it.'

FRIDAY 20 MAY

Crete, our last port of call. Sonia anxious to
spend the last hour of daylight on the beach.
She had slowed down, as always, towards the
end of the day, and joked about 'sleepwalking'
as I steered her through traffic and away from
lorries thundering by. I wondered if she was
taking medication which made her drowsy in
the evenings.

She believes in beta waves, which she
claims control consciousness, for instance when
going off to sleep. She claimed to have 'slept
standing up' on the crowded bus that took us
to the beach. She was often completely in a
world of her own, yet occasionally pulling me
into it. A particularly irritating conversation in
a little food shop. 'You really should try
yoghurt, you know.'

'But I don't like it at all.'

'Well, it's very good for you. I like it. It's
the intelligent thing to do, to eat things that
are good for you.'

I remind her that I'm not a child.

Tension between us, and I find it
increasingly difficult to go along with the ritual

of sitting down immediately inside a monument or historic site, while Sonia rubs lotion laboriously into her hands, cleaning them, she says.

After a trip to Knossos Palace, an extraordinary thing happened. We walked up the hill in stifling heat to find the house where British archaeologists had lived and worked. It was completely deserted but the doors were open. An ancient caretaker was asleep in the garden. We walked in and realised the house was empty, nothing to see. Sonia disappeared for at least forty minutes, and when she finally reappeared said she had slipped into a bathroom and had a cold shower.

Very sunburnt, but prone to cold sores on her mouth. She said this was a good thing. It was better for germs to be dealt with there, before reaching your throat.

She went to her room early, and did not reappear for supper.

SATURDAY 21 MAY
To Phaestos by bus in the morning – our last full day. Sonia wanted to see the archaeological site, then go for a swim. She reiterated her belief that it was important to understand men like Hitler, and reiterated her hope that I would not see Sutcliffe in this light.

She talked about Jesus Christ, and said some people believed he was not a holy man, the son of God, but a schizophrenic with mysterious powers.

I asked was Sutcliffe schizophrenic in her view. She said it was 'more complicated than that, wider . . .'

She sat rubbing her hands over and over again with lotion, talking about her husband's victims. By being malicious to her over the years, they had showed themselves as they really were, embittered, and now lowering themselves still further – even harming themselves.

She talked about the waxworks chamber of horrors that Sutcliffe was said to have visited and revisited at Morecambe when on trips to see his sister, Anne. 'I didn't know if he'd ever been there, so I asked him about it. He told me he's only ever visited one waxworks, the Madame Tussaud exhibition at Blackpool, with me. He hadn't been gorified by the chamber of horrors. I don't know where that came from. His brother Mick used to go – but that was just like him.'

We spent a long hot afternoon on the beach. She swam quite a distance, and loved to lie in the sun. She had a good slim figure and looked tanned and healthy in a modest bikini. A sudden mood swing would make her irritable. I offered to lend her my sunglasses so she wouldn't squint in the sun. 'I'm not squinting. I don't do that.'

Walking along the shore later, barefoot in the shallow water, she told me how she admired her sister's musical talents. And then said they were descended from Wagner, on her mother's side, generations back, but could not remember the exact link.

She went to the ladies' loo as we waited for our bus home, and was away so long that I had to fetch her. She had mislaid her watch and was flustered. I gave her mine and told her to keep it. She still wears it today.

SUNDAY 22 MAY
Mass at the great church in Heraklion. Greek Orthodox priests in their black hoods and long grey beards. Sonia was fascinated by the ritual of the service. She stood for several minutes at a side altar where dozens of candles burned. She seemed transfixed by the lights and the music.

We said goodbye over lunch in the main square. I promised to ring her parents as soon as I got back to England, to tell them she was all right.

—— o ——

Later in 1988, in August, I met Sonia in Crowthorne village, Berkshire, less than half a mile from Broadmoor Hospital. She had spent the morning visiting her husband and had arranged for me to see him. Now she had come to meet me in the Prince Alfred pub, at lunchtime.

I was surprised to see her wearing make-up – bright red lipstick and mascara. She had dressed smartly for the occasion, for Sutcliffe, not for me. When I arrived she was being annoyed by a man drinking on his own in a corner of the lounge bar, and so was glad when I joined her. She refused to eat any lunch.

We walked up the hill to the hospital together, past the terraced houses where staff live. Sonia reassured me that Sutcliffe would be easy to talk to. She laughed in her sudden, giggly way when I asked what to talk to him about. She said he was the easiest person in the world to get on with. I had brought him a present, the biography of John Lennon, by Albert Goldman, published that day.

Sonia signed us both into the visitors' book. Then we walked over to a redbrick building where rows of brown boxes – like school tuck boxes – were lined up on a shelf. She put my book and some fruit from her into one of the boxes and filled in a label. She did it quickly and neatly, and I commented on that. As usual, when a personal remark was made, she snapped back: 'I don't know what you mean.

Why shouldn't I do it properly?'

We waited with a small group of others, then the official escort took us to Central Hall.

Sutcliffe came in last, smiling. He was plumper than I had expected. He came straight up with his self-conscious ambling gait, and kissed me, saying: 'How are you, luv?'

He had brought colour photographs of his paintings with him, and we all looked at them and discussed them. I was impressed, although much of the subject matter was bizarre.

He liked my joke when I asked for a gin and tonic from the canteen, but it made Sonia nervous. 'Oh, Pete. You can't get alcohol in here, can you?'

'No, luv,' he said. 'it's a joke, that's all.' In a way, I knew how he felt. Sonia does not have a ready sense of humour.

After our visit, we stood with other friends and relatives while the patients were called to their wards by the 'screws'. Anguish was etched on many faces. Some patients turned to give a last secret little wave. The sight of grown men being led away like that was to me odd, unnerving. I asked Sonia if this was the bit she hated most. 'I'd rather not say,' she said.

It was shortly after this that her own visits to Sutcliffe started to become less frequent. She told me that it was important not to give in to 'emotional blackmail', and to visit when she could, rather than when he put her under pressure.

Having told me, and him, on several occasions that she did not rule out the possibility of having other men friends some time in the future, she had by now developed a relationship with a man who was pressing her to go on holiday with him. In late summer 1988, she finally agreed, and the couple flew to southern Spain. Sonia, fiercely independent, had borrowed the money for the trip from her sister. On her return, she visited Sutcliffe and told him about the friendship, at the same time reassuring him of her continuing affection for him.

However, when I visited Sutcliffe at Broadmoor early in 1989, he was by then very anxious about his marriage. 'I just want to know what's going on,' he told me. 'If she wants to make a new life with someone else, I'd rather she just told me straight out. It's not knowing for sure that's upsetting me.'

He asked me to find out all I could about Sonia and her new friend, but I refused. Sutcliffe said he might ask a former Broadmoor patient to call at the man's house, but I told him that was not a good idea. As he continued to brood, I reassured him that I believed Sonia was not serious about anyone else. Her sister, Marianne, had told me that Sonia would never become as fond of anyone as she was of her husband. 'He's the only man in the world for her. He always has been and always will be,' she said.

By spring 1989, Sonia's preparations for her big libel claim against *Private Eye* magazine were coming to a head. She wrote to Sutcliffe saying she was too engrossed in the case to visit him. She told me later that 'the worst thing' she could do in court was to express any sympathy for or loyalty to him. Her new solicitor had advised her to break off her friendship with me, too, in order to disassociate herself from journalist acquaintances. She continued to see me, however, in the days leading up to the hearing in the High Court, and met me afterwards when *Private Eye's* appeal was pending.

The case lasted two weeks. Sonia was claiming that she had been 'brought into public scandal, odium and contempt' by two stories published in *Private Eye* – one on 30 January 1981, and the other on 11 February 1983. She was claiming damages for these two articles, and aggravated damages for the publication of a further story on 17 February 1989.

Most national newspapers carried articles about the opening of the case, heard before Mr Justice Michael Davies and a jury on Tuesday 16 May 1989. Then, for the subsequent two weeks of the trial, little information came out of the High Court. A great deal of Fleet Street's dirty linen was being washed in there and most newspapers chose not to hang it out in front of a wider public.

Sonia was at her most impressive during the gruelling hours in the witness box. She dressed each day in a tailored grey pinstripe suit, with a variety of different coloured shirts. She carried a briefcase and a sheaf of legal papers, and I saw her wearing reading glasses for the first time. She looked every inch the lady lawyer, a role I knew she relished.

The jury heard how *Private Eye* had made proposals to settle the action before coming to court. On 7 March 1989, they had written to Sonia's solicitors offering to publish an apology and a retraction of their earlier allegations – to make a substantial payment to a fund to benefit the surviving victims of her husband and the relatives of those who died – and to pay Sonia's reasonable indemnity legal costs. Their proposals were turned down.

CHAPTER NINE

Conspiracy

The setting was unremarkable – a picnic table in the beer garden of a Bradford pub. It was a mild and sunny September afternoon in 1986 and Sonia Sutcliffe sat in earnest conversation with a friend, outlining a plan she had thought out in great detail.

For the five years since her husband was imprisoned for murder Sonia had been living a solitary, reclusive life. She had endured loneliness and had been shunned by former friends and acquaintances. Now, one thing was on her mind – a reunion with her husband. Not the regular two hours of hand-holding and despair they shared during Broadmoor visits, but a full resumption of their married life.

In what must be the most remarkable twist in this extraordinary relationship between a mass murderer and his wife, Sonia Sutcliffe planned to help the Yorkshire Ripper escape from Broadmoor and find a way in which they could live together again in freedom.

By the time the two of them had worked out the details, Sonia knew she would have to enlist more help. She had never learned to drive, and a getaway car would be essential if the plan was to go through. She knew me quite well by then, but she did not turn to me. There was another journalist to whom she had grown close, and he was trusted by all the family. He was probably the only friend they had left.

Barry Askew, shrewd and personable, had made it his business to befriend Sonia Sutcliffe immediately after her husband's arrest. He was one of dozens of journalists beating a path to her door with offers of huge sums of money for her story. However, there was an important difference with him. He was not just another news reporter, he was the editor of the *News of the World*. He was also the only one to hang on in. Where cash offers failed to work, patience and understanding found a way.

While Sonia looked on other journalists as 'scum', she found Barry irresistibly courteous and charming. It was Barry Askew who sought out a senior police officer willing to guarantee Sonia's safe passage in and out of the Old Bailey during Sutcliffe's trial. It was he who provided transport for her and her mother as they dodged the attentions of other reporters and photographers. It was he who would listen to their endless tirade against the Press, the police and even the murder victims. And it was he who sat down that day at the picnic table with Sonia Sutcliffe, and listened with increasing astonishment as she explained how she planned to help her husband to escape.

———— o ————

'I'd had a gut feeling, as journalists do, that Sonia had asked to see me to discuss something special, something different,' he said. 'Her phone call to me had been secretive; she was convinced her phone was tapped. But it wasn't just that. I knew her well by then, and I'd listened to many hours of complaints from her. I just sensed this time was going to be something different.'

Nothing could have prepared him for the earnest proposal Sonia put to him that day. She leaned towards him and explained in a barely audible voice that she wanted him to help get Peter out. His part would be to have a car waiting on the main road between Broadmoor Hospital and the nearby village of Crowthorne, and to speed away with the Ripper towards a port on the south coast. From there, Sutcliffe would board a ferry, and Sonia would be waiting for him on the Continent.

'She told me how he and a fellow patient in the top security wing had worked out an escape route. They needed a hacksaw and grappling hooks, but she told me this was not a problem. Security at Broadmoor was quite informal, especially for visitors. The equipment, she said, could be taken in. Or it could be obtained at one of the hospital workshops and concealed in Sutcliffe's room.'

Sutcliffe and his co-conspirator had discovered a skylight which gave on to a flat roof. Patients at Broadmoor were locked in their rooms by late evening, giving them plenty of time to use the hacksaw. Once they had sawn through the iron bars at their windows during the night, they could climb through the skylight, crawl along the roof and scale the redbrick walls surrounding the hospital by using grappling hooks.

Sonia Sutcliffe was adamant that the escape would work. She said no security lighting played on the boundary walls at night, and many members of the staff and doctors, who lived on the Broadmoor Hospital site, could be seen walking through the grounds. Inmates wore their own clothes, so two men in civilian clothes strolling towards the main road would not arouse suspicion.

Sonia said that the skylight was in a doctor's room where only a handful of patients were treated. Sutcliffe and his friend were confident they could gain access to it.

Talking to me about this, years later, Askew said he was riveted. He had no doubt that Sonia was deadly serious. He said: 'Most people would laugh off such a plan as bizarre, ludicrous, impossible to mount and foredoomed to failure.' But he did not laugh. He listened closely and did some quick thinking. Askew had known Sonia well for five years. He knew that all hope of Sutcliffe's future freedom, all appeals procedures or the possibility of parole, were long since behind her. Ahead stretched a lifetime of incarceration for him; for her there was left only a burning need to be with him.

'She told me simply and forcibly that I was the only person in the world whom she could trust to help her. That was palpably true. I decided to respond positively, and began by suggesting that I should find a driver to make the journey between Broadmoor and the south coast. My intention throughout was to milk the escape bid of all its details, and to do that I needed to convince her I was her confidant and supporter. I actually found a man prepared to drive the so-called getaway car. He was a friend who had the physique, the nerve and the driving skills to pull it off. I discussed the whole thing with him, and the next step would be to introduce him to Sonia.'

Having listened to the fine detail, Askew says his firm intention was to drop it at the right moment like a hot potato. 'I was totally secure in the knowledge that without me Sonia would be incapable of pulling it off. She literally did not know anyone else in the world whom she could ask for help. Without me, it could not happen.'

At their next meeting, with Sonia's mother present, local maps were produced and routes to the coast discussed. 'My mind was reeling,' says Askew. 'What was to happen to Sutcliffe's inmate accomplice? How did she and her husband hope to live in freedom, knowing they would be the most wanted couple in Britain?'

He was told that Sutcliffe's friend would make his own way to London and go to ground. The two men would separate as soon as they were out of Broadmoor.

Alarm bells now rang for Askew. This was the moment, he said, to inform the authorities. 'We were now talking about a serious attempt by two highly dangerous men to escape to freedom. I returned to my home in Preston, picked up the telephone and spoke to the duty officer at Broadmoor, giving him full details.'

Years later, Sonia and her mother were to rebuke Askew for the way in which security appeared to have been stepped up at the hospital at that time. Peter Sutcliffe told them he was convinced the 'screws' had overheard their plans during visiting hours, but Sonia believed Askew's driver friend had leaked the escape plot. Either way, she insisted, the plan would have worked. It was a good and well-thought out scheme, she told Askew, but 'the shutters went down', and once Sutcliffe and other high risk patients had been transferred to Broadmoor's new wing, the whole thing became impossible.

Sonia was so deeply involved in the escape plot that she believed at one time that she was a target for unnamed people who were against it. She told Askew of an attempt on her life – a car travelling at high speed towards her as she walked through the grounds of Broadmoor on a visit to her husband, aiming at her but, instead, striking another pedestrian. Sonia ran to a nearby house for help, and an ambulance was called to the injured man. She said that as he lay on the pavement, his leg badly hurt and possibly broken, he gave her 'a look like thunder', and she wondered whether he had been involved in the attempt on her life. It is all highly fanciful, but nevertheless an indication of how seriously she took the escape plan.

Sonia also believed that a car accident Askew had around the same time might have been deliberate. 'I told her that was impossible. She put it to me that my friend, whom she believed was to have been Sutcliffe's driver, might have warned the authorities about the escape. I told her I thought that was unlikely.'

Barry Askew made a decision to tell me about this and much more. He explained that he had come to notice a change in Sonia Sutcliffe, which meant he now felt free of any loyalty towards her. He said that for several years he had retained a strong human desire to see her protected. She had struck him as vulnerable, almost fragile. In her he saw a woman virtually destroyed by the trauma of the wretched discovery that her husband was a mass murderer. 'I have waited very much longer than most journalists or authors to make any contribution to the Ripper debate. The reason I do so now, without feeling in the slightest hedged about by considerations of friendship towards Sonia, is that Ripper writing has become an industry. And it is arguably true that the person who has done most to foster that industry in Sonia Sutcliffe herself.'

He added that she had made much more money out of the process by her 'skilled, if dubiously motivated' litigation than any authors who had so far put pen to paper. 'There is, of course, another, more basic reason, for me to talk about these matters now. It is quite simply that I am a working journalist who set out on the trail of a story with the notion of one day telling it. That I am doing now.'

Askew said he had observed an 'unfortunate hardening' of Sonia Sutcliffe's attitudes, which had transformed her into a litigious, money-making machine. 'At one time it was possible to see her as a victim of the popular Press, hounding her for any knowledge she may have had of her husband's killings. It is almost as easy now to see the Press as victims of Sonia's own quest for financial reparation.'

Barry Askew and I are undoubtedly the two journalists, possibly the only two 'outsiders' in

Sonia Sutcliffe's life, to have come closest to her. She has mentioned little of him to me, and probably less about me to him.

On the last occasion he saw her, early in 1992, she had again spoken to him about the escape plan conceived six years earlier and repeated that she was quite certain it would have worked. She added that her husband already had a hacksaw in his possession at the time she and Askew first discussed the plan.

Askew asked her: 'Did you take it into Broadmoor for him?'

She laughed and said she would rather not reply. Later in the conversation, he pressed her again. He said: 'I bet you took that hacksaw in, didn't you Sonia?' She paused, laughed, and said she was not going to tell him whether she did or she didn't, but she did not deny it.

Askew's description of the plan to free Sutcliffe struck some chords in my own mind. I had known nothing of it previously, yet it coincided exactly with some information I had been given at Broadmoor in 1989.

At Sutcliffe's request, I had been paying regular visits to a friend of his called Ron Saxon, who had been incarcerated for nearly twenty years and had received no letters or visits from friends or family. Ron had told me of his colourful past, which included desertion from the army on two occasions.

He told me how he had lived successfully as a fugitive in Egypt and Italy for long periods. He had once been a stowaway on board a ship heading for South Africa and had jumped overboard when a police launch drew alongside and swum for the shore, hiding out for days before he was arrested. All this had given him something of a reputation as an escape artist, and when his clothes were searched on his admission to Broadmoor, the 'screw' found a hacksaw blade embedded in the sole of his shoe.

Ron told me how he and another man had once planned to escape from Broadmoor. They intended to climb on to a low roof then scale the boundary walls. He was convinced it might have worked. He said part of the plan was to take some rope from the chapel and use it to climb up to the roof. He had asked to attend chapel one Sunday and this had aroused suspicion as he had not been to a service there in nearly twenty years.

'When I got there on Sunday morning with this friend of mine, we found the place was wall-to-wall with "screws", all looking at us. We thought they must have overheard us talking about escaping. Anyway, it was impossible to do anything. From then on they seemed to be watching our every move,' he told me.

What Ron Saxon didn't tell me was that his 'friend' had been Peter Sutcliffe. Years later, hearing Askew's extraordinary story, I realised I had known one isolated piece of the jigsaw. He provided the rest and the whole picture was clear. In July 1991, Sutcliffe himself wrote to a friend of another patient's successful escape. He referred to the need for improved security in the old buildings, adding: 'There were one or two obvious weaknesses there that even an innocent like myself couldn't help noticing (tee hee), I suppose I will now be asked to sell my ideas, eh wot!'

Barry Askew knew, as I have always known, that Sonia Sutcliffe liked to play a dangerous game. She had been an entirely forgettable person before the label of Yorkshire Ripper's wife was imposed upon her. Now, although appearing to shun all attention from the Press, she was allowing herself to be charmed and befriended by some of the most ambitious journalists in Fleet Street.

It was not until 1988 that she began suing the media wholesale for allegedly blackening her character. One of her main complaints in litigation was that newspapers could dare to imply that she had benefited from being the Ripper's wife.

In the seven intervening years between Sutcliffe's conviction and his wife's launchpad case against *Private Eye*, she had accepted large sums of money from the *News of the World* via a tortuous route set up by Barry Askew and involving four other journalists.

When Sonia Sutcliffe walked into Court Fifteen

of the High Court, she knew that what had been said about her being willing to take money from newspapers was true. Yet she denied it in the witness box despite close questioning under cross-examination. Her good fortune on that occasion was that the defence called no witnesses.

Along with most other people, I did not know then that she had been paid £12,000 by the *News of the World*. I have learnt recently from Barry Askew that this money was paid, with her ready agreement, in a number of instalments through a third party. Payments were made by the newspaper to an agency which regularly supplied editorial material. Extra payments went to the agency to be passed on to Sonia Sutcliffe. She knew full well of these arrangements and was keen to conceal them.

It was the style of *Private Eye's* defence that, I believe, helped her to conceal this during the celebrated libel trial at which she was awarded £600,000. I was one of several possible witnesses subpoenaed to appear in court, and sat in the public gallery throughout the hearing. I was not called to the stand and neither were the others.

My financial arrangement with Sonia Sutcliffe over a book (arrangements which she reneged on) would have undoubtedly made an impact on the jury in that case. I did not volunteer the facts to *Private Eye*, but they came out later to contribute to the reduction of damages on appeal. *Private Eye* has since vilified me in several editions. The revelations they now read here should bring home to them how ill-prepared they were in their legal fight against Sonia Sutcliffe.

The whole issue of payments to the relatives of criminals became the subject of national debate during the Yorkshire Ripper trial itself in May 1981. A key witness, Trevor Birdsall, told the court he had been promised money by a newspaper. The mother of Jacqueline Hill – the murderer's last victim – wrote in desperation to Buckingham Palace, telling the Queen that she was outraged at the payment of 'blood money'. Unusually, she received a reply which told her that the Queen shared her distaste.

The result was censure for every national newspaper known to have made an offer to the Ripper's relatives.

It was in this hostile climate that Barry Askew was instructed by his proprietor, Rupert Murdoch, to with-draw the *News of the World's* offer of £130,000. However, the streetwise journalist in Askew prompted him to maintain the close links he had started to forge with the Ripper's wife. 'I knew that she and her husband were always going to be newsworthy. I knew that of all the journalists pursuing their story, the story of their life together during the Ripper hunt, I was one of the most likely to get it out of them. There could be world exclusive after world exclusive. Of course I wasn't going to drop Sonia.'

By that time, Sonia was regularly visiting his London home in East Finchley, using it as a staging post between Bradford and the Isle of Wight where her husband spent his first few years of imprisonment.

The two of them would sit up into the small hours, talking and drinking. Sonia's favourite nightcap was a glass of brandy, and she would share a yellow *chaise-longue* with Askew long after his wife had gone to bed.

'Of course, the inevitable questions were asked. "Was I becoming too close to Sonia?" "Was I sleeping with her?" The answer is "Yes", I was close to her but, no, I was not sleeping with her,' says Askew.

He was a journalist in a powerful position, he had personal charisma, a genuine concern for Sonia's plight as he saw it then, and he shared with her a mistrust of the police, having exposed police corruption himself in an award-winning series of articles.

Sonia saw herself and her husband as victims of police heavy-handedness. Askew used this. The two drew so close that at one time Sonia likened him to her husband, in that both were intelligent sons of strong mothers, now dead.

Askew turned his attention to the vexed question of whether Sonia could have known her husband was the Ripper. 'As I understand it, she had not the slightest reason for any suspicion. Firstly, there was her hostility towards any criticism of him at any stage. Secondly, I knew her husband had dealt with his bloodstained clothing himself in the washing machine I had seen myself in their kitchen. Thirdly, he had a job which explained his night-time absences and was a well-controlled schizophrenic who presented as normal to the outside world. Add to this her preoccupation with her life as a teacher and her obsession with their new house, and you have an explanation of her ignorance of her husband's secret life.'

However, Askew agrees that the question has never been totally resolved.

He often found her difficult to deal with. She would be withdrawn and silent for hours at a time. 'She had a facility for evasion of the central issues, an adroit way of switching to another subject whenever you were about to broach an important point. Overlaid on all this was a remote, almost bleak, attitude to life which seems to me to be an ethnic thing, springing from her background as the child of displaced East European refugees.'

He said he had made up his mind from the start to 'play a long game', a game of patience, with Sonia Sutcliffe, to set about the 'wooing' of her in a courtship he hoped would be consummated between the covers of a book.

He said what struck him most forcibly about her from the time they first met was the way she always spoke of Sutcliffe as if he were an innocent man. 'It was as though we were discussing, not the events surrounding a notorious killer who had butchered thirteen women, but rather the story of a blameless man grievously wronged by society. It felt as though we were talking about some third party unconnected with the horror story. Sonia clearly loved her husband dearly and deeply. She talked about him as if he were of unimpeachable character.'

Askew said she had a limitless capacity to see Sutcliffe as not only blameless, but almost as a hero. 'It was blind loyalty on a scale I had never previously encountered,' he says.

Askew was baffled. Today, even though he has known her for so long, he admits she is still an insoluble enigma.

CHAPTER TEN

Broadmoor

At 9.00 p.m. the reinforced steel door clangs shut; a key scrapes the bolt. For the rest of the night, the only link with the outside world is a tiny spyhole in the door, and the black sky and the shapes of trees and buildings that he can see from his barred window. A full bottle of his favourite mineral water stands on a bedside table next to a rubber plant.

Briefly, Sutcliffe stretches out on his bed in the corner of the room, warm and safe, enclosed once more in that world of his own where he can never be reached. Not by the nurses or the doctors, nor their drugs and potions; not by any bad feelings of guilt or remorse; nor by any painful memory or realisation of the misery and suffering he has caused, for he has explained all that away to his own total satisfaction. All that remains for him to do now is to take each day as it comes and somehow survive the knowledge that he is here in Broadmoor Hospital for the rest of his life.

The days are noisy and busy, with all the other patients, some of them severely disturbed, upsetting and annoying him. Now at last he can have some peace and settle down for the night, alone. However, he is not entirely alone, for out of the walls, the low ceiling, even through the barred windows, comes the sound that filters through all waking and sleeping. The 'voices' are speaking to him again. The familiar Quaker tone rings in his head: 'Thinkest thou that thou has dispensed with us? That thou can escape us? Thou art wrong, and when the time cometh again, we will speak and instruct thee as before.'

Sutcliffe believes the voices are a phenomenon outside himself, audible to others as sensitive and suggestible as himself. He will not accept that they are inside his head and part of his madness. 'I'm still hearing them. Still getting the messages from them. But I control them now,' he says. 'They don't control me any more.'

— o —

Sutcliffe is aware of what he calls the 'regal lifestyle' he enjoys at Broadmoor, joking about being there at Her Majesty's pleasure, but at the same time remarking what a waste of time and money it is to keep him locked up. 'My mission is over now,' he says. He received his last set of 'instructions' when he was in Parkhurst prison, and says it means 'I'll never have to kill again'.

For three years he was treated like other lifers in Parkhurst, the notoriously tough prison on the

Isle of Wight. He refused all medication, as is his legal right, and was by all accounts a model prisoner who did not behave in any unpredictable or violent way. There was a clash once with authorities when Sutcliffe refused to accept a legal notice served on him in relation to bankruptcy proceedings against him. After an argument with prison warders, he was taken to the governor's office and persuaded to accept the documents, but still claims to have intimidated his captors before giving in. 'I gave in when I felt like it, not because I was frightened of them,' he says. 'They were frightened of me.'

It was at Parkhurst that Sutcliffe's talent as an artist was first discovered, when he sat down with paints and a canvas for long solitary hours, producing impressive copies of old masters, as well as original work of his own. He told me how he persuaded the 'screws' to let him have old bed sheets to tear up into squares and stretch on a frame to make a canvas.

Meanwhile, psychiatrists reported that he was becoming increasingly 'florid' and disorientated – telltale signs of his deteriorating mental condition. At one time, he told doctors, he felt a presence in his cell, believing that one of his murder victims, Emily Jackson, was there with him. A highly controlled schizophrenic, he was never subject to obvious attacks and gave little away to fellow prisoners, but expert examination revealed that he was a full-blown paranoid schizophrenic and should be moved to a hospital.

While Sutcliffe's future was being considered, he came under attack from another prisoner. One day, as his back was turned towards the door while he washed at a handbasin, fellow inmate Jimmy Costello, who was serving ten years for armed robbery, lunged at him with the jagged edge of a glass coffe jar he had smashed. Sutcliffe was slashed across the face several times and needed eighty-four stitches to wounds above the left eye and across his chin and neck.

When Costello, aged thirty-five, appeared at Newport magistrates' court on the Isle of Wight, on a wounding charge, Sutcliffe was the key witness. Appearing in public for the first time since his trial, his performance in the witness box was a clue to the self-righteousness which has now completely overtaken him.

He announced: 'There is a lot wrong with society today. It's depraved. All they think of is money and finances. There are no moral values.'

Asked about his mental health, Sutcliffe shrugged his shoulders and said he was not 'the right person' to answer those questions. But he added that he was still hearing voices. 'They give me advice when I am depressed.' He was asked if he was unpopular with other prisoners, and if they tried to provoke him. Sutcliffe said: 'They just don't understand. It's difficult – nobody likes being called nasty names. But I don't harbour any grudges.'

He wore the same grey suit he had worn for his murder trial two years previously. The case was conducted amid heavy security. Everyone coming into court was searched, and fourteen officers lined the courtroom. Sutcliffe described how Costello had lunged at his face. He said the attack was 'very nasty, totally unprovoked'.

'Before I had time to defend myself it had sunk twice into my face. The glass fell to the floor and some smashed. I put my hand up and hurled him away and then I just kept my arm up for protection. I simply had no time to avoid the attack. I've no idea what it was all about. I had not spoken to this man before. A hospital orderly came to pull us apart.'

Costello was transferred to Broadmoor Hospital before the court case.

Four months later, after further reassessment, Sutcliffe was also moved secretly to Broadmoor to continue his sentence. A short statement read in the House of Commons was the first the public knew of the transfer.

The Ripper was suffering from what the then Home Secretary, Leon Brittan, described as grave mental illness. He was seen as posing a serious danger to prison staff and others, and required treatment that could be given only in hospital.

The Home Secretary ordered the transfer after reports from Dr John Hamilton, Broadmoor's Medical Director, and Dr Bryan Cooper, Principal Medical Adviser at Parkhurst, which concluded that Sutcliffe was a paranoid schizophrenic. Mr Brittan said he was satisfied that Sutcliffe's mental condition had deteriorated seriously. Reports showed that he believed he was hearing voices. He had no understanding of his own condition and would not accept medical treatment, which prisoners could not be compelled to do. Mr Brittan said he was satisfied that stringent security precautions would be taken at Broadmoor.

In conditions of great secrecy, Sutcliffe was taken from Parkhurst the day before the Home Secretary's statement. He travelled to Broadmoor in a police van, guarded by six prison officers. A police car drove in front of the van and another drove behind it throughout the journey. When Sutcliffe arrived at Broadmoor, few of the nursing staff were aware of his transfer.

His move not only vindicated the doctors who had insisted at his trial that Sutcliffe was mentally ill, but served also to vindicate Sutcliffe, who could now crow that his plea of manslaughter due to diminished responsibility should have been accepted by the Crown. Yet he has never admitted to any kind of madness, remaining convinced that his acts of murder and attempted murder were due to the 'temporary mental aberration' he suffered.

Sutcliffe still hopes for a retrial on 'theological' grounds, and is pressing for an appeal, for although judges have already ruled out an appeal hearing, he is entitled in law to present his case to them again. 'I know it wouldn't make the slightest difference to my life sentence or chances of ever being released,' he says. 'I'd just like the satisfaction of putting the record straight.'

Like other patients at Broadmoor, he is entitled to an annual tribunal at which his progress is assessed, and has used one of these hearings to press for a move to Park Lane Hospital, Liverpool, without success. There is no Parole Board hearing for patients, and Sutcliffe's case, like all others, is subject to continual assessment by doctors.

His work on legal documents, and the many letters he writes daily, are his reasons for having opted for a job on the ward where he lives. He is held in Taunton Ward, in the top security wing of Somerset House, along with other high-risk patients, among them Ronnie Kray, the notorious East End gangster who has been at Broadmoor for more than twenty years.

While most of the thirty patients in Taunton have daily jobs that take them away from the ward and over to the kitchens or one of the workshops, Sutcliffe's job is to clean out the toilets and bathrooms, a distasteful task which earns him about

£8 a week, plus overtime. It is the only way, he says, in which he can have sufficient time to answer all his correspondence. 'I just couldn't keep up with my letters to friends, if I worked all day,' he says.

On days when he has no visitors, he may not leave the stuffy, unhealthy ward on the third floor of the Victorian red-brick block at all. At other times, he is escorted to the patients' canteen across the yard, to buy sweets, chocolates and personal items. Once, while he was in dispute with the prison authorities over his overtime payments, he complained to me that he could not afford to buy 'essentials'. Soap and toiletries, unless brought in by visitors, must come out of his wages. He suffered a facial rash caused by cheap soap bought at the canteen, and complained about it. He insists on buying good quality soap powder, as the hospital issue contains bleach, he says, which ruins his clothes.

Patients are encouraged to wash some of their own clothes and Sutcliffe is almost obsessive about hygiene, anyway. He is self-conscious about clothes, too, and was known as something of a sharp dresser back in the Bradford pub-crawl days, wearing a number of garish suits and colourful ties. Today, he wears jeans nearly all the time, and trainers, often with a black sweater or cardigan, or a track suit top. He complains that Sonia no longer bothers to buy him new clothes. She used to bring in jeans and sweaters and shirts she thought he would like. He told me his sizes as a general hint once, but I ignored it.

Sutcliffe has always been enthusiastic about personal cleanliness. Once I waited twenty minutes for him to arrive for a visit in Central Hall, having been told that he was 'soaking in the bath' and would be late. On another occasion he wrote to say he had seen me driving away from the car park after a visit, while he was standing in the shower.

On an earlier occasion I had been taken in by his manipulative skills and went out looking for some cassette tapes he told me he wanted but which were impossible to buy. I found them in the first record shop I entered, of course, and he told me how 'touched' he was. I learnt later that he had built up quite a collection of old rock songs and ballads by gaining the sympathy of his visitors and throwing out a discreet challenge by saying the tapes were unavailable.

Institutionalised as he is, he has turned his room on Taunton Ward into a home from home. He has his music and books, the rubber plant and his letters and photographs in a private box. Of course, the 'screws' or the doctors could go through his belongings at any time, but Sutcliffe enjoys the privacy, the secrecy, of the collection locked away in the box which he bought by mail order. Like all other patients, he regularly reads the mail order catalogue brought round to the wards, and can spend his earnings from his Broadmoor job on pretty well anything he likes. His friend, Ron, whom I visited many times, bought Christmas presents for me from the catalogue, and said many patients sent gifts home or bought clothes for themselves in this way.

Others, in a safer category than Sutcliffe, are taken on shopping outings. When the new regime came in at Broadmoor, with the introduction of the Special Hospitals Authority, Sutcliffe actually believed he might be allowed on outings. That was totally unrealistic of him but, generally speaking, he is realistic about the rules.

His superior frame of mind means he is sometimes contemptuous of other patients on the ward. Broadmoor's all-out favourite television programme, for example, is the series about London police officers' daily working life, *The Bill*. If Sutcliffe wants to see something more 'intellectual', it is impossible for him to change channels on the ward's TV set and he will sneer at the others. At the same time, he dreads TV or newspaper material based on his crimes, or even a passing mention of them. This always means a backlash of one kind or another – particularly from those patients who dislike him anyway.

Ronnie Kray, a veteran of Taunton Ward, will have nothing to do with him, but he is close to Sutcliffe's friend, Ron. Waiting in Central Hall on one occasion, while Ron was being brought over from the ward, Kray waved to me from the other end of the room, then sent a tray of tea over to me. Another time, a 'trusty' came over with a box of Dairy Milk Tray chocolates 'with the compliments of Mr Kray'. The Central Hall at Broadmoor suddenly had the flavour of a smart cocktail bar where a strange man in the corner had sent over a glass of Pimms for me. I smiled and waved back.

Kray still had something of his old style and I had to smile at it. He had cans of Barbican low-alcohol lager stacked up in front of him at the start of every visit, the most adventurous drink he was ever going to be allowed in this particular cocktail bar. He had a visitor on every occasion I visited Broadmoor. Ron Saxton, by contrast, had none at all until Sutcliffe persuaded me to see him. He has been there for over twenty years and still swears that he has not been institutionalised. He told me he had warned Sutcliffe against taking part in hospital activities like weekly socials and escorted sessions to the sports field. Ron himself would have no home comforts in his room. He said there were bare essentials there and nothing more. He would have no plants or pictures. He wasn't going to 'give in' to 'them' and accept that he was staying there for good.

He was in his sixties, but looked fitter than Sutcliffe. Although he refused to join in the sports afternoons – 'they count you out one by one, and count you back, like animals' – he said he took exercise by doing gymnastics in his room with the help of conveniently placed water pipes. His was a corner room, and he was very proud of it. There was a wash-basin, the water pipes he valued so much, a view across the grounds, and a family of pigeons who visited his windowsill several times daily for the bits of bread he put out for them.

Like Sutcliffe, Ron carried many of his personal papers – letters he'd received many years earlier, and family photographs – with him continually. They were worn and dog-eared with constant handling. He would put them on the table between us, then slide an envelope containing a note from Sutcliffe discreetly towards me, his eyes never leaving either me or the table, warning me that the 'screws' were looking and it was against the rules to pass letters in this way. Of course the 'screws' knew it was going on. They knew everything that was going on. They knew the rules and they knew how best to enforce them. They knew that patients like Ron, who hardly emerged from his ward except to walk to the hospital shop or to Central Hall for my visits, had no real knowledge of the outside world.

Once, I arrived rather late for a visit and explained that I had been held up in traffic on the M4. Ron gave me a blank look – the M4 wasn't built when he came to Broadmoor. Similarly, when

I had no money on me to pay for our canteen tea and biscuits, I apologised and said I hadn't got to the bank and the cash-point 'hole in the wall' machine wasn't working. Blank looks again. Ron has never seen a credit card, and knows nothing of cash-points. It was all old money when he came to Broadmoor.

Broadmoor allows patients five weekday visits each month, and visits every Saturday and Sunday, each visit, morning and afternoon, lasting for two hours. Sutcliffe has more visitors – and many more letters – than any other patient. Like Ronnie Kray, who was once attacked in Central Hall by an old adversary, Sutcliffe has insisted on a restricted list of visitors vetted personally by him, and turns down many more requests for visits then he accepts.

Other patients are distrustful of him, and dislike his smug and 'Christ-like' pose. One of them confided to me that at one stage Sutcliffe appeared to believe he *was* Christ, and, with crucifixes and holy pictures covering all the walls of his room, he spent many hours in silent meditation. When mixing with others, he would offer words of homespun wisdom, while adopting a superior, sanctimonious, sometimes disapproving attitude. His letters at that time echoed this, being full of platitudes and homilies with a religious overtone.

At least two of his women friends are taking instruction in the Catholic Church, and whereas many patients openly use the opportunity to mix with friends at Mass on Sunday in the Chapel, Sutcliffe spends his time in deep silent prayer. In 1991 he claimed to have found the Catholic religion 'hypocritical' and said it did not follow the Bible truthfully. It was at this stage that he became involved with the Jehovah's Witnesses.

In many ways he sees himself as an example to others, and will take on a tone of despair when discussing the sorry state of the outside world. He wrote to me: 'No matter how cruel and unscrupulous people have been over the past seven years or so, I am not bitter! I just feel very sorry about their ignorant and misguided attitude. The irresponsible Press is directly a cause of the state of our society. Oh, where have all the moral values gone? Smothered by greed I expect.' And another time: 'I am a person of 100 per cent sincerity, so you can see that all that has happened has indeed been pretty terrible.'

He has talked of being 'let down' by Sonia when she failed to turn up for a visit, and when she told him she was seeing another man, he talked of 'the torture of being in limbo', not knowing if Sonia would continue to be loyal to him. He wrote that she 'has no idea how it hurts me when she breaks a promise to see me. It takes very little effort to put someone's mind at rest – a little consideration costs nothing'.

In the early part of 1989, he knew that Sonia was regularly cancelling visits because of her action against the magazine *Private Eye*. She had accumulated sufficient funds in out-of-court settlements against the *Yorkshire Post* to enable her to launch a major libel suit over an article which had appeared six years previously, accusing her of negotiating deals with a national newspaper.

I was subpoenaed, among others, to appear as a witness for the defence, an extraordinary situation given that I was regularly visiting and interviewing Sutcliffe, and in close contact with Sonia. In between sitting in on the trial hearing, and doing my work at my office a few hundred yards from the High Court, I was visiting Sutcliffe and keeping him up to date with the case. He was extremely anxious about Sonia putting herself in the public gaze, and at times almost desperate to get word to her to pull out of the case. Part of his reasoning was that he always got a hard time from other patients, and some of the warders too, when his name came up in the Press.

No witnesses were called for the defence in the *Private Eye* trial, despite the fact that several of us had vital evidence to give from the witness box. Sonia was awarded record libel damages of £600,000. Several people asked me where I was on the morning when the damages were announced. I'd been sitting in the public gallery throughout the case, but I wasn't there that morning. I was at Broadmoor, waiting with Sutcliffe to see what the outcome would be. He was right to fear the worst in his own situation: he reckoned a pay increase for his job on the ward was withheld as a result of his wife's huge payout.

During the subsequent months of controversy, *Private Eye* launched an appeal against the amount of damages. The hearing went ahead, but before the Law Lords could announce a more reasonable amount, Sonia's lawyers had come to an agreement with *Private Eye*: the total she was to receive – including a sum for aggravated damages – was £160,000. However, some of the evidence she had given in her sensational court action was to lead to accusations of perjury the next time she appeared at High Court.

In an outburst after several visits had been cancelled by Sonia, Sutcliffe wrote of the 'anticlimax which was like a slap in the face... Sonia does not realise how it feels to be constantly treated so shabbily and she ought to be told in no uncertain terms that it is not done when you care for someone. I mean if she doesn't stick to her next promise of a visit, then I will never be able to take her seriously again'.

Begging me to contact her for a chat along those lines, as he hated to put his feelings in writing, in letters that would be censored before they left the hospital, he said: 'It's useless to put it in letters for everyone to sneer at and gloat over, and it's damned private really. It's a sickness, this paranoia over people's letters when it's the only contact they have in most cases. It's the government's fault really because mail censoring has been abolished by Strasbourg – they said the censoring of prisoners' mail is illegal, and the excuse that it is in the interests of psychiatry is nonsensical and a limp-wristed excuse when we ought to be using the telephone anyway. It shows where the paranoia lies! And it's quite unnecessary, this censorship of letters, when people can say what they like on visits, which rubbishes the whole issue of censorship – quite apart from the "illegal" aspect.'

Along with other high-risk patients, Sutcliffe has all his incoming and outgoing mail censored by the hospital authorities. Letters from him are accompanied by a pale blue form, 134-1A, headed Broadmoor Hospital, Mental Health Act 1983, which declares: 'This packet has been opened and the contents inspected pursuant to the provisions of Section 134 (4) of the Mental Health Act 1983. Nothing has been removed from the packet – this form has been inserted in the packet before re-sealing and posting to meet the requirements of regulation 17 (1) of the Mental Health (Hospital, Guardianship and Consent to Treatment) Regulations 1983.'

Most of his letters contain a philosophical message intended to comfort either himself or the reader – for example, the first letter he ever sent to me had a postscript: 'I'll be 42 on Thursday. What a place to spend it on one's tod, eh? Ah well, stop countin' the years, eh?'

Once, I was astonished to receive a postcard from Blackpool from him. 'Hi!' it read. 'Well, what a coincidence bumping into you of all people at Blackpool! (Tee Hee!!)'

Remembering that I had recently been up to Blackpool while reporting a party political conference, Sutcliffe was enjoying a little joke he's used many times since. Using picture postcards sent to him over the years, he pastes over the back with plain card, and neatly prints 'HANDMADE CARDS' at the top. I have a collection from the Tipton Canal at Birmingham, one from Ingleton Falls, another from Shakespeare's Parish Church in Stratford-upon-Avon, one from St George's Chapel, Windsor, and another from Cambridge, showing the gates of several university colleges.

In addition, there are examples of his attempts to manipulate in the letters or cards he writes. In a collection of almost fifty such messages, I have been asked by him to write to or meet other patients he wants to impress; to attend Mass in the Chapel; to write to and meet friends of his outside the hospital; to help friends who want to move to

London, and perhaps offer them somewhere to
stay; to find out what Sonia is doing and where
she is staying; and to send messages to her on
his behalf, or put pressure on her to visit him.
Each 'do-me-a-favour' message is accompanied
by fulsome thanks for some past helpfulness, and
expressions of great affection. Sutcliffe, the Agony
Uncle of Taunton Ward, is undoubtedly a great
'user', as his doctors and his priest have realised.

The Catholic priest from the nearby Holy
Trinity Church, in Crowthorne, conducts a short
and simple Mass with Holy Communion at 9 a.m.
each Sunday. He invites patients to come up and
read the lessons, and there are familiar hymns,
sung touchingly well by the odd assortment of men
and women in the small congregation. The priest
delivers a short address, standing in front of the
plain altar also used by Church of England vicars
for their Sunday service. He wears a formal black
cassock and dog collar over his blue jeans and
open-necked shirt. The organist who accompanies
the hymns is accomplished. She is a middle-aged
lady with greying hair, who makes the trek up to
the hospital grounds early every Sunday morning
and is the first to take her place among the handful
of us who have turned up for Mass.

During the ceremony an unusual little scene
is regularly played out: the Catholic Mass now
includes a 'greeting' between strangers, and those

taking part turn to their neighbour and shake hands, or even exchange kisses on the cheek.

While the Broadmoor Mass is said, the inevitable single file of 'screws' stands guard, looking rather embarrassed throughout, on either side of the chapel. One patient, a bearded, stooping man, marches over to the 'screws' at this point in the Mass, and insists on shaking hands with each. I've hidden a smile when it happens, but everyone else seems to dismiss it as just another manifestation of the quirky things that happen in this strange place.

The priest walked back to the entrance gates with me once, and was keen to know when Sonia would visit again. He'd been worried about Sutcliffe, he said. He had seemed 'almost suicidal' at one stage when Sonia failed to turn up. He was clearly sympathetic in his professional, pastoral way, but he hastened to add that Sutcliffe took some pleasure in his special status at the hospital, and warned me that he was 'an arch manipulator'. I didn't really need the warning. I'd seen many of the games Sutcliffe likes to play.

On an extremely unsubtle level, he enjoys evoking emotion in others. His squabbles with a Scottish girlfriend, who visits and writes to him, is an example, with Sutcliffe playing the part of the jealous lover in order to elicit reassurance and expressions of loyalty from her.

Once I told him that, having helped another

patient to contact his family, I had discovered that his teenage son had committed suicide, and asked Sutcliffe how the sad news could be broken to him. On my next visit I found that he had taken it upon himself to pass on the information, despite my having asked him not to, and I suspected that he rather relished the role he had been able to play.

Sutcliffe insists that he is not becoming institutionalised at Broadmoor, but he is no rebel and is inevitably ruled by the many restrictions. He takes part in some social activities, especially the get-togethers on Monday evenings in Central Hall where he can chat with Marion, a girlfriend in the female wing, but avoids other organised events, like bingo games or the hospital's amateur dramatic performances. 'I don't want to mix with too many people I don't know,' he says. 'I'm never sure what their attitude is going to be.'

He is right to be wary, some patients will have nothing to do with him. Ronnie Kray, with his gangster's code of ethics, refuses to mix with him, and Kray's crimes are somehow more acceptable to other patients than Sutcliffe's.

Kray, who has a 'privileged' room on the ward, occasionally holds a Broadmoor-style dinner party, sending out for food from a local restaurant and inviting a handful of other patients, sometimes from other wards. Sutcliffe is never invited. Sutcliffe has a small circle of friends, and is the most talkative among them, enjoying his celebrity status, emphasised by the sheaf of letters he receives daily. He attracts friendship in others by reading or writing for them, and drawing a good likeness on pieces of card or scrap paper.

He has not been offered a 'privileged' room, and has never asked for one. 'It would only get out in the Press, and then everyone would be nasty about me again,' he says.

The main privilege attached to rooms like Ronnie Kray's is that the door is left open for him to enter and leave during the daytime. For Sutcliffe and most others, their doors are unlocked at 7.30 a.m. and locked against them at 1 p.m. They go back, to be locked in, at 9 p.m. During the morning they can go in and out of their rooms as they wish, but during the afternoon and evening they are confined to the day-room – a large open-plan area where they can watch television, read newspapers or books, smoke and move freely about to talk to friends.

Patients can cook eggs or other kinds of food they have bought in the hospital shop, or that have been brought in by friends or relatives, if they don't want to eat hospital food. Sutcliffe describes the meals on Taunton Ward as 'swill', but does not do any of his own cooking. He likes to receive fruit juice or jars of Nescafé coffee from outside, as he dislikes the coffee served on the ward. He put on weight soon after coming into the prison system, and has attempted to diet at Broadmoor, despite his natural greediness. He will munch steadily at Jaffa Cakes and other food during visiting hours, saying it is much better than meals on the ward. He takes no physical exercise and looks increasingly unhealthy, his naturally sallow skin suffering from the lack of fresh air on the ward.

Despite his catalogue of complaints about life inside, he admits that he and other patients are free from much of the stress of the outside world. 'We don't get any bills, and it's always warm and comfortable. We don't have to rush anywhere, so there isn't really any stress except petty conflicts with each other that flare up from time to time.'

He realises that the families of the women he killed must hate him for what he did, and resent the fact that he is leading a safe and secure life now, at the taxpayers' expense. 'I thought about writing to them, trying to explain about myself. Why I did what I did, and why they ought to try and understand me. I'd like them to know I'm not a monster.'

When a girlfriend sent him information about Jehovah's Witnesses, he became interested for a while in the idea of rejecting Catholicism and joining them. 'Then I realised that the Jehovahs take over your life, telling you what to think and what to eat and drink. I didn't fancy that,' he said. It was through Jehovah's Witnesses he came to accept that the 'missions' he believed he was on must have been controlled by the Devil, not by God. This is what prompted him to want to write to his victims' families, but he didn't do it. 'The Press would get hold of it, and make me suffer more.'

He has acknowledged that he acted wrongly, but still remorse never comes. 'I believed I were doing the right thing, and I had to do it. Nobody seems to realise what it took out of me. Now I have to forget about this life, and just look at the one after this.' Self pity seems to be the strongest emotion that washes over him. The worst aspect of life in Broadmoor for him is missing his wife. 'It's the same for all of us in here. It's really difficult to deal with sexual frustration. They offer you bromide and stuff like that, but I won't take it. Some of them do, to suppress their natural instincts. A lot of others read sexy magazines that come into the ward from time to time, and masturbate. I don't do any of those things. I'm completely in control of myself. That's how I go on from day to day.'

Sutcliffe lies on his bed, looking at the black sky outside the barred window, listening to Sixties ballads on his cassette player, telling the 'voices' that he is in complete control now.

CHAPTER ELEVEN

Sutcliffe's Women

A shaft of winter sunlight makes specks of dust dance around the reverently bowed heads of the tiny congregation as solemn chords from the chapel organ mark the moment when Catholics believe the bread and wine are turned to Christ's body and blood. Holy Communion is to be distributed to a sad, shuffling group of worshippers who file respectfully up to the altar rails. Among them is Peter Sutcliffe, the Yorkshire Ripper murderer, hands clasped in front of him as he kneels in silent prayer beneath a statue of Our Lady, the Immaculate Conception. He takes the host, and walks back to his place at the rear of the chapel, a look of serene piety on his face.

Walking beside him is a blonde woman for whom these moments are vitally important. Here in the chapel at Broadmoor, she can spend half an hour in close physical contact with Sutcliffe. Indeed, she first took instruction in the Catholic faith at his urging.

When their relationship began, she was a patient in the secure unit of a psychiatric hospital in Kent. Today she is in the female wing at Broadmoor, and is so attached to Sutcliffe that she claims she 'could not go on living' without him.

At least ten other women write to him, visit him, and believe they are in love with him.

—— o ——

Marion is an attractive thirty-five-year-old, held at Broadmoor because other hospital units have not been able to contain her. A chronic depressive, controlled by tranquillising drugs, she is a high-risk potential suicide who has escaped from other institutions where she was being treated. She is completely in love with Sutcliffe and writes him daily notes in the internal post, to which he replies daily with letters intended to cheer her up and encourage her to go on with life.

They meet twice a week: once at Sunday Mass in the chapel, where the sexes can mingle, and then on the next evening at the socials held in Central Hall where patients from all over the hospital can talk together and share soft drinks. In the summer months, men and women patients can also meet on the sports field where some of them play cricket and other games.

Sutcliffe told me once with relish how couples sometimes split off from the rest of the crowd watching a cricket match on a sunny afternoon, and wandered off behind the sports pavilion to have sex. He was certain couples went 'all the way', and once said there was a rumour about a woman patient getting pregnant. Gossip among patients is rife, and occasionally there is a real scandal at Broadmoor – patients paying the 'screws' for favours, for example –but no more was seen or heard about the pregnancy. It was Sutcliffe's enthusiasm for the idea that worried me most.

He said most couples who attended Mass treated it as a social, rather than a religious, occasion. Girls could hold hands with their boyfriends, and he and Marion were not the only couple regularly to exchange love letters in the internal post. When Sutcliffe renewed his request for a move to Park Lane Hospital in mid 1991, he told friends he was sure Marion could move there with him.

Knowing that I was in contact with Sonia, he may have been holding back about details of his friendship with Marion, but she had no such reticence when talking to me. She said she lived for the Sundays when she could be near him during Mass, and for the Monday evenings when they could talk for hours together.

There is strict supervision by hospital staff, and during the occasional discotheque evenings, couples may be separated if it is felt they are getting too friendly. Understandably, many of them have become emotionally dependent, and Marion talks openly of how much she cares for and needs Sutcliffe.

It was he who asked me to meet and befriend her, for although his own mental condition means that his emotions are limited, he enjoys manipulating others and encourages his various 'friends' to meet one another.

I felt drawn to Marion on our first meeting, finding her intelligent and sweet-natured. She told me she was receiving substantial doses of Librium and other tranquillisers, which affected her speech, another side effect being that she walks awkwardly, inelegantly, and sometimes needs help from a nurse.

She began writing to Sutcliffe when he was in Parkhurst prison, feeling she wanted to get to know him, and continued writing when he was transferred to Broadmoor. In 1987 she was sent there herself. 'It was a few weeks before Christmas, I'd spent a lot of my life in psychiatric hospitals, and I knew this was the ultimate one. I'd tried to kill myself at least twice, and I'd escaped from the last place they put me in. I attacked one of the doctors, too. I escaped with a friend who gave himself up, and I got caught. They thought Broadmoor was the only place for me after that.'

Marion has a nice, philosophical way of putting things. She told me how she was too depressed, and a bit nervous, to write to Sutcliffe when she first arrived. 'Then I decided to send him a Christmas card in the hospital's internal post. I just put:

"Guess what. I'm here too!"'

Soon they met up, and Marion found herself hopelessly attached to Sutcliffe. Her early family life had been deeply unhappy, and she realises that as a result she is free with her emotions, her psychiatric condition demanding attention, friendship and affection. She told me: 'I'm a lucky girl to have Peter. He's one of my dearest friends. I love him dearly. I cannot picture life without him. I would do anything he asked me. I do love my Peter so much.'

If she had three wishes, she said, she would ask to spend the rest of her life with Sutcliffe; for both of them to be free; and to complete her own 'mission'. For she, too, believes she has a mission, requiring revenge against those who she claims persecuted her in past years. Like Sutcliffe, she hears 'voices', although, unlike Sutcliffe's her schizophrenia is palpable, for she has not achieved his level of control and finds it impossible to master her feelings. Also unlike him, she accepts medication.

Marion and Peter have pet names for each other. He calls her Poppy, because she was born on Poppy Day, 11 November, and she calls him Pee Wee. She remembers calling out for him when she was being anaesthetised before being given electro-convulsive therapy to relieve a bout of depression. 'I heard my own voice calling from the end of a long tunnel. I was screaming his name.'

The bizarre relationship, known and watched by Broadmoor authorities, can never develop into anything deeper. Marion is very sick, and to be pitied. Any hope of a normal life outside Broadmoor is for the moment non-existent, although, like all patients, she is entitled to a tribunal hearing once a year in which her case is re-examined. If she was released into the community, it would be under controlled conditions. However, all of Sutcliffe's other women friends are on the outside, living apparently normal lives.

Psychiatrist Hugo Milne, the doctor most familiar with Sutcliffe's case, has declared himself 'absolutely fascinated' by the notion of women, in particular, befriending Sutcliffe and developing deep affection for him. 'I know more or less all about him, but I would be very interested in knowing more about them.'

Much of Sutcliffe's notoriety – and the cause of much of the hatred directed against him – is inspired by the sadistic and deliberate debasement of his victims after death, many having been left in attitudes that made them look 'cheap and disgusting', in the murderer's own words. Their blouses or sweaters were often pulled up to expose their breasts, which he had slashed; and their skirts or trousers would be pulled down, their legs parted. Sutcliffe would have draped their battered bodies with a coat or some other covering, in an attempt to demonstrate that he had 'saved their souls' by killing them, and was now covering them up for the sake of decency. It is all the more extraordinary that it should be mostly women who have sought him out since his arrest and trial.

One of these friends, who continually turned up at Broadmoor skimpily dressed and would wave her hand in the direction of Sutcliffe's barred window in Taunton Ward as she drove from the car park, was eventually banned from visiting him.

Others have written from France and Holland. Two women travel down from the West Midlands to see him, lodging at boarding houses near the hospital in order to spend a whole day or more in his company.

One of them, a former Catholic nun, has talked of the 'profound peace of mind' inspired in her by Sutcliffe, and says she is devoted to caring for him for the remainder of her life. There have occasionally been cross words between her and another woman she introduced to Sutcliffe, and neither of them wishes to share the visits, although three people are allowed to see a patient at one time.

Apart from members of his own family and Sonia's family, there are sixteen visitors on Sutcliffe's restricted list at Broadmoor, of whom six are married couples, and the rest women who write and visit as often as they can.

One of them told me she spent as much spare

time as possible with him, despite being unemployed and hard up for cash. She works on a voluntary basis with homeless people in a Midlands city, and Sutcliffe asked Jimmy Savile to help her. Savile was persuaded to take on his *Jim'll Fix It* role for Sutcliffe's friend, and donated £500 to a project she was running for handicapped people. This was not one of the projects selected for television viewers, however: it was probably considered best left unpublicised, although the funds were undoubtedly going to a good cause.

I spent some time in the company of Maggie, a woman who had only recently joined Sutcliffe's list of visitors, but who was keen to visit as often as possible. She told me that a past love affair had ended in a broken engagement, and that she spent all her time trying to help the homeless find shelter. She was serious, almost depressed, but seemed to be gaining something from her trips to see Sutcliffe. I watched them together a few times, her leaning towards him, her shoulder-length hair streaked with grey, and him appearing to be reassuring her, trying to cheer her up. He told me he used to make fun of her, which she enjoyed, clearly playing her off against her friend who also cherished the regular visits.

I puzzled over how their days could be lightened by this pilgrimage which I found so profoundly depressing. Occasionally one or other of the two women would accompany Sutcliffe to Mass in the chapel at Broadmoor. It was something they said they wanted to 'share' with him, despite the fact that they must keep to the visitors' special pews, and that Marion, an inmate herself, was at his side throughout.

All of the women whom I met wanted to know more about Sonia and were frankly jealous of her special relationship with the murderer. Bizarrely, she would sometimes be staying at nearby lodgings – fixed by the Friends of Broadmoor Hospital at about £8 a night – while other women were staying at lodgings elsewhere. Sutcliffe was never short of visitors, and he particularly enjoyed the mischief-making of getting them to meet up with each other, believing their sole topic of conversation was him. Sadly, I think he was probably right. He would smile and enjoy every moment of a conversation in which I was asked what had been said about him by one or other of them. He would also endeavour to arrange visits so that we would all be thrown together.

Sutcliffe enjoys this mingling of interests. There is an echo of truth in his own half-joking assessment of the friendship offered by women strangers: 'I think for some of them it's loneliness. Probably they couldn't get a man in the outside world to sit down and listen to them for two hours at a time!'

He is certainly flattered by the attentions of

these women, many of whom, he claims, wrote to find out what sort of man he was, saying they couldn't believe that he was really a monster. 'They got to know me gradually, and they realise they were right. I'm not a monster. I'm a good, caring person. It's just that something went tragically wrong for me and it's all been terrible. My friends know this and I'm grateful for their loyalty and support.'

One dark-haired, attractive girl in her twenties, Marie, is particularly special to him although, being unemployed and living in Scotland, she is unable to visit frequently. She suffers depression from time to time and says that Sutcliffe helps her through it with his letters; she is deeply attached to him. 'I'd do anything for that man, anything. Sometimes we have little arguments, misunderstandings. He'll write and demand to know why I haven't written, and accuse me of seeing other men. I hardly ever go out, and I don't have other boyfriends. I write back and reassure him, and we make it up.'

Sutcliffe has pressed me to befriend her, too, and we talked several times on the telephone and met up once. Afterwards he wanted to know everything she had said, especially about him. He would like her to live nearer to Broadmoor so that he could see her more often, and it was she on Christmas Day 1989, instead of Sonia, who received his once-yearly telephone call.

Like all the others, she has sent him photographs of herself and her family. He showed them to me and I noticed his handwriting on the back of several. A picture in which she is dressed in a glamorous black outfit, is marked 'yum yum' on the back. He calls her Babykins in his letters. Not surprisingly, her parents are appalled at her friendship with Sutcliffe, and have pleaded with her to end it, but the letters go on. Sutcliffe is so taken with her style of writing that he has copied it closely. Like her, he now draws little faces under the many exclamation marks he uses and also incorporates a great deal of Sixties language, such as 'looking 4ward 2 seeing U'.

His women friends know, of course, that any real relationship is fantasy and nothing more. They will never have sex with him, and there is no longer any need to fear him as he will never be released. Perhaps the thrill of being close to him, even of having 'tamed' him, is the turn-on. For some of them, the friendship with Sutcliffe is the nearest they have had to a close friendship with any man and, certainly, unlike many men, he has the time to sit and listen. Easily amused, and amusing himself on an unsophisticated level he is practised in the art of small talk, and perhaps his 'specialness' in the small, mad world of Broadmoor Hospital appeals to them.

His letters are full of homespun advice about

'taking each day as it comes' and 'keeping your chin up, gal'. How admirable it must seem, to some of them, that he is able to keep his own chin up despite his grim surroundings and lack of a future; how minute are their stresses and strains, compared with his, and what a strong and unselfish person he is, a model for them to admire and emulate. They truly believe that Sutcliffe is enriching their lives. He has been misunderstood in his time, and perhaps they, too, feel misunderstood and therefore drawn to him.

A more understandable reaction to Sutcliffe was that of a girl who was sent to prison in 1985 for failing to complete jury service in a court case unconnected with the Ripper trial. She received a letter from Sutcliffe congratulating her on her stand, in which he wrote, 'As one human being to another, gal – justice is always clouded by bias and innuendo.' Scared and horrified, she threw the letter away.

Among the huge pile of correspondence he receives each week there are occasionally letters from graphologist Diane Simpson, from Chester, who was called in by West Yorkshire police during the Ripper hunt to study the handwriting in the letters sent by a hoaxer to police chief George Oldfield. Later, she helped to prepare for Sutcliffe's Old Bailey trial by studying his handwriting in the daily log sheets he filled in as a lorry driver. She has visited him in Broadmoor, and Sutcliffe, claiming they are friends, has agreed to interviews with some of her trainees.

Sonia, of course, knows of her husband's friendships with the women who write and visit, but has done nothing to prevent them, confident that her own visits take priority over all others. Sutcliffe will always cancel an arrangement with someone else, even when Sonia decides to see him at the last moment. Her name is at the top of his restricted list, with members of his own family, who rarely visit. There are no names of friends or acquaintances from the past. No one who knew him before he became the Yorkshire Ripper has ever come to see him.

It is as if he is in the third and final phase of his life. First there was Peter Sutcliffe, the nobody from Bingley, West Yorkshire; then there was Sutcliffe the Ripper murderer; today there is Sutcliffe, the celebrity patient from Taunton block – smug, sanctimonious, martyred, incurable.

Epilogue – The Trial

Sonia stood stiffly in the witness box, staring fixedly at the twelve men and women on the jury bench and sipping her glass of water every thirty seconds or so. The court usher brought her a fresh decanter. This was not a new experience for Sonia Sutcliffe, for she was a courtroom veteran after her lengthy and successful action against the satirical magazine, *Private Eye*. This time, however, she looked nervous and uncertain, perhaps fearing she had been matched against the wrong adversary, someone who could and would demolish her case.

———— o ————

Court Thirteen, on the first floor of the Royal Courts of Justice in the Strand, is small, dark and oppressive, with little natural light coming through mullioned windows just below the high ceiling. The court is panelled with oak, the benches narrow, uncomfortable and squeezed together in tight rows.

On the afternoon of Monday 3 December 1990, Court Thirteen was the last place in the world I wanted to be. For more than a year I had known I was to be dragged into Sonia Sutcliffe's libel suit against the *News of the World*, but until I actually sat before the judge's bench there had been a faint hope that she might see sense and pull out.

Now I sat in mute fury as her counsel, Geoffrey Shaw, opened his case by repeatedly describing me as 'a close friend' who had betrayed Sonia. The truth was that I had been on the fringes of a story which had appeared in the *News of the World* and greatly upset her.

In December 1988, the headline 'Sonia Loves A Ripper Double' had appeared on the front page of the *News of the World* above a story about her relationship with Greek tour guide George Papoutsis, whom she had met while on holiday with me. Photographs of Papoutsis and Sutcliffe, set side by side, showed a remarkable similarity between the two men, emphasised by the identical beards both wore. Sonia had never admitted to Papoutsis that her husband was the Yorkshire Ripper and that she was still loyal to him, visiting him at Broadmoor Hospital.

I had watched the relationship between the two deepen, listening as Sonia opened up to George, telling him her innermost thoughts and feelings. She had given him her address and telephone number in Bradford – her most closely guarded secrets. When months later quite by chance, George was to discover who she really was, he was very upset. In his excitable, temperamental way, he felt he had been duped, and both his pride and feelings were hurt.

George decided to sell his story, and I said I would help although it was not a story my newspaper would be interested in. I thought he should go to a Sunday tabloid which specialised in such 'kiss and tell' revelations, and I put George in touch with an agency which would look after him. I also arranged for him to be interviewed by a freelance journalist, who was a friend of Ian Parry, the young photographer who had taken pictures of Sonia during the Greek holiday. My only further participation was to allow payment for the story to go through my bank account to George Papoutsis and to Ian Parry.

After the writ arrived, *News of the World* executives decided to draw in everyone and anyone who had the slightest involvement in the story. My peripheral role did not emerge immediately, and it was not until mid-1990 that my part in the selling of the story was made public.

The agency had already been made a third party in the case, as had George Papoutsis. In plain English that meant that if the *News of the World* had to pay substantial damages to Sonia Sutcliffe, the newspaper would turn on the third parties to recoup as much of the money as possible.

On the afternoon of 4 July 1990, I became the third third party. Called to the reception desk of my newspaper, I was presented with the writ, along with a bunch of flowers, by an anonymous-looking man wearing a shabby raincoat. I threw away the flowers – a ruse to lure me from my desk – and studied the writ, aware that it was the prelude to months of anxiety, resentment and legal expense I could not afford. I was to run up lawyers' bills of £8,500 before being warned I would have to pay more than ten times that amount if I were to be represented during the trial itself. It was devastating news which left me in a state of near panic. At one point I considered declaring myself bankrupt and submitting to the judgment of the court without putting up a fight.

However, my attitude changed during a weekend with my parents. Seeing how worried I was, and despite knowing none of the details, they offered me their life savings to fight the case. I was grateful, and at the same time angry at the thought of their hard-earned money being swallowed up by an implacable and voracious system which worked against natural justice and the individual. It was a turning-point. I decided I would fight my own corner, with off-the-record advice from two lawyers who saw a principle at stake and encouraged me to represent myself. On 17 October 1990 I served Notices of Intent to Act in Person on the court, and on the other parties in the case.

In the six weeks leading up to the trial itself, I

had to deal with demands for documentation, with summonses whose wording I barely followed, with sleepless nights and endless speculation.

I learned how to swear affidavits and serve them on others and how to decipher the jargon and untangle the red tape surrounding the case. I was driven to tears while duplicating sheaves of documents to be passed out to the court once the hearing was underway. The process of issuing a summons was the most time-consuming and frustrating of all those I became familiar with. The job is normally done by clerks, with whom I queued one morning outside offices on the second and third floors of the High Court, only to find that my first port of call should have been the Fee Room, where £15 was payable on each summons I had neatly typed out the night before. I eventually came away from the Fee Room, my home-typed documents transformed into the real thing by the official red stamp, and presented them to yet another clerk in yet another office. Copies were made, and some lodged there for the judge; the others I served personally on the other parties in the case. It was just one of many days when I felt dwarfed and infuriated by the relentless legal machine.

Yet the frustration of the paper chase was nothing compared to my feelings when I first appeared before the judge who was to try the case. At a pre-trial hearing, in chambers, without the press or public present, I appreciated the real difficulties of being a litigant in person for the first time. I didn't know when to stand up or sit down; I lost my place in my notes every time I looked up at the judge; and he cut me short as I stumbled through my application for documents I wanted from Sonia Sutcliffe and the *News of the World*.

I left Court Thirteen that day more worried than ever about the trial to come. But it was too late to back out now. To lose the case would be to lose everything – not only my home and my car and all other belongings, but also my reputation as a working journalist.

———— o ————

Nervous as I was on the first day of the trial, there was an initial skirmish I simply had to try and win. George Papoutsis had provided a lengthy and detailed statement about his relationship with Sonia Sutcliffe, which was vital evidence, but might not be admitted by the judge because Papoutsis was not willing to appear before the court in person. The solicitor advising me, Raz Mireskandari, had spent hours with me studying the Civil Evidence Act 1968, which provided my only hope of convincing Mr Justice Drake that the statement should go before the jury.

I argued as best I could. George Carman QC,

acting for the *News of the World*, said he would not oppose it, while Geoffrey Shaw, acting for Sonia Sutcliffe, fought vigorously to keep it out. To my intense relief, after long minutes of nail-biting anxiety, Mr Justice Drake ruled in my favour. The first battle had been won, and I began to believe there was a chance I might be taken seriously. When the moment came for me to confront Sonia, I had prepared a list of questions which would take nearly two days to cover.

She was more nervous than I had ever seen her. George Carman had riled her by reminding the court of the enormous amount of money she had won from various newspapers in libel and copyright actions, and had tried to draw her out on her feelings for her husband since his conviction as a mass murderer. Sonia had not risen to the bait then, but I knew that it would be my most revealing line of questioning.

'Do you think it is right for your husband to be called the Yorkshire Ripper?' I asked.

She paused: 'Well, in view of the fact he was born in Yorkshire . . . as for the Ripper, it would suggest that people were either ripped or tortured. My view of this, and also in this instance there is police research, is that when my husband killed these people – some were prostitutes, perhaps some were not – he was in the belief that these people were immoral and he had a mission, and he was saving their souls, from leading the sort of lives they were leading...'

At that point the judge intervened: 'I'm not sure the question has any particular point.' However, Sonia went on, 'I think not the Ripper because my husband believed he killed them humanely, in that when he took a hammer to the back of their heads they died instantly and he did not torture them when they were alive. That was his understanding, that is what he thinks.'

I put the original question again: 'Do you think it is right for your husband to be called the Yorkshire Ripper?'

She replied simply, 'No.'

It was the first of many answers she would give which left the court stunned at the matter-of-fact way in which she spoke of her husband's murder victims.

Helen Rytka, by all accounts, was the prettiest of the prostitutes so brutally killed by Peter Sutcliffe. The Ripper himself has admitted that he had sex with Helen before murdering her, but it was a confession I knew Sonia could never face. I put it to her that her husband had had sex with the girl and that Sonia could not face that 'unpalatable truth'. She replied that Sutcliffe 'had not penetrated' Helen Rytka.

Then began her second chilling monologue. In a flat, disinterested voice she said: 'The situation I

have been told is that my husband picked up this
prostitute with the intention of terminating her life.
To put off the physical encounter he did not wish
to go through, he told her he was going to the toilet
– not a public toilet. He got out of the car. She also
did. She had practically undressed by now. She
started to undress him, or something, then the idea
was for them to go to the back of the car. My
understanding is that penetration did not actually
take place.' She added: 'I have gone into very full
detail, that means I have faced it... I am not
running away from it. It is not palatable, but I am
not shunning it.'

She seemed completely unaware of the reaction
in court. One of the nine women on the jury put
her head in her hands, and in the public gallery
there were audible gasps.

I was to put another unpalatable truth to Sonia
– that her husband had caught venereal disease
from another woman and not, as she had insisted
to me, 'from a still-warm toilet seat'. In court I
suggested to her that no intelligent, informed
person would believe that was possible. It was 'an
old wives' tale'. She clung to her own version of
events.

The most significant of all the unpalatable truths
with which I confronted her was the relationship she
had had with George Papoutsis. 'You did have a
close romantic relationship and took advantage of

that to leave him with two hotel bills to pay, didn't you?' I asked her.

'That is a total untruth. He was not the sort of man I could fancy at all, if I was capable of fancying somebody,' she replied.

Later, in an address to the jury, I accused Sonia of using Fleet Street newspapers when it suited her; but now I put it to her specifically that she had travelled to New York at the expense of the *News of the World* in July 1981, just three months after her husband's conviction. Once again, she tried to dodge the question and, to laughter in court, claimed that she went abroad 'to get a mortgage on my house'.

The judge, with a look of irritation, pressed her to explain and I took his cue to ask her whom she had seen in New York. Back came the half-answer: 'A lady.'

'What did that lady do for a living?' I asked. Finally, I got the answer I sought. The lady in question was a publisher, and Sonia had been trying to sell her life story.

The whole process had been like pulling teeth, but now I felt that at last the truth about Sonia Sutcliffe's relationship with the Press was beginning to emerge. She would court the media when it suited her, and sue them when they intruded.

By the time she stepped from the witness box, the public image of Sonia Sutcliffe had changed.

The woman who had once been seen as a victim of her husband's notoriety had now shown herself to be indifferent to the suffering of the women he had killed and maimed, and unwilling to believe that the crimes were truly monstrous. Later, George Carman was to describe her as having 'danced on the graves of her husband's victims'.

I left the eloquent statements to him. My strength was in edging Sonia towards the point where she demonstrated by her own speeches how unfeeling she was towards these women and their families. Cross-examining her, I felt irritated by her evasive answers, but notes passed to me by my student son, Matthew, who was in court as my unofficial clerk, and by my friend and expert witness, former *Daily Mail* executive Bob Hill, reminded me to stay calm.

George Carman himself advised me in a whispered conversation during an adjournment, 'Go on riling her; don't let her rile you.' Grateful for any advice, I heeded the words, and on renewing my cross-examination on Monday 10 December, I took care to remain unflustered.

I tackled Sonia over an issue at the very heart of the case. Why, I asked, had she gone on holiday with me in May 1988? I put it to her that she had been paid money as part of an agreement to work together on a book about the Ripper and his crimes, reminding Sonia that I had taken out a personal bank loan of £15,000 in May 1987, and that, six weeks later, when she said she needed a further £10,000 to save her house, my newspaper the *Mail on Sunday*, had taken over the investment in exchange for first option on serial rights to the book. 'In short, by early 1988, had you given me anything at all in return for £25,000?' I asked.

'Well, as I recall it, you telephoned me several times and persuaded me it would be good for my health to go away to the sunshine.' I was having great difficulty in getting Sonia to address the key question of why she had accepted the money.

It was essential to my case that she should be reminded of her willingness to accept money in return for work with me on the book project, and now two receipts – one signed by her mother for £15,000 and one signed by Sonia for £10,000 – came back to haunt Sonia in front of the libel jury. I produced them both in evidence and asked her to examine them. When the usher took them to the witness box and handed them up to Sonia, she could barely bring herself to touch them. 'Do you recognise these pieces of paper?' I asked.

Experience had shown that Sonia found it difficult to give a simple answer to any questions, and even now, confronted with hard evidence of her earlier willingness to collaborate with me, she tried to baffle the court with complicated and convoluted explanations. Of the receipt signed by her mother:

'I knew nothing about that before we went on holiday.' Of the second, in her own handwriting: 'It's a nonsense, just rubbish. We both agreed it was rubbish at the time.'

Sonia's capacity to infuriate had been known to me since our first meeting. Now she was performing before a larger audience, and the irritation in court was palpable. In the face of repeated questioning, she refused to tell the jury she had accepted the money in return for her participation in the book.

In his summing-up, the judge was to tell the jury: 'You must ask yourselves whether it is likely that a working journalist like Miss Jones would have offered Mrs Sutcliffe £25,000 as a loan from a friend, or whether it is more likely that the money was advanced for her participation in a book about her husband.'

The receipts themselves, which came to be of such crucial importance in the case, were placed in a bank vault for safety during the trial, and they remain there to this day.

Sonia spent several days in the witness box. Court rules prevented her discussing the case at that time with anyone, including her own lawyers. On the second day of her cross-examination by George Carman, the court heard from Sonia's counsel, Geoffrey Shaw, that he had an 'urgent matter' to talk over with his client, and, after a whispered conversation between Mr Shaw and Mrs Sutcliffe, the jury was told that she had agreed to pay £4,000 to a witness.

With the benefit of hindsight, she may now regard that deal as a cardinal error, for the witness, Mike Gold, a former business partner of George Papoutsis, showed scant respect for the court or the woman who had paid him so handsomely. It soon became clear he'd come to court with one purpose – the destruction of my credibility and reputation.

Before he was called to the witness box, Sonia had a temporary change of heart, even she having realised that paid testimony might be worse than useless. She sent a secret note to the judge, saying she had been agonising over whether to call Gold or not, and 'thought it was probably wrong to pay for evidence'; she was therefore reconsidering her decision to call Gold 'even though he could demolish all my opponents'.

However, her reservations were short-lived, for Mike Gold swaggered into the witness box to describe the proceedings as 'this load of old rubbish'. He told the court that his partnership with Papoutsis had ended as a result of the publicity which followed the *News of the World* story. He said he didn't think George had been having a romance with Sonia Sutcliffe and, in describing an evening when he saw them together in close conversation in his bar on Paros island, he commented: 'If he was trying to chat her up he wasn't having much luck. She looked utterly miserable.'

Geoffrey Shaw asked him if he had ever tackled George about the relationship with Sonia. He replied: 'I asked him if he was screwing Sonia Sutcliffe. He said "No".'

Mr Shaw then asked him: 'Did you ask George about his relationship with Barbara Jones?'

Gold replied, 'Yes. I asked him if he was screwing her.'

Geoffrey Shaw: 'And what what his reply?'
Gold: 'He said yes.'

It was my turn to cross-examine Gold. Once more I had been forced to listen in silent fury while lies were told about me in open court, and now I took the most dignified course available to me. I did not cross-examine him about his false accusation. There were nine women on the jury and they were all looking at me. I was sure some of them felt for me, too, at this moment.

Out of respect for them and myself, I ignored Gold's most insulting allegations and instead asked him about the break-up of his business partnership with George Papoutsis, about which he had expressed bitterness. He admitted they were still in dispute over financial matters, and also admitted that at one stage he had offered to give evidence for the *News of the World* for a large sum of money. I sat down after only a few moments, feeling honour had been satisfied.

In his summing-up, the judge referred to Gold as the first 'rent-a-witness' he had seen in his many years at the High Court, and reminded them that I had said his evidence could be coloured by the dispute he still had with George Papoutsis.

The next day I called myself into the witness box for, as a litigant in person, I had to play both advocate and defendant. I had given Sonia Sutcliffe a grilling; now I must submit to one myself.

I felt the *News of the World* might not give me too hard a time, for I had not grilled either of their witnesses, reporter Morven Kinlay and executive Bob Warren, both of whom had given evidence with some dignity. I hoped to do the same.

First, I had to offer my own evidence. I told the jury how I had come to know Sonia Sutcliffe, how we had ended up on holiday together, and about the instant attraction I had seen between her and George Papoutsis. The relationship was not just a holiday romance, I said, but something more permanent.

Asked by the judge if the holiday had been successful, in that I had collected sufficient information for my book, I remembered how difficult and often downright unpleasant my fortnight with Sonia had been. I recalled, in particular, a heated row with her about, of all matters, the Hitler death camps.

We had been driving along a rough mountain road when a car with German registration plates overtook us on a bend. I said the driver was a roadhog, and Sonia chided me for 'hating Germans', lecturing me in a patronising way. As the sermon continued, she said the Germans were a fine race and that I should understand Hitler's motives in wanting to keep his nation pure.

How the conversation had taken this bizarre turn I wasn't sure, but once Sonia had sought to justify the Final Solution I could barely constrain my anger. 'It is not right to call Hitler evil. He was driven by noble motives. After all, the Jews were an intruder race. He thought it was right to use them for medical experiments.' Under cross-examination, I was pressed by Geoffrey Shaw to say that the Hitler conversation never took place, but unfortunately for his client, I had a detailed note of it in my own holiday diary written at the time and produced by me in evidence. Sonia, to this day, denies that she has ever supported Hitler's views.

The final stages of the case were fraught and frustrating. I listened as Geoffrey Shaw attempted to suggest I'd planned the romance between Sonia Sutcliffe and George Papoutsis. He accused me of mud-slinging and duplicity, and to my mute anger he tried to suggest that I had been sleeping with

George Papoutsis. In his closing speech, during which I was repeatedly called a liar, I clenched my hands and stared at the jury as the attacks continued, hoping they had not been swayed against me.

There was even an attempt to prevent me delivering my own closing speech to the court, Mr Shaw arguing that I did not have the right as a third party in the case and that the main action was between his client and the *News of the World*. The judge would have none of it, ruling that I had the same right to address the jury as George Carman and Mr Shaw himself.

I kept my speech brief, simply reiterating the main points that had emerged in the trial.

On the fourteenth day in court, Mr Justice Drake began his summing-up.

The jury went out the following afternoon. They were to return twice before delivering their verdict. Court Thirteen positively buzzed with anticipation while the jury deliberated, taking six and a half hours of court time, and an overnight adjournment, to arrive at a unanimous decision.

While they were out, journalists crammed the press bench and spilled over into the bench where I sat in front of the judge. Others joined the public in the benches behind me, where there was standing room only. I tidied up my files, talked to reporter friends and experienced a kind of fateful relief that at least it was over, no matter what the verdict.

When the jury came back into court for the third and final time, I wished it didn't matter so much to me. After all, if they found for Sonia Sutcliffe, I still had a strong case with which to defend myself against the *News of the World*. I had hardly started even to prepare that case, yet if there was an adjournment now, until after Christmas, I felt the wait would be intolerable.

I did not have to worry. After interminable minutes, the jury foreman was asked if they had found for the plaintiff or for the defendant. 'The defendant,' she said, and I wanted to hear her say it over and over again. I felt grateful that the truth had won and that I would not be out on the streets with the clothes I stood up in and nothing more. Tears started, but didn't persist. I leaned towards Raz and whispered: 'I think I'll say it's a great day for British justice and a great day for me. Is that OK?'

He looked absolutely horrified. 'No,' he said. 'Don't say anything. The judge won't like it!'

I laughed for the first time for a long time. He thought I was going to get up there and then to make a victory speech, whereas I had only been thinking out loud what to say to the press waiting outside.

We left court in a small team. Friends offered to carry the heavy boxes containing my files, being taken home for the last time, but I insisted on carrying them myself, remembering the way I felt on the day I'd first carried them in.

A group of about forty journalists were at the High Court gates. One of them, Keith Hatfield from ITN, asked me: 'How would you describe your relationship with Sonia Sutcliffe now?'

I thought for a second, then answered with relish: 'Over!'